FROM PIXELS TO PROFITS

A Comprehensive Guide to Play-to-Earn Gaming and Virtual Economies

CRAIG SOLACE

ISBN: 9798304439923

TABLE OF CONTENTS

PART I: THE FOUNDATIONS OF PLAY-TO-EARN 1

Chapter 1: The Evolution of Gaming and the Rise of Play-to-Earn *1*
    A Brief History of Gaming Economies   3
    The Blockchain Breakthrough   6
    Defining Play-to-Earn   9

Chapter 2: Understanding the Core Technologies: Blockchain, NFTs, and Tokens *17*
    What is Blockchain?   17
    Non-Fungible Tokens (NFTs): Unique Digital Assets   21
    Fungible Tokens and In-Game Currencies   25
    Smart Contracts and Ownership   27

Chapter 3: Value Creation in Virtual Worlds *37*
    Rarity, Utility, and Community Consensus   38
    Play-to-Earn vs. Traditional Models   40
    Player Governance and Community Influence 44

PART II: GETTING STARTED WITH PLAY-TO-EARN 58

Chapter 4: Essential Tools and Setup *58*
    Digital Wallets: Your Gateway to the Blockchain 58
    Exchanges and Marketplaces: Acquiring and Trading Assets   62
    Security and Best Practices: Protecting Your Assets   67

Chapter 5: Choosing the Right Play-to-Earn Game 83
    Evaluating Game Mechanics: Matching Your Playstyle 83
    Analyzing the Tokenomics: Ensuring Long-Term Sustainability   87
    Checking the Roadmap and Team Credentials: Gauging Reliability and Vision   89

Community and Social Proof: The Power of a Thriving Player Base   92

Practical Steps to Narrow Your Choices   97

Case Studies: Applying the Criteria   99

Long-Term Considerations: Beyond the Initial Choice 101

Balancing Profit Motive with Fun and Ethics 102

Preparing for the Future: Diversification and Exit Strategies
     103

Chapter 6: Gameplay Strategies for Maximizing Earnings 106

Advanced Tactics to Further Boost Earnings 122

Common Pitfalls and How to Avoid Them   126

Case Studies: Putting Strategies into Practice 127

PART III: EVALUATING GAME TOKENS AND DIGITAL ASSETS 132

Chapter 7: Tokenomics 101 ....*132*

Beyond the Basics: Advanced Considerations in Tokenomics
     149

Real-World Examples and Case Studies   153

Practical Steps for Evaluating a P2E Token's Viability   155

The Future of P2E Tokenomics   157

Chapter 8: Identifying Valuable NFTs *161*

Scarcity and Provable Ownership   163

In-Game Utility   169

Branding, Partnerships, and Lore   175

Secondary Market Considerations   180

PART IV: UNDERSTANDING THE BROADER VIRTUAL ECONOMIES 189

Chapter 9: The Metaverse and Interoperability...*189*

Expanding the Metaverse: Additional Dimensions of Interoperability   203

Challenges and Limitations   206

Cultural and Social Implications   209

The Road Ahead: Future Outlook   210

Chapter 10: Virtual Real Estate, Land Sales, and Renting Models.216

    Land Ownership in Virtual Worlds   217
    Leasing and Fractional Ownership   222
    Commercialization Opportunities   227

Chapter 11: DeFi, Staking, and Yield Farming Within Games 242

    Merging Gaming and DeFi   244
    Game Tokens as Collateral   250
    Risks and Rewards   256

Chapter 12: Regulatory Landscapes and Tax Considerations 272

    Navigating Legal Gray Areas   275
    Tax Implications   280
    Staying Informed: Avoiding Surprises in a Fluid Environment
    285

Chapter 13: Market Cycles, Speculation, and Sustainable Play 294

    Volatility in Crypto Markets   297
    Investment vs. Entertainment   300
    Building a Diversified Portfolio   304

Chapter 14: Ethical and Social Considerations 314

    Fairness and Accessibility   315
    Bots, Exploits, and Cheating   317
    Future of Work and Leisure   319
    Environmental Impact and Sustainability   322
    Child Participation and Gambling-Like Mechanics   324
    Best Practices and Policy Recommendations 325

PART VI: THE ROAD AHEAD 330

    Chapter 15: Emerging Trends and Future Predictions   *330*
    NFT Interoperability Protocols   331
    Layer-2 Solutions and Scalability   334
    AI and Procedural Content   336
    Potential Risks and Challenges   338
    Visions for the Next Decade of P2E   340

Charting a Sustainable Path Forward   341

Chapter 16: Cultivating a Mindset for Success 362
    Continuous Learning and Adaptation   363
    Networking and Community Building   366
    Contributing to the Ecosystem   369
    Bringing It All Together: The Holistic Mindset372
    Overcoming Common Psychological Barriers373
    Real-World Anecdotes and Success Stories 374
    Practical Steps to Foster a Success Mindset 376

Appendices..379

The play-to-earn revolution represents a paradigm shift where leisure, work, investment, and creativity converge in digital realms. As new players, developers, investors, and communities embrace these virtual economies, gaming transforms from a pastime into a platform for value creation and financial empowerment. The journey will not be without challenges—navigating technical complexity, regulatory uncertainty, and market volatility requires careful thought and adaptability. Yet, for those who understand the mechanics, maintain a long-term perspective, and engage ethically, the rewards can be substantial. May this guide serve as your compass as you venture boldly into the vibrant world of play-to-earn gaming and virtual economies.

PART I: THE FOUNDATIONS OF PLAY-TO-EARN

Chapter 1: The Evolution of Gaming and the Rise of Play-to-Earn

In the early days of gaming, few would have predicted that this fledgling entertainment medium—initially limited to simple pixels flickering on rudimentary screens—would evolve into a multi-billion-dollar industry with complex global markets, thriving communities, and expansive virtual worlds. But that is precisely what has happened. Over the course of several decades, video games have transformed from niche curiosities found in arcades and living rooms into massive cultural and economic ecosystems. The appeal of games now transcends geographic, cultural, and demographic boundaries. Gamers from all walks of life engage with titles on PCs, consoles, smartphones, and virtual reality headsets, connecting through shared experiences and collective challenges that unfold entirely within digital environments.

Yet, beyond their entertainment value, these virtual spaces have also given rise to new forms of economic activity. While many gamers initially played purely for fun, the concept of virtual economies began to emerge once the internet enabled players to interact with each other. Over time, items, characters, and in-game currencies took on perceived value in the eyes of players. Some began exchanging these digital goods for real money, paving the way for new economic opportunities, albeit in often informal and unregulated ways.

In the last few years, a dramatic new shift has occurred. With the advent of blockchain technology, decentralized finance (DeFi), and non-fungible tokens (NFTs), a robust infrastructure has emerged, allowing game developers and players alike to integrate genuine economic value directly into the fabric of virtual worlds. Instead of merely buying a disc or downloading a game, players can now own assets that hold verifiable, blockchain-backed scarcity. The result is a new paradigm known as "play-to-earn" (P2E), where players are not just consumers of digital entertainment but active participants in fully fledged virtual economies. These ecosystems reward players for their time and skill, blurring the lines between hobby, investment, and profession.

This chapter explores the evolution of gaming economies and the pivotal breakthroughs that enabled the play-to-earn model. We will examine the early informal grey markets that formed around online games, delve into the blockchain revolution that provided the technological backbone for transparent, decentralized ownership of digital assets, and finally define what play-to-earn truly means. By understanding where gaming economies came from and how they evolved, we gain a clearer picture of why the rise of P2E is not merely a trend, but a fundamental milestone in the ongoing transformation of digital entertainment and work.

A Brief History of Gaming Economies

From Leisure to Livelihood (The Early Landscape)

In the earliest era of video gaming—think the late 1970s and early 1980s—arcade cabinets and home consoles existed primarily to entertain. The concept of an "in-game economy" was almost non-existent. Players inserted coins into arcade machines, aiming for high scores and little else. Earning real money from these activities was unheard of. The transaction was simple: you paid for entertainment and, at the end of your session, you left with nothing but the memory of having played.

In the 1990s, console games like the Super Mario series and The Legend of Zelda offered more complex worlds, yet these experiences remained firmly single-player or local multiplayer affairs. The games sold millions of copies and generated huge profits for developers and publishers, but players themselves couldn't trade anything of tangible monetary value. While certain elements—like rare Pokémon on the Game Boy—became cultural phenomena, their trade or sale for real money outside the game was minimal and largely frowned upon. The underlying economic model was simple: you buy a game, you play, and the monetary value goes only one way, from the player to the game's publisher.

MMORPGs and the Birth of Virtual Economies

The birth of the internet as a mainstream communications platform changed everything. In the late 1990s and early 2000s, Massive Multiplayer Online Role-Playing Games (MMORPGs) like Ultima Online, EverQuest, and later World of Warcraft introduced persistent virtual worlds where thousands or even millions of players coexisted, adventured, and interacted in real-time. These games had fully functioning in-game economies, complete with currencies, items of varying rarity, and marketplaces where players could buy and sell virtual goods using the game's internal currency.

What developers did not initially anticipate was that these in-game assets would start to accumulate real-world value in the eyes of the players. A powerful sword, a rare mount, or a high-level character account could save a player dozens or hundreds of hours of tedious "grinding." This perceived value led some players to trade these assets for real money on external websites. A cottage industry of "gold farmers"—players or groups who spent their time collecting valuable in-game resources to sell to other players for real-world cash—sprang up, often concentrated in regions where labor was cheaper. Even though game publishers forbade these transactions in their terms of service, a grey market flourished. Entire economies formed around these digital assets, with middlemen, brokers, and auction sites appearing almost overnight.

The Informal "Grey Market" Era

For much of the 2000s and 2010s, the informal trade of virtual items was a kind of open secret in the gaming community. Websites like eBay temporarily listed virtual currencies or rare in-game gear, and specialized forums and marketplaces emerged to facilitate deals. Players sold their high-level World of Warcraft characters for significant sums, or their rare skins in games like Counter-Strike: Global Offensive for sometimes hundreds or thousands of dollars. The inherent problem was trust and security: these trades were often conducted outside the game's official infrastructure. There was always a risk of fraud—buyers paying for an item that was never delivered, or sellers handing over their property only to receive no payment. Additionally, because these transactions violated the game's terms of service, players risked having their accounts banned if caught.

Despite these hurdles, the mere existence of these grey markets proved a critical point: virtual items can have real-world value, and many people are willing to pay substantial sums for digital goods that save them time, enhance their in-game status, or provide unique experiences. The challenge was a lack of formal mechanisms to recognize and secure this value. Without official developer support or robust technology to guarantee item authenticity and ownership, the system remained precarious, limited, and often exploitative.

Evolving Player Expectations and the Seeds of Change

As players spent more and more time in virtual worlds, they began to see these environments not just as games but as social spaces and creative platforms. Virtual real estate in Second Life could be rented out or sold; elaborate costumes in MMORPGs fetched real dollars. The demand for legitimate ways to profit from gaming activities intensified. If players were putting in countless hours to acquire special items, why shouldn't they have a secure, transparent way to monetize their efforts?

Moreover, new monetization models, such as free-to-play games, reshaped the landscape. In free-to-play titles, players can download the game at no cost but are encouraged to purchase cosmetic items, boosts, or expansions. This shift meant that digital items already had official, developer-backed monetary values. Players got used to the idea of spending real money within a game's ecosystem. The leap to players also earning money within these ecosystems was a logical next step—what was missing was a technology that could ensure fairness, transparency, and authenticity.

The Blockchain Breakthrough

Decentralization and Trustless Transactions

Enter the blockchain. Invented as the backbone technology for Bitcoin in 2008, blockchain introduced a revolutionary way of recording and verifying transactions without relying on a centralized authority. Instead, multiple nodes in a distributed network validated each transaction. This made it possible to have a tamper-proof, transparent, and secure ledger of ownership. In the context of gaming economies, this was nothing short of a revelation.

Before blockchain, virtual goods were, from a technical standpoint, merely entries in a database controlled entirely by the game's publisher. If the publisher decided to ban an account, close the server, or create more copies of a rare item, they could do so unilaterally. With blockchain-based systems, digital assets could exist independently of any one entity's control. Ownership records would be public and impossible to forge, and scarcity could be mathematically enforced. The era of trustless transactions had arrived, making it possible for players to truly own their in-game items without relying on the goodwill of the developer.

Non-Fungible Tokens (NFTs) and Digital Scarcity

One of the key innovations that bridged the gap between decentralized finance and gaming was the creation of non-fungible tokens (NFTs). Unlike cryptocurrencies such as Bitcoin or Ethereum, which are fungible (each token is identical and interchangeable), NFTs represent unique digital items. Each NFT has distinct attributes recorded on the blockchain, ensuring provable authenticity and scarcity.

For gamers, NFTs meant that an in-game sword, a piece of armor, or a virtual plot of land could exist as a one-of-a-kind asset. Its rarity would be transparent to anyone who cared to look at the blockchain data. This assurance of scarcity and provenance upended old dynamics. Instead of relying on the developer's database entries, the value of an item could now be guaranteed by cryptographic proof. This opened the door to trusted secondary markets where players could buy, sell, or trade items with confidence.

Cryptocurrencies as In-Game Currencies

In addition to NFTs, blockchain-based games could use cryptocurrencies for their in-game economies. Players could earn tokens as rewards for completing quests, defeating enemies, or winning tournaments. Because these tokens exist on the blockchain, they could easily be traded on external cryptocurrency exchanges. This meant players could convert their in-game earnings into widely recognized cryptocurrencies like Ethereum or even into fiat money, such as U.S. dollars, through various exchanges.

What started as a technological curiosity—blockchain gaming experiments running on the Ethereum network—quickly gained momentum. Early projects like CryptoKitties demonstrated that people would spend significant sums of money on purely digital collectibles, while newer, more game-like experiences followed. Developers experimented with governance tokens that allowed players to influence game development decisions, further blurring the line between player and stakeholder.

Building Trust and Legitimacy

By leveraging blockchain, developers offered something that the grey markets of old could not: trust and legitimacy. Because ownership and transactions were recorded on a public ledger, disputes were minimized. If a player bought an NFT representing a rare sword, the blockchain's records could verify the authenticity instantly. The risk of fraud diminished, and the notion of true digital ownership crystallized.

The integration of blockchain technology also attracted attention from regulators, investors, and mainstream institutions. While the legal landscape surrounding cryptocurrencies and NFTs continues to evolve, the infrastructure and interest level have matured considerably. Venture capital poured into blockchain gaming startups, major brands released their own NFT collections, and leading game publishers explored integrating blockchain assets into their titles. The stage was set for a new era where gaming and real-world economies would merge seamlessly—setting the foundation for the play-to-earn phenomenon.

Defining Play-to-Earn

From Entertainment to Economic Activity

Traditional video games typically follow a simple model: players pay a fee (either upfront or through in-app purchases) and receive entertainment in return. In this model, the player is always a consumer, never a producer, and rarely, if ever, a beneficiary of the game's economic success. Play-to-earn (P2E) games invert this model. Instead of merely consuming content, players actively contribute to the game's ecosystem. Their time and skill in defeating enemies, crafting items, or building virtual infrastructure generate valuable digital assets that they can own, trade, and monetize.

In a P2E model, the player's activities produce something of tangible value—whether it's a token that can be sold for cryptocurrency, an NFT item that can be auctioned off, or even passive income from virtual land rented out to other players. By rewarding players for their participation, P2E games align incentives in a way that was previously impossible. The player isn't just a customer; they're a partner in the economic ecosystem, potentially profiting from the success of the game and the community that forms around it.

The Elements of a P2E Ecosystem

At its core, a successful P2E ecosystem has several key components:

1. **Blockchain-Based Assets:**

Whether through NFTs for unique items or fungible tokens for in-game currencies, these blockchain-based assets are the economic backbone of P2E games. Because they are decentralized and transparent, they provide the trust and legitimacy needed for healthy markets to form.

2. **Ownership and Control:**

In P2E games, the player truly owns their assets. These are not just digital objects in a server that can be deleted at a developer's whim. Instead, they are entries on a blockchain that can be stored in a player's crypto wallet. Players can move these assets outside the game's ecosystem, selling them on external marketplaces or holding them as investments.

3. **Interoperability and Portability:**

While still an emerging concept, interoperability—where a player's NFT item could be used across multiple games or virtual worlds—is a defining vision of the future P2E space.

This portability enhances the value of digital assets and encourages larger, interconnected metaverses rather than siloed gaming experiences.

4. Community Governance and Participation:

Many P2E games offer governance tokens, which grant players the right to vote on game updates, economic policies, or development directions. By decentralizing decision-making, these games empower players to shape the experience in which they have invested time and money.

5. Player-Centric Economies:

Instead of developers dictating prices or creating arbitrary item distribution, P2E economies often let market dynamics, supply, and demand determine value. Players become entrepreneurs, traders, and investors within the game's ecosystem, responding to incentives and market signals.

Implications for Players and Developers

The rise of P2E gaming means that players can potentially turn their gaming hours into income. Consider regions where traditional job opportunities are limited, or players who have honed their skills over years in competitive games. These individuals can now leverage their expertise to earn a living wage by engaging in digital economies. Already, we've seen examples of players in developing countries earning more from

P2E games than from their local jobs—an unprecedented trend that challenges conventional notions of work and leisure.

For developers, P2E introduces both opportunities and responsibilities. Building a sustainable virtual economy is no simple feat. Developers must carefully manage token issuance, ensure that gameplay remains balanced, and maintain fairness so that the economy doesn't collapse into inflationary chaos or degenerate into pay-to-win scenarios. Successful P2E games often have intricate tokenomic models and robust governance structures. The developers become equal parts game designers, economists, community managers, and financial architects.

The Blurring of Lines Between Virtual and Real

What does it mean when players can earn real money from virtual worlds? For one, it challenges the notion of what constitutes "real." If a virtual sword can be sold for a thousand dollars, does that make it any less real to the buyer or seller than a physical object of the same price? The value now lies not in the physical matter but in the utility, scarcity, and social capital that the digital asset confers within a community. This value transfer between digital and physical realms is ushering in a world where time spent in virtual spaces can be as economically meaningful as time spent in traditional workplaces.

With P2E, the lines between gamers and investors, between hobbyists and professionals, start to blur. Someone who began playing for fun may find themselves owning a portfolio of NFTs worth thousands of dollars. Conversely, a savvy investor might enter a game's economy purely for profit, employing skilled players or purchasing in-game assets to earn passive income. The societal and economic implications of these shifts are profound. We may soon see a rise in what some call the "metaverse workforce," people who earn a living entirely within virtual environments.

Potential Challenges and Criticisms

The P2E revolution, while exciting, is not without its criticisms and challenges. Critics argue that putting monetary incentives front and center could degrade the pure fun and escapism that games have traditionally provided. They worry that focusing on profits might turn gaming communities into hyper-competitive and extractive environments. Additionally, the volatility of cryptocurrencies and NFTs raises questions about financial risk. A player's hard-earned digital assets could lose significant value if the market turns or if the game's developers fail to maintain player interest.

There are also concerns about regulatory frameworks. How do governments classify these earnings? Are they considered income or assets? What happens if players use these platforms for money laundering or other illicit activities? The legal and ethical landscape is still in flux.

Developers must also ensure that their tokenomics are sustainable. Without carefully balanced supply-and-demand mechanisms, P2E economies could experience "pump and dump" cycles, where early investors profit at the expense of new players. Ensuring long-term stability and fairness requires transparency, governance, and ongoing community dialogue.

The Dawn of a New Era

Despite these concerns, the rise of P2E is part of a broader movement toward digital empowerment and decentralized ecosystems. It aligns with trends in decentralized finance, creator economies, and the metaverse. For players who have spent decades investing time and effort into virtual worlds without any financial return, P2E represents recognition that their digital labor and creativity have real value.

As blockchain technology continues to evolve—improving scalability, reducing transaction costs, and facilitating greater interoperability—P2E games will likely become more accessible, more stable, and more fun. Just as we've seen with earlier technological shifts, the initial learning curves, early volatility, and skepticism will give way to more refined models, best practices, and widespread adoption. The concept of playing a game to earn money will no longer be a novelty or a niche interest; it may well become a standard feature of the gaming landscape.

Conclusion

The evolution of gaming economies has been a slow but steady journey from simple entertainment to complex ecosystems that mirror and even surpass aspects of the real world. From the earliest arcade cabinets that offered no economic dimension, to the emergence of MMORPGs that unknowingly set the stage for grey market trades, to the blockchain breakthroughs that finally made secure digital ownership and trustless trading possible, we've seen gaming transform into something far bigger than what its pioneers could have envisioned.

Now, with the advent of play-to-earn gaming, we stand at a pivotal moment. The technology to enable these economies—blockchain, NFTs, decentralized marketplaces—already exists and is improving rapidly. Players and developers are experimenting with new models of engagement and compensation that challenge traditional boundaries between work and play. While challenges remain—regulatory, economic, and cultural—the foundational shift is undeniable.

Play-to-earn is not just a feature; it's a fundamental shift in how we perceive and interact with digital worlds. As we move into a future where gaming, finance, and social interaction merge seamlessly, the potential for innovation and empowerment is vast. These new paradigms invite us to reconsider long-held assumptions: What is value? How should it be distributed? Who creates wealth, and who benefits from it? In exploring these questions, the rise of play-to-earn gaming has the potential to redefine not only the gaming industry, but the nature of economic activity and the meaning of leisure itself.

As the journey of this book continues, we will delve deeper into the specifics of how to get started in play-to-earn gaming, how to evaluate digital assets, and how to navigate the broader virtual economies that are emerging around these worlds. But first, by understanding the historical context and the technological revolutions that led us here, we ground ourselves in the reality that the transformation of gaming economies is no mere fad—it is a lasting evolution that will shape the future of both entertainment and commerce.

Chapter 2: Understanding the Core Technologies: Blockchain, NFTs, and Tokens

The world of play-to-earn (P2E) gaming is built upon a foundation of innovative technologies that enable true digital ownership, secure transactions, and transparent governance. To fully grasp the potential of these emerging virtual economies, it is essential to understand the underlying frameworks that make them possible. The trio of blockchain technology, Non-Fungible Tokens (NFTs), and fungible tokens—often managed by smart contracts—forms the technological core that allows in-game assets to carry real-world value.

This chapter delves deep into these core technologies. We will unpack the concept of blockchain and explain how its decentralized, immutable nature establishes trust and authenticity. We will then explore NFTs, the unique digital assets that bring scarcity, identity, and provenance to the virtual realm. Lastly, we will look at the role of fungible tokens as in-game currencies and how smart contracts automate the rules of these new digital ecosystems. By the end of this chapter, readers will have a robust understanding of the technical frameworks that underpin the play-to-earn revolution.

What is Blockchain?

A Brief Introduction to Blockchain Concepts

Blockchain technology emerged in 2008 as the foundational data structure supporting Bitcoin, the first decentralized cryptocurrency. At its core, a blockchain is a chronological series of data blocks linked together using cryptographic principles. Each block contains a batch of transactions and references the previous block, creating a verifiable and tamper-resistant chain. This simple yet powerful structure ensures that once a block is added to the chain, altering it becomes computationally expensive—if not practically impossible—due to the need to recalculate subsequent blocks and achieve consensus with the rest of the network.

The hallmark of blockchain lies in its decentralization. Instead of relying on a single authority, like a bank or a tech giant, blockchains are maintained by a distributed network of computers (often called "nodes"). These nodes collectively validate and record transactions according to predefined rules coded into the blockchain's protocol. This approach eliminates the need for intermediaries, creating a trustless environment where no single entity wields unilateral control over the database.

Key Principles of Blockchain Technology

1. **Decentralization:**

Traditional databases are typically controlled by a single organization. With blockchain, the ledger is maintained simultaneously by multiple independent nodes. No single node has absolute authority. If one node fails or attempts to cheat, the other nodes will reject its modifications, ensuring the ledger's integrity.

2. Immutability:

Once data is written to a blockchain and validated by the network, altering it is extremely difficult. Changing a past transaction would require controlling the majority of the network's computing power to rewrite the blockchain from that point forward. This immutability is crucial for building trust in systems where participants may not know or trust each other.

3. Transparency and Public Verifiability:

Most public blockchains, like Bitcoin and Ethereum, allow anyone to view all past transactions. Although participants are usually represented by cryptographic addresses rather than their real names, the record of activity is open and transparent. This radical transparency differentiates blockchain networks from traditional, opaque financial or gaming databases.

4. Security Through Consensus:

Blockchain networks rely on consensus mechanisms— protocols that nodes follow to agree on the state of the ledger. The most famous consensus mechanism is Proof of Work (PoW), used by Bitcoin. Another popular method is Proof of Stake (PoS), which many modern blockchains use to achieve similar security and consensus with lower energy consumption. The consensus ensures that all nodes trust the state of the network without trusting each other individually.

Blockchain's Relevance to Gaming

Before blockchain, digital items existed solely in proprietary databases controlled by game developers. If a developer banned your account or shut down the server, your items could vanish instantly. Blockchain disrupts this model by introducing secure, player-owned assets. In the context of gaming, several features of blockchain stand out:

1. **True Player Ownership:**

When a virtual item or currency is represented as a blockchain token, the player holds it in a personal crypto wallet. The developer cannot confiscate or replicate it at will. This shift empowers players, granting them unprecedented agency over their in-game belongings.

2. **Preventing Duplication and Fraud:**

A crucial problem in traditional virtual economies is the risk of duplication. Players might hack or exploit bugs to create multiple copies of a rare item, diluting its value. Blockchain ensures that each item can be tracked on the ledger. If the supply is limited to 10 items, the blockchain guarantees there are no hidden duplicates.

3. **Interoperability and Composability:**

Blockchain-based assets, like NFTs, can potentially move between different games and platforms that recognize the same standards. This creates a more open ecosystem where virtual assets have utility beyond a single game's borders.

Ultimately, blockchain provides the technological backbone that enables a global marketplace for digital goods, where items

are scarce, verifiably authentic, and securely owned by players—
not just the game's central authority.

Non-Fungible Tokens (NFTs): Unique Digital Assets

Defining NFTs

Non-Fungible Tokens (NFTs) emerged as a solution for representing unique digital assets on a blockchain. While cryptocurrencies like Bitcoin are fungible (one Bitcoin is interchangeable with another), NFTs are distinct. Each NFT carries its own specific set of attributes, metadata, and identity recorded in a blockchain's ledger, making it one-of-a-kind.

Think of fungibility as a property of uniform assets. A $10 bill is fungible because it holds the same value as any other $10 bill; they are interchangeable. By contrast, a one-of-a-kind painting by a renowned artist is non-fungible because you can't simply replace it with another painting of equal value—its uniqueness and provenance are integral to its worth. NFTs bring that same concept of uniqueness and verifiable authenticity into the digital realm.

Attributes of NFTs

1. **Uniqueness and Scarcity:**

   Each NFT has a unique identifier often encoded into the token's metadata. The blockchain's public ledger records the NFT's entire transaction history, proving its authenticity and origin. By enforcing limited supply—be it one-of-a-kind art pieces or a finite set of game items—NFTs introduce scarcity, a key driver of value.

2. **Indivisibility:**

While certain frameworks allow fractional ownership, most NFTs are indivisible at their core. You can't pay for half of an NFT unless the asset has been tokenized into fractional shares. This indivisibility often makes sense for representing items that are conceptually whole, like an in-game sword or a virtual plot of land.

3. **Interoperability and Transferability:**

NFTs are generally minted on open blockchain standards such as Ethereum's ERC-721 or ERC-1155. These standards ensure compatibility across marketplaces, wallets, and applications. For gamers, this means NFTs can be traded on various platforms, displayed in galleries, or potentially used across multiple games, provided developers integrate them.

4. **Proof of Ownership and Provenance:**

The blockchain-based record of ownership (provenance) is critical. This record shows who created the NFT, all previous owners, and the current holder's address. This transparency builds trust. Gamers can verify that a rare skin or a special artifact was indeed minted by the official game developers and not a counterfeit.

NFTs in Gaming

NFTs revolutionize in-game economies by providing a robust framework for digital collectibles, characters, skins, weapons, and even parcels of virtual land. Prior to NFTs, "owning" an item in a game often meant having access to a line of code in a centralized database. With NFTs, players genuinely possess these assets. This ownership enables a host of possibilities:

1. **Real Ownership of In-Game Assets:**

If your character wields an NFT sword, it lives in your crypto wallet. Even if the game shuts down, you still have cryptographic proof of owning that asset. While its utility might vanish if the game no longer exists, its collectible or sentimental value could persist—and if other games or platforms integrate the same NFT, it might retain functionality there.

2. **Secondary Market Opportunities:**

NFTs can be bought and sold on decentralized marketplaces. Players who earn rare items through skill or luck can monetize their achievements by selling these NFTs. This dynamic turns gaming time into a potential income stream, contributing significantly to the play-to-earn model's appeal.

3. **Upgradable and Evolving Assets:**

Some NFTs can evolve over time based on player achievements. For instance, a base-level NFT sword might gain special attributes or visual enhancements as the player completes quests. Each improvement adds to the sword's history and potentially its market value.

4. **Branding and Collectibility:**

Limited-edition items released by game developers, eSports teams, or famous gaming personalities can become coveted collectibles. Over time, these unique assets can appreciate, offering players long-term investment potential.

Standards for NFTs

The Ethereum blockchain pioneered many NFT standards, with ERC-721 being the most famous. ERC-721 defines a minimum interface for smart contracts, enabling the creation, ownership, and transfer of unique tokens. Other standards, like ERC-1155, allow for both fungible and non-fungible tokens under the same contract, providing more flexibility for game developers who might want to issue large batches of items—some unique and some fungible.

While Ethereum dominates the NFT space, scalability and transaction costs have been challenges. Alternative blockchain platforms and Layer-2 solutions, like Polygon or Immutable X, offer lower fees and faster confirmations, making it more practical for games that process numerous in-game transactions.

Criticisms and Challenges

The NFT boom hasn't been without controversy. Critics argue that many NFTs sold as "rare" collectibles lack intrinsic value or that the hype cycle leads to speculative bubbles. Environmental concerns also emerged around blockchains using Proof of Work, where energy consumption runs high. However, the gradual shift to more energy-efficient consensus mechanisms and the maturing of the NFT space suggest that NFTs are evolving from speculative novelties into functional tools, especially in gaming contexts.

Fungible Tokens and In-Game Currencies

What Are Fungible Tokens?

Fungible tokens represent digital assets where each unit is interchangeable with another. Cryptocurrencies like Bitcoin, Ether, or stablecoins (tokens pegged to a real-world currency) are fungible. They serve as a medium of exchange, a store of value, or a unit of account. In gaming, fungible tokens often represent in-game currencies or reward points. Unlike NFTs, which are unique, fungible tokens are uniform and identical. One token is equal in value and properties to another, making them suitable for representing currencies and other divisible resources.

Role of Fungible Tokens in P2E Games

1. Medium of Exchange:

Fungible tokens can serve as the in-game currency. Players earn these tokens by completing tasks, winning battles, or trading items. They can then use the tokens to purchase NFTs, upgrade their gear, or pay for services within the game's ecosystem. Because these tokens live on a blockchain, they can also be traded on external exchanges for other cryptocurrencies or even fiat money.

2. Liquidity and Market Dynamics:

The availability of a fungible, tradable token creates liquidity within the in-game economy. If players can convert their earnings into widely recognized cryptocurrencies, they gain real-world value for their time and skill. This liquidity also incentivizes more players to join, fueling a virtuous cycle of economic growth within the game.

3. Tokenomics and Game Balancing:

Developers must carefully design the supply and distribution of fungible tokens to maintain a healthy economy. If tokens are too easy to earn, inflation may devalue them. If they are too scarce, players may feel frustrated. Balancing these dynamics requires thoughtful "tokenomics" to ensure long-term stability. Some games introduce "token sinks," mechanisms that encourage players to spend or burn tokens, maintaining scarcity and value.

4. Integration with DeFi (Decentralized Finance):

Because fungible tokens are blockchain-based, they can interact with the broader decentralized finance ecosystem. Players might stake their tokens to earn passive income, or game developers can form partnerships with DeFi protocols to offer liquidity pools, lending platforms, or yield farming opportunities. This integration bridges gaming and finance, enhancing the economic dimension of play-to-earn ecosystems.

Token Standards and Platforms

On Ethereum, fungible tokens commonly follow the ERC-20 standard, which defines the functions needed to create a fungible token that can be transferred and managed uniformly. Like NFTs, fungible tokens can also be minted on other blockchains. The choice of blockchain often depends on transaction fees, scalability, and the community of users and developers.

Real-World Examples

In the popular play-to-earn game Axie Infinity, the main in-game fungible token is Smooth Love Potion (SLP). Players earn SLP by battling monsters and other players. SLP can be used to breed new Axies (the game's creatures, represented by NFTs), creating a cycle of production and consumption. Players who accumulate excess SLP can sell it on cryptocurrency exchanges, turning their in-game efforts into tangible real-world income.

Another example is Gala Games, a gaming ecosystem that uses the GALA token. Players earn GALA by playing games in the ecosystem and can spend it on NFTs, participate in governance, or cash out by trading on external exchanges. This model empowers players to become stakeholders, not just consumers.

Smart Contracts and Ownership

Defining Smart Contracts

A smart contract is a self-executing piece of code running on a blockchain network. It executes certain actions automatically when predefined conditions are met. Unlike traditional contracts—where enforcement depends on trusted intermediaries and legal systems—smart contracts are enforced by cryptographic rules and the consensus of the blockchain network.

For example, consider a simple smart contract that releases an NFT to the player's wallet if the player sends a certain amount of the in-game currency to the contract's address. Once the conditions are fulfilled (i.e., the payment is confirmed on the blockchain), the smart contract transfers the NFT. There is no need for a middleman or escrow service; the code itself ensures fairness and transparency.

How Smart Contracts Enable Fair and Transparent Ownership

1. **Automated Execution:**

Smart contracts eliminate the need for human intervention once they're deployed. This means that the rules of the game economy—like how players receive rewards—are enforced automatically and cannot be arbitrarily changed or corrupted. If a player completes a quest, the contract triggers the release of a reward token.

2. **Verifiable Conditions:**

The conditions encoded in a smart contract can be verified on-chain. For instance, if a player must hold a specific NFT in their wallet to access a special in-game area, the contract can easily check the blockchain's ledger to confirm ownership. This cryptographic verification reduces fraud and ensures that only eligible players gain rewards.

3. **Trustless Environments:**

In traditional gaming environments, players must trust game developers and centralized servers to deliver their rewards. Smart contracts remove this necessity. Because the code is visible and immutable once deployed (assuming best practices are followed), players can trust the protocol rather than any single party. This trustless mechanism forms the bedrock of play-to-earn economies.

4. **Programmatic Scarcity and Rules:**

Smart contracts can also define scarcity rules. For example, a contract can limit the minting of a certain NFT collection to only 100 units. Once those 100 units are created, the contract cannot mint more. This programmatic enforcement of scarcity underpins the economic value of these assets.

Examples of Smart Contract Use Cases in Gaming

1. **Quests and Rewards:**

Suppose a play-to-earn RPG requires players to defeat a certain monster to earn a rare NFT weapon. The conditions—monster defeated, verified on-chain—trigger the smart contract to deliver the NFT to the player's wallet. No human intervention, no disputes over fairness: the contract enforces the rules.

2. **Item Rentals and Time-Limited Access:**

A player might want to rent out their rare NFT mount to another player for a fixed period. A smart contract can escrow the asset and release it to the renter's control for the agreed-upon time. After that period, the NFT returns automatically to the original owner. The payment is also handled trustlessly through the same contract.

3. **Governance and Voting:**

Some gaming ecosystems issue governance tokens that grant voting rights. A smart contract can tally votes automatically, preventing manipulation. It can instantly enact changes approved by a majority, whether adjusting token rewards, altering game difficulty, or adding new features.

Ensuring Security and Reliability

While smart contracts offer numerous benefits, they must be carefully audited and tested. Bugs in smart contract code can lead to exploits, theft of assets, or unintended behavior. This risk highlights the importance of professional audits, bug bounties, and security best practices. As the industry matures, standard libraries, frameworks, and formal verification methods are emerging, making smart contracts safer and more reliable.

Legal Considerations and Dispute Resolution

Unlike traditional contracts, smart contracts are not interpreted by lawyers and enforced by courts. Their interpretation is literal, based solely on the code. This can cause complexities in edge cases or disputes not anticipated by developers. Some projects use hybrid approaches—where smart contract execution is automated, but certain aspects of dispute resolution or governance might involve human decision-making, often through decentralized organizations. As the technology evolves, new frameworks will emerge to handle more complex legal and social scenarios.

Bringing It All Together: The Technological Ecosystem of P2E

The Synergy of Blockchain, NFTs, and Tokens

When combined, blockchain, NFTs, fungible tokens, and smart contracts form a powerful, synergistic whole. Consider a fully-fledged P2E ecosystem:

- **The Blockchain Infrastructure:**

A public blockchain like Ethereum hosts the in-game asset records, token balances, and smart contract logic. Layer-2 scaling solutions might be employed to reduce transaction fees and improve speed.

- **NFT Assets for Uniqueness and Ownership:**

Players own unique NFT characters, skins, and equipment that they can trade freely on marketplaces. These NFTs confer advantages, status, or aesthetic appeal within the game. They also hold collectible value, potentially appreciating over time.

- **Fungible Tokens as a Currency Layer:**

Players earn a fungible in-game token by completing quests, participating in tournaments, or contributing to the game's ecosystem. This token circulates as the currency for buying NFTs, upgrading items, or accessing special content. Its exchangeability with other cryptocurrencies gives it real-world liquidity.

- **Smart Contracts to Enforce Rules:**

All game logic—such as quest completion, reward distribution, and governance proposals—runs through smart contracts. Players know that if they fulfill the required conditions, they will receive their rewards automatically, without requiring any human intermediary.

Examples from Existing Ecosystems

- **Axie Infinity:**

One of the most notable P2E games, Axie Infinity uses NFTs (Axie creatures) and two fungible tokens (AXS and SLP). Smart contracts handle breeding mechanics, marketplace transactions, and reward distribution. Players earn SLP by playing, and can sell it on exchanges. This interplay of technologies underpins the entire ecosystem's economy.

- **The Sandbox:**

A virtual world where land parcels are represented as NFTs, The Sandbox uses its SAND token as the in-game currency. Creators build experiences on their NFTs, and users can buy and sell these assets on marketplaces. Smart contracts ensure that ownership rights and revenue splits are enforced automatically.

- **Alien Worlds:**

Alien Worlds is a decentralized metaverse running on blockchain, where fungible tokens (TLM) and NFTs representing tools or lands interact. Smart contracts define mining rules, resource extraction, and rewards. Players stake tokens, vote in planetary governance, and earn a share of the ecosystem's income.

The Future of P2E Infrastructure

As blockchain technology improves, we can expect increased scalability, cheaper transaction costs, and more intuitive user interfaces. Layer-2 solutions, sidechains, and new generation blockchains are reducing the technical barriers that once made blockchain-based gaming cumbersome. This progression will make P2E ecosystems more accessible, efficient, and feature-rich, attracting a wider player base.

Interoperability standards, such as EIP-2981 for royalty management or EIP-2535 for modular smart contract upgradability, will simplify the development process and enhance user trust. In the future, players might carry their NFT avatars, items, and currencies across multiple virtual worlds, games, and social platforms—an interconnected metaverse of value, commerce, and play.

Overcoming Challenges and Criticisms

Usability and User Experience

For newcomers, dealing with blockchain transactions, private keys, and crypto wallets can be intimidating. Gas fees (transaction fees on networks like Ethereum) may also deter casual players. Developers are working on abstracting these technical complexities, allowing players to interact with the game much like a traditional app while the blockchain operates under the hood.

Security and Fraud Prevention

While blockchain ensures authenticity and scarcity, hacks and exploits in smart contracts or bridges (connections between different blockchains) remain a challenge. Rigorous testing, professional audits, insurance protocols, and vigilant community oversight reduce these risks. As infrastructure matures, improved standards and best practices will further secure P2E environments.

Regulatory Uncertainty

As P2E games blur the lines between gaming, investment, and work, regulatory scrutiny is increasing. Are these tokens securities? Are earnings taxable income? Different jurisdictions have varying approaches, and developers must stay informed to maintain compliance. Over time, clearer guidelines and frameworks will emerge, but in the interim, participants should exercise caution and seek professional advice when dealing with significant investments.

Market Volatility and Sustainability

The value of in-game tokens and NFTs can fluctuate wildly. Early investors and players may reap significant rewards, but speculative fervor can create boom-bust cycles that leave latecomers with worthless assets. Sustainable game design, balanced tokenomics, and community-driven governance aim to mitigate these risks. Ultimately, P2E ecosystems that provide genuine utility, compelling gameplay, and long-term value propositions are more likely to endure.

Conclusion

Understanding the core technologies powering play-to-earn gaming—blockchain, NFTs, fungible tokens, and smart contracts—is essential for anyone looking to participate effectively in these new digital economies. Blockchain's decentralized ledger eliminates trust issues and provides a secure, transparent foundation for in-game assets. NFTs introduce uniqueness, scarcity, and genuine digital ownership, allowing items to gain real-world value as collectibles, investments, and functional assets. Fungible tokens serve as the currency driving in-game trade and liquidity, connecting the virtual world with the broader global economy. Finally, smart contracts ensure fairness and automation, transforming game rules into unambiguous code and enabling sophisticated interactions without intermediaries.

These technologies, working in harmony, create a landscape where players transcend their traditional role as consumers. They become stakeholders, investors, creators, and entrepreneurs in vibrant virtual ecosystems. While challenges persist in the form of usability, security, regulation, and sustainability, ongoing innovations and industry maturation promise a bright future. As we venture deeper into the world of P2E, understanding the technical underpinnings of these innovations will empower players and developers to navigate opportunities and risks, ultimately driving the continued growth and evolution of this groundbreaking sector.

By building on the foundations explored in this chapter, readers will be well-prepared to engage with the next stages of the P2E journey—evaluating game tokens, assessing digital assets, and strategically participating in the economies that are reshaping the relationship between play, work, and value creation.

Chapter 3: Value Creation in Virtual Worlds

One of the most revolutionary aspects of play-to-earn (P2E) gaming is the opportunity for players, developers, and investors to participate in the co-creation and distribution of value within virtual ecosystems. Historically, games were closed environments where all the economic benefit flowed toward publishers and developers. Gamers were, at best, consumers— often paying for additional content, expansions, or cosmetic items and receiving nothing but entertainment in return.

The advent of blockchain-based, play-to-earn paradigms has upended this model. Virtual worlds now facilitate the creation, exchange, and appreciation of digital assets, and these economies are shaped by rarity, utility, community consensus, and decentralized governance. The interplay of these elements determines the worth of items, currencies, and even the underlying platforms themselves.

In this chapter, we'll explore the fundamental principles behind value creation in these virtual worlds. We'll examine how scarcity, item utility, and community perceptions influence asset values; how the play-to-earn dynamic challenges and reconfigures traditional business models; and how player governance mechanisms, often enacted through Decentralized Autonomous Organizations (DAOs), foster a more participatory, equitable, and value-enhancing environment.

Rarity, Utility, and Community Consensus

Value in any market—physical or digital—rests on a combination of factors. For virtual economies, three pillars often determine asset worth: rarity, utility, and community consensus. Understanding these factors helps players, developers, and investors identify promising opportunities and navigate a complex and rapidly evolving landscape.

1. Rarity: Scarcity as a Driver of Value

Scarcity lies at the heart of economics. If something is limited and in demand, it generally acquires value. Before blockchain-based gaming, digital items were easy to replicate. Developers could generate infinite copies of a special sword, mount, or skin, diluting any sense of real scarcity. With NFTs (Non-Fungible Tokens) and verifiable ownership recorded on the blockchain, game developers can enforce strict supply limits. When a piece of virtual land is coded to exist in only 1,000 copies, the players know that no additional land parcels can be conjured at whim.

This scarcity instantly triggers a more traditional economic framework. Consider the difference between a widely available cosmetic skin and a once-in-a-lifetime NFT collectible minted as a reward for winning a prestigious tournament. The latter might hold substantial market value, not just as a game item, but as a badge of honor, a limited edition collectible, or even a status symbol in the community.

Yet rarity alone does not guarantee lasting value. Speculative bubbles can form around rare assets if players believe others will pay more later. Without real underlying reasons for continued demand, such bubbles eventually burst, devaluing the asset. To achieve long-term stability, rarity must be accompanied by other factors, most notably utility and community consensus.

2. Utility: The Real-World Functions of Virtual Assets

An asset's utility refers to how effectively it can be used to accomplish goals within the game or ecosystem. Utility might mean:

- **Functional Utility:** A weapon that increases a player's chances of winning battles or an NFT character that grants access to exclusive quests.

- **Productive Utility:** Virtual land that can be leased out to other players, generating yield. A plot of digital real estate might be used to host events, advertise brands, or mine resources that translate into game tokens.

- **Social Utility:** Items that signal status or identity, much like luxury fashion in the real world. Owning a rare avatar skin could grant access to elite social circles or guilds within the virtual community.

A piece of land in a virtual world like Decentraland or The Sandbox can appreciate if it's in a high-traffic area where players gather for events, concerts, or community hangouts. The utility arises because that land can generate foot traffic, attention, and potentially rental income. Similarly, a special NFT mount that increases movement speed in a sprawling game world has tangible value for players who need to travel quickly. The greater the in-game advantages or productivity an item provides, the more it is likely to command a stable, enduring price.

3. Community Consensus: Perception and Cultural Capital

Beyond scarcity and utility, community consensus—what players collectively believe—is a fundamental value driver. In many ways, this parallels the way cultural context shapes the value of art, fashion, or collectibles in the real world. A painting's worth is partly determined by critics, institutions, and the community of art lovers who agree that it is significant.

In virtual worlds, community is a powerful force. It determines which assets are considered valuable, which games gain traction, and which tokens hold prestige. Memes, lore, influencers, and narrative building contribute significantly to the perception of value. For example, if a well-respected influencer in the gaming community endorses a particular NFT collection, demand may surge. If the player base rallies behind a certain asset as a symbol of early adopters or top-tier competitors, that asset gains cultural importance.

This communal aspect makes digital assets akin to social currencies. People don't just buy these items for their in-game advantages; they buy them because owning them means something within the community. As virtual worlds grow more socially rich and interconnected, consensus-based value formation will become even more pronounced.

Play-to-Earn vs. Traditional Models

The traditional video game market often revolved around a clear-cut relationship: developers produce content, and players consume it. Players pay upfront for a game or purchase recurring subscriptions and cosmetic items. Apart from rare exceptions—like secondary markets for in-game gold in MMORPGs—no official mechanism returned value to players.

Play-to-earn ecosystems turn this model on its head. Players can earn tokens, NFTs, and other valuable digital goods simply by playing. This shift introduces a new set of incentives, reshapes the developer-player relationship, and redefines what it means to "play."

1. The Old Paradigm: One-Way Value Flow

In traditional gaming ecosystems, the flow of value is primarily one-directional:

- Players purchase the game or pay ongoing subscriptions.

- Players buy cosmetic items, expansions, or boosts directly from the developer or publisher.

- Any secondary trading of items is often against the terms of service and unauthorized.

The result is a closed economy where the developer and publisher receive all the monetary gains. Players might enjoy entertainment value, community, and personal accomplishments, but they rarely see financial returns. Their time and effort in the game world primarily benefit the company's bottom line.

2. The New Paradigm: Two-Way (or Multi-Directional) Value Flow

In P2E environments, the situation changes fundamentally:

- Players can earn in-game tokens by completing quests, winning matches, or contributing to the ecosystem in meaningful ways.

- These tokens, often fungible and tradeable, can be sold on external cryptocurrency exchanges for other cryptos or fiat currency.

- Players can also acquire rare NFTs either through gameplay or purchasing them early and then resell them later if their value increases.

- Developers may still earn revenue from initial asset sales, marketplace fees, or token distribution. However, a significant portion of the economic value is now available to the player community itself.

This new system incentivizes players to invest time and skill into the game because their efforts directly translate into financial opportunities. Over time, a balanced and sustainable P2E model can create stronger, more engaged communities. Players have a stake in the success of the game: if the player base grows and the game's economy flourishes, asset values rise, benefiting everyone.

3. Implications for Game Design and Player Motivation

The shift from a traditional to a P2E model influences game design. Developers must think carefully about balancing economic incentives with enjoyable gameplay. If earning becomes too easy, the in-game currency might inflate and lose value. If it's too hard, players might not feel rewarded enough to continue.

Moreover, not all players will focus solely on profits. Many still want fun, narrative depth, creativity, and community. In a well-designed P2E ecosystem, the enjoyment of the game and the potential to earn value should coexist symbiotically. One without the other risks alienating portions of the player base. For example, a game that focuses purely on yield farming and token generation may attract short-term speculators who leave once profits dwindle. On the other hand, a rich gameplay experience with minimal economic incentives might fail to stand out in an increasingly competitive market.

4. Attracting and Retaining Players Through Value Creation

When players know their time and skill can result in real value, they may be more invested in the game's long-term success. This leads to a more stable and dedicated player community. It also means that developers need to maintain player trust and ensure fairness. Any perception that the developer is manipulating the economy or playing favorites can lead to a loss of faith and a decline in the asset values.

By aligning incentives—where developers earn by making a better product, and players earn by actively participating—P2E can create a virtuous cycle of growth. Developers are motivated to create engaging content because it keeps players active, which sustains the economy and maintains or increases asset values. Players, in turn, are motivated to contribute positively, attract new players, and foster a healthy community, as these efforts raise the overall prosperity of the ecosystem.

Player Governance and Community Influence

A hallmark of many blockchain-based games is the decentralization of decision-making. Instead of top-down control where developers unilaterally decide every update and change, P2E ecosystems often distribute power to players through governance tokens and DAOs (Decentralized Autonomous Organizations). These structures allow the community to influence game direction, token economics, and other key aspects of the ecosystem.

1. What Are DAOs and Governance Tokens?

A DAO is a decentralized organization governed by the collective votes of its token holders. Instead of traditional corporate hierarchies, DAOs rely on smart contracts— transparent, automated rules on the blockchain—for proposals, voting, and decision implementation. Governance tokens represent the voting power within the DAO. The more tokens you hold, the more influence you have over decisions.

In a gaming context, a DAO might influence:

- Economic policies: Adjusting token emission rates, rewards distributions, or fees.

- Content priorities: Choosing which game features to develop first.

- Community rules: Setting guidelines to ensure fair play, handling disputes, or banning exploitative behavior.

- Treasury management: Deciding how to use funds collected from marketplace fees or other revenue streams for community benefit.

2. How Governance Increases Value

Giving players a voice in shaping the game fosters a sense of ownership, accountability, and community pride. When players believe their opinions matter, they are more likely to remain engaged, invest time and resources, and advocate for the game to others. This involvement can enhance the game's reputation, attract new players, and increase demand for the game's tokens and NFTs.

Moreover, a well-functioning DAO can adapt quickly to changing market conditions. If the game's economy experiences inflation, the DAO can vote to introduce token sinks or reduce rewards. If players find certain features unfair, they can propose and vote on solutions, thereby continuously improving the ecosystem's sustainability and fairness. This responsiveness can stabilize asset values and maintain trust.

3. Balancing Developer Vision and Community Input

While DAOs empower players, developers still have an important role. They build the initial infrastructure, set the initial token distribution, and guide the ecosystem's vision. A healthy balance is crucial:

- **Foundational Control:** Early in a game's lifecycle, developers may retain a larger share of governance tokens or employ a more centralized decision-making structure to ensure that the original vision is realized and not derailed by immediate community whims.

- **Progressive Decentralization:** Over time, as the community matures and demonstrates competence, developers can gradually relinquish control. This "progressive decentralization" allows the ecosystem to become more player-driven without descending into chaos.

This delicate dance ensures that both the developer's long-term vision and the community's evolving desires are accounted for. When done right, this synergy can enhance the game's value proposition.

4. Avoiding Governance Pitfalls

DAOs and governance systems are not without challenges:

- **Voter Apathy:** If only a small fraction of token holders vote, decisions may not reflect the community's true will. Incentivizing participation is crucial—perhaps through rewards for voting or reputation systems.

- **Whale Influence:** Large token holders (often called "whales") can disproportionately sway outcomes. Mechanisms like quadratic voting or token lock-ups can mitigate such imbalances.

- **Complexity and Education:** Players accustomed to traditional games may find DAOs confusing. Providing user-friendly interfaces, educational materials, and transparent communication can lower the barrier to participation.

Despite these hurdles, player governance aligns deeply with the ethos of decentralized economies. By involving players directly in decision-making, the ecosystem becomes more resilient, transparent, and community-driven—enhancing overall value and trust.

Case Studies: Value Creation in Action

To understand how these principles manifest in real-world scenarios, let's consider a few examples where scarcity, utility, community consensus, play-to-earn models, and player governance converge to create value.

1. Axie Infinity: Breeding, SLP, and Community Governance

Axie Infinity, a pioneer in P2E gaming, revolves around Axies—NFT creatures that players breed, train, and battle. Several key aspects drive value:

- **Scarcity and Utility:**

Each Axie is unique, with distinct genetic traits. Breeding Axies requires Smooth Love Potion (SLP), a fungible token earned through gameplay. Rare traits can make Axies more valuable, as they can win battles or produce desirable offspring.

- **Play-to-Earn Incentives:**

Players earn SLP by battling in the game. As demand for breeding Axies grows, the value of SLP can rise, allowing skilled players to profit from their efforts.

- **Community Consensus and Culture:**

Axie Infinity's community strongly influences which Axie traits are most prized. Over time, certain lineages or cosmetics become status symbols.

- **Governance Tokens (AXS) and Player Influence:**

AXS, the governance token, gives holders a say in the game's future development and treasury management. As the community participates in governance decisions—such as adjusting SLP emissions—they help maintain economic stability, thereby preserving asset value.

This interplay of factors has seen Axie Infinity NFTs and tokens achieve substantial market value at various times, reflecting how carefully orchestrated scarcity, utility, and community-driven economics can succeed.

2. The Sandbox: Virtual Land and User-Generated Content

The Sandbox is a virtual world where land parcels, represented by NFTs, form the basis of its economy.

- **Rarity and Utility of Land:**

The world's land supply is finite, enforcing scarcity. Land is not just a decorative asset—it's a platform for creators to build games, host events, or run virtual businesses. This tangible utility, combined with scarcity, drives land value.

- **Play-to-Earn Incentives Through Content Creation:**

While not all players "play" in a traditional sense, creators earn by building engaging experiences that attract visitors, potentially generating income through in-game currency (SAND) or renting their land to others.

- **Community Consensus and Cultural Significance:**

The community's perception matters. Land parcels near high-profile partners or popular creators can fetch premium prices. Just as in the physical world, location and neighborhood reputation matter.

- **Governance and Decentralization:**

Over time, The Sandbox plans to increase player governance. As landowners and SAND holders guide development choices, the community shapes the direction of this metaverse. Active involvement can sustain a vibrant economy and maintain or even increase asset values.

3. Decentraland: Social Spaces and DAO Governance

Decentraland is a fully decentralized virtual world governed by its users. Here, scarcity, community involvement, and governance come together:

- **Scarcity of LAND NFTs:**

Virtual land (LAND) parcels are finite. Owning prime real estate in popular districts can provide both social prestige and economic opportunity. LAND can host art galleries, virtual stores, games, or events, each with its own revenue potential.

- **Social Utility and Consensus:**

Many players value Decentraland not just for formal gameplay but as a social platform. Communities form around districts dedicated to art, music, or education. The cultural life of these areas influences land values.

- **Play-to-Earn Elements:**

While Decentraland isn't a combat-based P2E game, players can earn from activities like play-to-earn casinos, events that distribute tokens, or selling items created using the builder tools.

- **DAO Governance:**

Decentraland's DAO enables the community to vote on policies, land usage guidelines, and treasury allocations. This player-driven governance ensures that changes to the world reflect collective preferences, bolstering trust and long-term stability.

The Interplay of Economics, Culture, and Technology

Value in virtual worlds is not merely a product of technical constraints or game mechanics; it's a rich interplay between economics, culture, and technology.

1. Economic Factors

Supply and demand drive fundamental economics. If a game carefully limits the supply of rare assets while demand grows, prices rise. If a game's tokenomics ensure balanced emission and consistent token sinks (ways for tokens to be spent or removed from circulation), the currency can maintain or increase its value. Proper economic design requires careful analysis, iterative testing, and responsiveness to player feedback.

2. Cultural and Social Dynamics

The success of P2E games and their economies is also cultural. Memes, lore, social influencers, and narratives can drive demand for certain items. Just as sneaker collectors covet specific limited-edition shoes due to cultural significance, gamers might chase after NFT collectibles linked to celebrated players, historical in-game events, or famous partnerships.

Communities often form subcultures within these worlds, each with their own value systems and traditions. Some players might value efficiency and gameplay advantages, while others appreciate rarity, artistry, or historical significance. The convergence of these perspectives forms a vibrant, ever-evolving marketplace of tastes and trends.

3. Technological Infrastructure

None of this is possible without robust technological infrastructure. Scalable blockchains, user-friendly wallets, intuitive NFT marketplaces, and secure smart contracts are crucial. High transaction costs or unreliable networks can deter players, reducing demand and value. Ongoing improvements in Layer-2 scaling, interoperability standards, and gaming-focused blockchains are lowering friction and increasing reliability, making value creation more accessible to a broader audience.

4. Regulatory and Ethical Considerations

As virtual economies grow, real-world governments and institutions take notice. Regulations around digital assets, taxation, anti-money laundering measures, and consumer protection could shape the future of P2E gaming. If players face onerous regulations or if the game's legal status becomes uncertain, confidence—and thus asset value—could suffer.

Ethical considerations also matter. Are play-to-earn models exploiting players by turning leisure into labor? Are developers designing economically manipulative systems? Transparency, fairness, and community involvement can address some of these concerns, ultimately supporting a healthier, more valuable ecosystem.

Sustaining Value in a Competitive Landscape

The surge of interest in P2E gaming has led to a crowded market. Dozens of projects launch every month, each vying for player attention and investment. How do ecosystems maintain and grow their value over time amid such competition?

1. Continuous Content and Feature Updates

Stagnation is the enemy of long-term value. Successful P2E worlds continually introduce new features, content updates, gameplay modes, and item releases. This steady drumbeat of innovation keeps the community engaged and attracts new players, thus sustaining demand for assets.

2. Balancing Speculation and Stability

Speculation can be a double-edged sword. While hype can drive prices up, it can also create volatility and risk. Long-term value stems from genuine utility and community attachment. Games must find a balance between celebrating rare collectibles and ensuring that speculative mania does not overshadow the core gameplay and community spirit.

3. Educating the Player Base

Players who understand the game's economics, governance mechanisms, and long-term roadmap make more informed decisions. Education—through guides, tutorials, workshops, and community AMAs—fosters trust and encourages responsible participation. Informed players are more likely to stay engaged, invest thoughtfully, and contribute positively.

4. Interoperability and Partnerships

As the metaverse concept expands, games that collaborate with others, share assets, or allow NFTs to move between ecosystems can create added value. When players can use the same NFT avatar across multiple worlds, the NFT's utility broadens, increasing its overall worth. Partnerships with major brands, influencers, or other blockchain projects can also bring attention and credibility to a game's economy.

The Ethical Dimension of Value Creation

As virtual worlds become places where people earn a livelihood, questions of ethics and fairness arise. This is not a trivial matter—value creation in gaming intersects with issues of labor, wealth distribution, community governance, and digital rights.

1. Equitable Access and Inclusion

If valuable assets become exorbitantly expensive, newcomers may feel excluded. Scholarship programs, where asset-wealthy players lend NFTs to newcomers in exchange for a share of earnings, have emerged as a way to lower the barrier to entry. Such initiatives can broaden participation and distribute value more equitably.

2. Preventing Exploitation

In some cases, players might be lured into an ecosystem by promises of quick earnings, only to find a harsh reality where early entrants reap outsized rewards, leaving latecomers as "exit liquidity." Responsible developers and communities must strive to create sustainable, merit-based systems that reward skill, creativity, and ongoing participation rather than just speculation or timing.

3. Balancing Fun and Profit Motives

Not every player wants to treat gaming as a job. Many value gaming as a form of entertainment, relaxation, or socialization. If the economic dimension overshadows the fun, the game could lose its cultural spark. Ethical design means offering various playstyles: those who want to focus on earning can do so, while those who just want to explore, create, and socialize can also find their niche.

4. Environmental Considerations

The environmental cost of blockchain technology, especially those using proof-of-work consensus, has been a point of controversy. As the industry moves toward more efficient proof-of-stake and Layer-2 solutions, games must consider their environmental impact. A community that cares about sustainability may value assets and platforms that align with greener practices, indirectly affecting perceived asset value.

Looking Ahead: The Evolving Landscape of Digital Value

We are still in the early stages of understanding and shaping value in virtual worlds. What might the future hold?

1. Greater Interoperability and Metaverse Integration

As multiple virtual worlds connect, assets like NFTs could function as universal digital passports. A rare character skin earned in one game might serve as a status symbol in another. Interoperability standards could create a broader network of value, where items gain utility and recognition across the metaverse, not just within a single platform.

2. More Sophisticated Economic Models

Future games may integrate advanced economic theories, artificial intelligence-driven market mechanisms, and dynamic tokenomic adjustments to maintain equilibrium. These models could result in stable, predictable growth rather than boom-bust cycles, attracting more mainstream users who crave reliability.

3. Cross-Pollination with DeFi and Creator Economies

We're already seeing overlaps between gaming and decentralized finance. As these sectors mature, players might stake their gaming tokens in DeFi protocols, use gaming NFTs as collateral for loans, or earn interest on their in-game currency. Similarly, creator economies—where artists and developers profit from user-generated content—will merge with P2E, enabling creators to earn royalties every time their NFT assets are resold.

4. Real-World Consequences

As virtual economies grow, they will influence the real-world economy. Players in developing countries might rely on P2E games for income. Virtual goods could become part of personal investment portfolios. Digital fashion, real estate, and art might command prices comparable to their physical counterparts. This shift demands that we think carefully about regulation, consumer protection, taxation, and the broader socio-economic implications.

Conclusion

Value creation in virtual worlds is a multidimensional process shaped by rarity, utility, community consensus, decentralized governance, and sustainable play-to-earn models. These factors collectively redefine what it means to participate in a game. Players are no longer mere consumers; they are stakeholders, investors, creators, and sometimes employees or business owners within digital ecosystems.

The traditional separation between "real" and "virtual" value is eroding. Digital assets are proving their worth not only as entertainment but also as economic resources, cultural artifacts, and instruments of social identity. As these ecosystems mature, the interplay between technology, economics, culture, and ethics will determine their trajectory.

By understanding how value is created and maintained within virtual worlds, we equip ourselves to navigate this new era of gaming, finance, and community-building. Whether you're a casual player looking to understand why certain items command eye-popping prices, a developer striving to design a stable economy, or an investor assessing the long-term potential of a blockchain-based world, these foundational insights are crucial. Virtual value is here to stay, and its importance—both within gaming and beyond—will only continue to grow as the metaverse expands and intertwines with our everyday lives.

PART II: GETTING STARTED WITH PLAY-TO-EARN

Chapter 4: Essential Tools and Setup

Embarking on your journey into play-to-earn (P2E) gaming and the expansive world of blockchain-based virtual economies requires a robust set of tools. Unlike traditional video games, entering P2E ecosystems often involves handling cryptocurrencies, navigating decentralized applications (dApps), and securely managing digital assets with real-world value. Understanding how to set up your digital wallet, choose reliable cryptocurrency exchanges, and maintain rigorous security practices will lay a strong foundation for long-term success and peace of mind.

In this chapter, we'll explore the essential tools you need to participate in P2E games and virtual economies. From selecting and configuring digital wallets to learning how to buy and sell tokens on exchanges, we'll cover the practical steps that transform your gaming sessions into economically meaningful experiences. We'll also delve into best practices for safeguarding your assets, mitigating risks, and ensuring that your journey remains both profitable and enjoyable.

Digital Wallets: Your Gateway to the Blockchain

Why You Need a Digital Wallet

In traditional gaming, your items, achievements, and progress are stored on the developer's servers. You have no direct control over these records; at best, you access them via your account credentials. In contrast, blockchain-based games rely on decentralized ownership. Your in-game currency, NFTs, and other digital assets exist on a blockchain, secured by cryptography and accessible only through your private keys. A digital wallet is the software tool that allows you to hold, send, receive, and interact with these blockchain assets.

Software Wallets vs. Hardware Wallets

There are two primary categories of digital wallets you need to be aware of:

1. **Software Wallets (Hot Wallets):** These are applications installed on your computer or mobile device. They are often user-friendly and convenient, allowing quick access to your assets. Because they are connected to the internet, software wallets are considered "hot." While they provide ease of use, they are potentially more vulnerable to online threats.

2. **Hardware Wallets (Cold Wallets):** Hardware wallets are physical devices resembling USB drives. They store your private keys offline, providing an extra layer of security. To sign transactions, you must physically connect the hardware wallet and confirm actions on the device itself. Hardware wallets are less convenient but far more secure, making them a preferred option for storing large amounts of valuable tokens and NFTs.

Popular Wallet Choices

- **MetaMask:**

One of the most widely used Ethereum-based wallets, MetaMask is a browser extension and mobile app that seamlessly integrates with decentralized applications. Many P2E games run on Ethereum or compatible networks, making MetaMask a go-to choice. Its user-friendly interface and widespread support across blockchains and dApps ensure you can engage with NFTs, game tokens, and governance platforms effortlessly.

- **Trust Wallet:**

A mobile-only wallet, Trust Wallet supports multiple blockchains, including Ethereum, Binance Smart Chain, and others. It's known for its ease of use, built-in dApp browser, and integrated NFT support. For players on the go or those preferring a mobile-first experience, Trust Wallet is a strong contender.

- **Phantom, Keplr, and Others:**

Different blockchain ecosystems have their own native wallets. For example, if you're playing a game on the Solana blockchain, you might use Phantom. For Cosmos-based ecosystems, Keplr is popular. The choice depends on the network hosting your chosen P2E game.

Setting Up Your Digital Wallet Step-by-Step

Let's walk through the general process using MetaMask as an example:

1. **Installation:**

Visit the official MetaMask website or your browser's extension store. Follow the prompts to install the extension or mobile app.

2. **Creating a New Wallet:**

Once installed, open MetaMask and click "Create a Wallet." Set a strong password. The app will then generate a seed phrase (also called a recovery phrase), typically 12 to 24 random words.

3. **Securing Your Seed Phrase:**

Write down the seed phrase on paper and store it offline in a secure place. Never share this phrase with anyone. If you lose it, you lose access to your wallet; if someone else learns it, they can access and steal your funds.

4. **Confirming the Seed Phrase:**

MetaMask will ask you to confirm your seed phrase by selecting the words in the correct order. This ensures you've recorded it accurately.

5. **Ready to Go:**

With your wallet created, you can now receive tokens or NFTs. You can also connect MetaMask to various P2E games and marketplaces that support browser wallets. When a site requests permission to interact with your wallet, carefully review the permissions and confirm only if you trust the site.

Connecting Your Wallet to a P2E Game

Most blockchain games feature a "Connect Wallet" button. Clicking it triggers a request in your wallet to confirm the connection. Review the request to ensure the correct site is connecting, then approve. Once connected, the game can read your wallet's public addresses (but not your private keys) and access the NFTs or tokens you own, allowing you to interact seamlessly.

Exchanges and Marketplaces: Acquiring and Trading Assets

Why Use Exchanges?

The P2E model often requires you to hold cryptocurrencies to get started. For example, you might need ETH to buy in-game NFTs or a game's native token to participate in certain earning activities. Cryptocurrency exchanges allow you to:

- Convert fiat currency (USD, EUR, etc.) into crypto.
- Swap one cryptocurrency for another.
- Sell your in-game earnings back into fiat if you wish.

Exchanges serve as gateways, letting you move between traditional finance and the blockchain ecosystem. They provide liquidity, making it easy to enter and exit P2E ecosystems.

Centralized vs. Decentralized Exchanges

1. **Centralized Exchanges (CEXs):**

Examples include Binance, Coinbase, and Kraken. These platforms are managed by companies that oversee user accounts, custody of funds, and regulatory compliance. CEXs typically offer user-friendly interfaces, high liquidity, and multiple trading pairs. On the downside, using a CEX means trusting a third party with your funds, and some regions may have restricted access or require identification (KYC).

2. **Decentralized Exchanges (DEXs):**
3. DEXs like Uniswap, SushiSwap, or PancakeSwap are autonomous protocols running on blockchain smart contracts. They allow peer-to-peer trading without intermediaries. When using a DEX, you remain in control of your private keys, enhancing security and privacy. However, DEXs may have lower liquidity, less intuitive interfaces, and potentially higher transaction fees on certain networks.

How to Buy Your First Tokens

To illustrate the process, let's assume you want to buy Ether (ETH) on a centralized exchange and transfer it to your MetaMask for use in a P2E game:

1. **Create an Account:**

Sign up on a reputable CEX like Coinbase or Binance. Complete any required identity verification (KYC) steps.

2. **Fund Your Account:**

Deposit fiat currency using a bank transfer, credit card, or other supported payment methods. Once your account is funded, you can purchase ETH directly.

3. **Buy Crypto:**

Navigate to the trading section and select the appropriate trading pair (e.g., ETH/USD). Enter the amount you want to buy and confirm the trade. Your account balance will reflect the purchased ETH.

4. **Withdraw to Your Wallet:**

Locate the "Withdraw" or "Send" option on the exchange. Paste your MetaMask Ethereum address and confirm the withdrawal. After network confirmation, your ETH will appear in your MetaMask wallet.

Converting Game Earnings to Fiat

If you've earned tokens from a P2E game and want to cash out:

1. Transfer Tokens to an Exchange:

If your tokens are not directly tradable for fiat on a centralized exchange, you may first swap them for a widely accepted cryptocurrency like ETH or a stablecoin like USDT using a DEX. Then send the ETH or USDT to your CEX account.

2. Sell Crypto for Fiat:

On the CEX, convert your crypto to fiat currency.

3. Withdraw to Your Bank Account:

Finally, withdraw the fiat back to your chosen withdrawal method. Timeframes vary depending on your bank and the exchange.

NFT Marketplaces

Beyond buying and selling tokens, many P2E games rely on NFTs for in-game assets. While some games have their own internal marketplaces, many NFTs trade on general-purpose platforms. Two popular marketplaces are:

- **OpenSea:**

The largest NFT marketplace, supporting Ethereum and other chains. OpenSea allows you to browse collections, place bids, and trade NFTs using Ether or other supported tokens.

- **LooksRare, Blur, and Other Competitors:**

Multiple NFT marketplaces offer various incentives, such as lower fees or token rewards for trading. Keep an eye on where your particular game's community is most active.

Game-Specific Marketplaces

Some P2E titles, like Axie Infinity or The Sandbox, maintain their own integrated marketplaces. Here, you can buy game-specific NFTs directly without leaving the ecosystem. Such marketplaces often charge lower fees and ensure that the listed NFTs are compatible with the game.

Fees and Gas Considerations

When using exchanges and NFT marketplaces, be mindful of:

- **Exchange Fees:**

CEXs charge trading fees, usually a small percentage of the trade volume. DEXs often have lower protocol fees but can incur high network transaction costs.

- **Gas Fees:**

On Ethereum, each transaction costs "gas," which can be expensive during network congestion. Consider using Layer-2 solutions (like Polygon or Arbitrum) or alternative blockchains that offer cheaper fees. Many P2E games choose less congested networks to keep transaction costs reasonable.

Security and Best Practices: Protecting Your Assets

Why Security Matters

In the world of blockchain gaming, security cannot be overstated. Unlike traditional gaming items that can be restored by a developer if compromised, your blockchain assets are under your sole control. If someone gains access to your private keys or seed phrase, they can drain your wallet, and no central authority can reverse the transaction. Securing your assets is non-negotiable.

Seed Phrases and Private Keys

Your seed phrase is the master key to your wallet. It can restore your entire wallet, including all tokens and NFTs, if you lose your device. Consider the following best practices:

- **Never Share Your Seed Phrase:**

No legitimate support member, admin, or developer will ever ask for it. If someone does, it's a scam.

- **Offline Storage:**

Write your seed phrase on paper and store it in a secure location. Consider a fireproof safe or a secure deposit box. Do not store it digitally on your phone or computer, as hackers can access those environments.

- **Multiple Copies:**

If desired, create multiple written copies of your seed phrase and store them in different secure places. This reduces the risk of losing everything if one location is compromised.

Using Hardware Wallets

For those holding substantial value, hardware wallets like Ledger or Trezor offer unparalleled security. By keeping your private keys offline, they protect you from a wide range of online threats. To use one:

1. **Purchase from Official Sources:**

Buy hardware wallets directly from the manufacturer or authorized resellers to avoid tampered devices.

2. **Initialize the Device and Write Down the Recovery Seed:**

Follow the setup instructions, generate your seed, and secure it offline.

3. **Connect to Your Software Wallet:**

You can connect your hardware wallet to MetaMask or other interfaces, using it to confirm transactions. Your private keys remain on the hardware device, which you must physically approve to sign.

Phishing, Scams, and Social Engineering

Scammers often exploit the novelty of blockchain technology. Stay vigilant:

- **Check URLs:**

Always verify the URL of the website you're visiting. Phishers create copycat sites that look identical to legitimate ones but steal your info.

- **Use Official Links:**

Bookmark the official sites of your favorite P2E games, NFT marketplaces, and exchanges. Rely on these bookmarks rather than clicking random links in emails or chat messages.

- **Don't Rush:**

If you receive an urgent message claiming you must act immediately or lose funds, it's likely a scam. Take your time to verify the request through official channels.

- **Watch Out for Fake Airdrops:**

Airdrops are free token distributions. Scammers often advertise "too-good-to-be-true" airdrops, luring you to connect your wallet to a malicious dApp that drains your assets. Only claim airdrops from projects you trust and have verified independently.

Maintaining Operational Security (OpSec)

OpSec refers to the measures you take to prevent personal information leaks that criminals can exploit:

- **Anonymous Identities:**

Consider using a pseudonym or dedicated online identity for your crypto and gaming activities. The less personal information you share, the harder it is for scammers to target you.

- **Separate Devices:**

If possible, use a dedicated device (like an inexpensive second smartphone or a separate computer) for crypto transactions. This minimizes the risk of malware infecting your main device.

- **Regular Updates and Security Checks:**

Keep your wallet software, antivirus programs, and operating systems updated. Regularly run malware scans.

Irreversibility of Transactions

Blockchain transactions are irreversible. If you send tokens to the wrong address or approve a malicious contract, there's no recourse. Always double-check addresses, transaction details, and contract permissions before clicking "confirm."

Revoke Unused Permissions

When you connect your wallet to a dApp, you often grant permission to spend certain tokens. Over time, these permissions accumulate. Use tools like Etherscan's "Token Approvals" page or similar blockchain explorers to review and revoke unnecessary approvals. Reducing the number of dApps that can access your funds mitigates risk if one of them is compromised.

Beyond the Basics: Additional Tools and Considerations

Portfolio Trackers

As you diversify into multiple P2E games, NFT collections, and different blockchains, keeping track of your holdings becomes challenging. Portfolio trackers like Zerion, Zapper, or Debank aggregate data from multiple addresses and networks into a single dashboard. They show your token balances, NFT holdings, and sometimes even estimated asset values. Regularly checking your portfolio ensures you stay informed and can make timely decisions.

Gas Fee Optimization Tools

On networks like Ethereum, gas fees can spike due to congestion. Tools like Gas Now or Etherscan's gas tracker provide real-time fee data, helping you choose the optimal time to transact. Some wallets allow you to set custom gas fees or schedule transactions to save money.

Bridging Assets Between Blockchains

As P2E evolves, multiple blockchains may be involved. You might own NFTs on Ethereum but want to use them on a game running on Polygon. Blockchain bridges allow you to move assets between chains. Before bridging:

- **Check Legitimacy:**

Use only well-known, audited bridging solutions.

- **Understand Costs and Risks:**

Bridges may charge fees, and occasionally they can be exploited. Keep yourself informed.

Staying Informed About Updates and Security Patches

The blockchain and gaming industries evolve rapidly. Follow the official social media accounts, forums, or Discord servers of the games you play. Join community groups, read newsletters, and stay current with the latest news. Early awareness of upcoming features, migrations, or security patches can help you avoid hiccups and capitalize on opportunities.

Practical Tips and Strategies

Start Small and Learn Gradually

If you're new to blockchain gaming, don't invest heavily upfront. Begin with a small amount to learn the ropes. Experiment with wallet setup, buying and selling small token amounts, and maybe acquiring a low-cost NFT to understand how the process works. As your confidence grows, you can scale up.

Use Separate Wallets for Different Purposes

Just as you might have separate bank accounts for savings, checking, and investing, consider using multiple wallets:

- **Main Wallet (Cold Storage):**

Store valuable NFTs and large token holdings offline in a hardware wallet.

- **Spending Wallet (Hot Wallet):**

Keep a smaller amount of funds here for regular gameplay, trading, or testing new dApps. If this wallet is compromised, your losses are limited.

- **Experimentation Wallet:**

Use this wallet for trying out new games or platforms. Keep minimal funds here as it's your "testing ground."

Check Smart Contract Details

Many dApps, including P2E games, require you to interact with their smart contracts. Consider looking up the contract's details on a block explorer:

- **Verify Authenticity:**

Ensure you're interacting with the official contract.

- **Read Community Feedback:**

If a contract or project is suspicious, community forums or social media discussions often raise red flags.

Regular Backups of Your Seed Phrases

If you rely on a single piece of paper that could be lost, stolen, or damaged, you risk losing everything. Consider:

- **Multiple Secure Locations:**

Store duplicate copies in different secure places.

- **Protected Storage:**

Some people engrave their seed phrases on metal plates designed to withstand fire and water damage. This might seem extreme, but for large holdings, it's a worthy precaution.

Use Reputable Services

When dealing with exchanges, only trust well-established platforms with strong security records. Look for audits, insurance policies, or regulatory compliance. For NFT marketplaces, confirm that the platform is recognized and widely used by the community.

Understanding the Broader Ecosystem

Layer-2 Solutions and Sidechains

The Ethereum blockchain, while popular, can suffer from high fees and slow transaction times. Layer-2 solutions (like Arbitrum, Optimism) and sidechains (like Polygon) offer cheaper, faster transactions. Many P2E games opt to build on these networks to ensure that players can interact with the game frequently without incurring exorbitant costs.

Setting up your wallet to connect to these networks is usually straightforward. In MetaMask, for example, you can add custom RPC endpoints or use tools like Chainlist to quickly configure multiple networks. Once set up, you can easily switch networks at the top of the MetaMask interface.

Interacting With Decentralized Applications (dApps)

To fully participate in P2E games, you'll often need to interact with their dApps. This might mean signing transactions that:

- Approve a game to spend your tokens.
- Mint or transfer NFTs.
- Join liquidity pools or stake tokens to earn yields.

Always read the confirmation prompts carefully. If something looks off—like a request to spend an enormous number of tokens—decline and double-check.

DAOs and Governance Participation

Some P2E ecosystems allow token holders to participate in governance. Voting on proposals, treasury allocations, or new game features is part of the experience. To vote, you connect your wallet to the DAO's interface and sign a message or transaction that records your choice. While participating in governance doesn't necessarily require specialized tools, understanding how to sign messages securely and verify that you're on the correct DAO platform is important.

Managing Taxes, Compliance, and Legal Considerations

While not strictly a "tool," knowledge about the legal implications of P2E activities is essential. Depending on your jurisdiction, you may owe taxes on cryptocurrency earnings or profits made from selling NFTs.

- **Track Your Transactions:**

Use portfolio trackers, spreadsheets, or specialized tax software to record every trade, sale, or token swap. Detailed records make tax filing easier.

- **Consult Professionals:**

If you're earning substantial amounts, consider consulting a tax professional or accountant familiar with cryptocurrency regulations in your country. Being proactive can prevent headaches later.

- **Check Local Regulations:**

Some countries have strict regulations on cryptocurrencies. Ensure that playing P2E games and trading digital assets is legal and that you understand any restrictions on converting earnings to your local currency.

Handling Technical Issues and Troubleshooting

Common Problems and Their Solutions

- **Transaction Stuck or Pending:**

Sometimes transactions get stuck if gas fees are too low. Most wallets allow you to speed up the transaction by paying a higher fee. Alternatively, you can cancel the transaction if not yet confirmed.

- **Wrong Network Selected:**

If you don't see your assets, check if your wallet is connected to the correct network. For instance, your NFTs might be on Polygon, but your wallet is currently viewing Ethereum mainnet.

- **Connection Issues With dApps:**

If a site fails to connect to your wallet, try refreshing the page, clearing your browser cache, or reconnecting your wallet. Ensure you're using a supported browser or the correct version of the mobile app.

- **Unrecognized Tokens or NFTs:**

Some tokens or NFTs might not display automatically in your wallet. You can manually add them by inserting the token's contract address. This doesn't affect the asset's presence in your wallet, just its visibility.

Customer Support and Community Help

Blockchain technology and P2E games may lack traditional customer support. Instead, you often rely on community-driven forums, Discord servers, or Telegram groups. Approach these communities with caution:

- **Official Channels:**

Only trust official communication channels listed on the project's official website or social media. Scammers thrive in unofficial or copycat channels.

- **Public Queries Over Private DMs:**

Posting your question publicly allows other community members to verify the legitimacy of responses. Scammers often try to lure you into private chats to phish information.

- **Never Share Sensitive Data:**

Even if you believe you are talking to an admin or moderator, never share your seed phrase, private keys, or passwords.

Preparing for the Future: Scalability and User Experience Improvements

As P2E ecosystems evolve, so too will the tools and services that support them. Developers and entrepreneurs are working to improve user experiences and reduce complexity:

- **User-Friendly Wallets:**

Expect to see wallets that don't force users to manage seed phrases directly. Social recovery, hardware-based account abstraction, or smart contract wallets may make the onboarding process more intuitive.

- **Built-In Fiat Gateways:**

Future NFT marketplaces and P2E platforms may integrate fiat gateways, allowing you to buy assets directly with credit cards or bank transfers without separately using an exchange. This simplifies the user journey.

- **Gaming-Focused Launchers and Hubs:**

Imagine a hub application that integrates multiple P2E games, tracks your NFTs and tokens across them, and suggests new titles based on your interests. Such tools could streamline the entire experience.

- **Enhanced Security Standards:**

Industry standards and best practices will continue to mature, with regular security audits, open-source code reviews, and insurance funds becoming common. This collectively reduces the risk of scams and exploits.

Conclusion

Setting up essential tools and securing your digital assets form the bedrock of a successful and rewarding experience in the world of P2E gaming. By understanding how to choose and configure wallets, interact safely with exchanges and NFT marketplaces, and follow strict security protocols, you protect your hard-earned value and can confidently explore new opportunities in virtual economies.

The early stages of any new technology come with learning curves, and blockchain gaming is no exception. The processes described in this chapter—installing a wallet, navigating an exchange, verifying contract addresses—might feel intricate at first. However, with practice, these steps become second nature. Over time, you'll develop a personal workflow that aligns with your risk tolerance, investment goals, and gaming preferences.

As the ecosystem grows, more user-friendly solutions, better documentation, and clearer guidelines will emerge, further simplifying the on-ramp for newcomers. For now, careful due diligence, ongoing education, and deliberate security measures will ensure that you can focus on what truly matters: playing, earning, and enjoying the vibrant metaverse of blockchain-based gaming.

Key Takeaways from Chapter 4:

1. **Digital Wallets Are Essential:**
   - A wallet stores your tokens and NFTs.
   - Keep your seed phrase secure and never share it.
   - Consider a hardware wallet for substantial holdings.

2. **Exchanges and Marketplaces Bridge Fiat and Crypto:**
   - Use reputable centralized or decentralized exchanges to buy and sell tokens.
   - Explore NFT marketplaces for in-game assets, always verifying authenticity.

3. **Security is Paramount:**
   - Protect your private keys and seed phrases.
   - Beware of phishing scams, fake airdrops, and suspicious links.
   - Regularly review and revoke unnecessary token approvals.

4. **Additional Tools for Management and Safety:**
   - Use portfolio trackers, gas fee trackers, and bridging services wisely.
   - Stay informed about network conditions and game updates.

5. **Continuous Learning and Caution:**
   - Start with small amounts, practice on less valuable assets, and grow as you gain confidence.
   - Engage with official community channels, verify information, and be patient.

By mastering these essentials, you equip yourself with the capabilities to thrive in the P2E landscape. Your digital wallet, chosen marketplace, and security toolkit form a powerful triumvirate enabling you to navigate blockchain games' economic dimensions confidently. As you proceed to the next chapters, you'll build upon these foundations to strategize, evaluate tokenomics, and engage more deeply with the virtual economies that promise both entertainment and tangible rewards.

Chapter 5: Choosing the Right Play-to-Earn Game

With hundreds of play-to-earn (P2E) games emerging across various blockchain networks, choosing the right one can feel overwhelming. Each project promises something unique—be it a cutting-edge metaverse, a skill-based competitive arena, or a rich narrative-driven world with rare NFT collectibles. But not all titles are created equal. Some offer sustainable ecosystems, while others may be short-lived experiments or even scams dressed in attractive marketing.

Your choice of P2E game can profoundly impact your experience and long-term profitability. The most rewarding games align with your interests, skill sets, and risk tolerance. They also have sound tokenomics, transparent development roadmaps, trustworthy teams, and vibrant communities. In this chapter, we'll delve into the criteria you should consider before committing time, effort, and capital to a play-to-earn platform. By doing due diligence and carefully evaluating candidates, you improve your odds of finding not just a great game, but a sustainable and enjoyable ecosystem where your digital assets—and personal engagement—can grow over time.

Evaluating Game Mechanics: Matching Your Playstyle

1. Start with Genre and Gameplay Preferences

Before diving into whitepapers or tokenomics, consider what kind of game you genuinely enjoy. Are you drawn to strategic turn-based combat, fast-paced action, collectible card battling, immersive role-playing, casual farming simulations, or esports-level PvP? The genre and fundamental gameplay loop will profoundly influence how you earn and what kind of rewards are possible.

- **Strategy Games:**

Turn-based strategy or real-time tactics games often reward careful planning and resource management. These titles might offer NFTs representing units, equipment, or territory. If you excel at thinking ahead and executing long-term plans, a strategy-based P2E might be rewarding both financially and personally.

- **Role-Playing Games (RPGs):**

RPGs allow you to develop characters over time, enhance their stats, and acquire rare gear. P2E RPGs might reward grinding or quest completion with valuable tokens or NFTs. If you love story, character progression, and world-building, RPGs can provide a more narrative-rich environment for earning.

- **Collectible Card Games (CCGs):**

In CCGs, strategic deck-building and understanding card synergies are key. Rare cards often become valuable NFTs.

If you enjoy the intellectual challenge of card strategy and trading rare collectibles, a CCG-based P2E could be ideal.

- **Simulation and Idle Games:**

Farming, city-building, or idle games reward consistent engagement over time. They might distribute tokens for completing daily tasks or yield NFTs for constructing special buildings. These games are often less skill-intensive and more about time management, making them suitable for players who prefer a relaxed, low-stress approach.

- **Esports and Competitive PvP:**

If you crave competitive adrenaline, look for P2E games that lean into esports. High skill players can earn significant rewards from tournaments, ranked matches, and seasonal leaderboards. This is riskier—your earnings depend on your performance—but potentially very lucrative if you excel.

2. Identifying Core Earning Loops

Different genres reward players in various ways. Understanding these loops clarifies if a game's earning potential aligns with your strengths:

- **Grinding and Farming:**

RPGs or simulation games might let you "farm" tokens by completing routine tasks—such as harvesting crops, defeating common enemies, or exploring dungeons. This can create a steady trickle of income if you invest enough time.

- **Trading and Speculation:**

Collectible card and NFT-heavy games might rely on you flipping valuable assets. If you have a knack for predicting market trends and enjoy the thrill of trading, consider games with robust NFT marketplaces and collectible scarcity.

- **Strategic Dominance:**

Strategy or MOBA-style P2E games may funnel earnings to top players or those controlling valuable in-game territories. Here, skill and planning lead to big rewards.

- **Crafting and Creation:**

Some virtual worlds emphasize player-generated content. Building structures, designing skins, or crafting rare items might earn you tokens. Artistic or creative players can monetize their talents in these environments.

3. Enjoyment vs. Profit Motive

While the focus in P2E is often on earnings, don't ignore the importance of enjoyment. If the gameplay loop bores you, sustaining long hours to earn tokens becomes a chore. Over time, only games that you genuinely enjoy—regardless of earnings—are likely to keep you engaged and motivated, especially if market conditions turn unfavorable.

Analyzing the Tokenomics: Ensuring Long-Term Sustainability

The long-term viability of a P2E game hinges on tokenomics—the financial architecture underlying its in-game currencies, NFTs, and reward systems. Sound tokenomics strike a balance between rewarding players and maintaining asset value. Conversely, poorly designed tokenomics can lead to inflation, reduced earnings, and a mass exodus of players.

1. Understanding Token Issuance and Utility

Ask these questions when evaluating a game's tokens:

- **How Are Tokens Created or Earned?**

Are tokens minted as rewards for completing tasks, winning matches, or staking NFTs? A sustainable model usually limits token issuance or ties it to skill-based achievements rather than simple time spent.

- **What Is the Token's Utility?**

Tokens should have meaningful uses within the game: buying NFTs, crafting items, breeding characters, entering tournaments, or influencing governance decisions. A token with no purpose beyond speculation will struggle to retain value.

- **Are There Token Sinks?**

A token sink is a mechanism that permanently removes tokens from circulation—such as spending them to upgrade NFTs or pay for entry fees. Without sinks, endless token issuance could cause inflation and devalue earnings.

2. Inflation vs. Deflation: Balancing the Economy

If too many tokens flood the market, their price will drop, diminishing player earnings. Conversely, if tokens are too scarce, players may feel the economy is inaccessible. Sustainable tokenomics implement careful balance:

- **Algorithmic Adjustments:**

Some games dynamically adjust token rewards based on player counts or token prices, maintaining equilibrium.

- **Multiple Token Systems:**

Complex ecosystems may use two tokens: one for governance and another for utility/rewards. For example, Axie Infinity uses AXS (governance) and SLP (utility), allowing for separate economic levers that stabilize prices.

- **Transparent Token Allocation:**

Check how tokens are distributed at launch. Are huge percentages reserved for developers or early investors? Such allocations can create selling pressure down the line. A more even distribution often indicates a fairer, more stable economy.

3. Reviewing Whitepapers and Litepapers

Most serious P2E projects release detailed whitepapers or litepapers outlining their tokenomics. Study these documents thoroughly:

- **Roadmap for Token Emission Reductions:**

Over time, many games plan to reduce reward rates to control inflation. Ensure the project has a clear schedule and rationale for such adjustments.

- **In-Game Economics:**

The whitepaper should explain how players use tokens within the ecosystem. Are there upcoming features that will add new utility to the token? Are partnerships or integrations planned that increase demand?

- **Developer Communication:**

Developers who are transparent about tokenomics, open to community feedback, and responsive to economic issues are more likely to steer the game through market volatility.

Checking the Roadmap and Team Credentials: Gauging Reliability and Vision

A promising concept and fancy website aren't enough. The real test lies in the project's roadmap—its step-by-step plan for growth—and the track record of the team behind it. Before investing time and resources into a P2E game, scrutinize the developers' professionalism, experience, and commitment.

1. A Realistic and Transparent Roadmap

A good roadmap should be publicly available, either on the official website, within the whitepaper, or on the project's social channels. Look for:

- **Clear Milestones:**

Does the roadmap list specific development stages: closed beta, open beta, mainnet launch, additional features, new NFT drops, marketplace expansions? Vague promises signal potential disorganization or lack of direction.

- **Feasible Timelines:**

Unrealistic deadlines raise red flags. Complex blockchain integrations and well-polished gameplay experiences take time. A roadmap that acknowledges potential delays or provides quarterly rather than weekly targets may be more credible.

- **Evidence of Progress:**

Has the team already delivered on initial promises? Check if the game has an alpha or beta version. Working prototypes, gameplay previews, or testnet trials indicate active development rather than pure hype.

2. The Team Behind the Project

P2E games involve complex elements: blockchain development, game design, economic modeling, and community management. Evaluate whether the team has the necessary expertise:

- **Credentials and Backgrounds:**

Look up the LinkedIn profiles of core team members. Do they have experience in the gaming industry, blockchain, or entrepreneurship? A seasoned developer or a known game designer adds credibility.

- **Advisors and Partnerships:**

Established advisors from reputable projects or partnerships with known brands (game studios, blockchain foundations, eSports organizations) can signal that the project passed some due diligence.

- **Transparency and Communication:**

Teams that show their faces, give interviews, host AMAs (Ask Me Anything sessions), and remain active on social media are generally more trustworthy. Anonymity doesn't automatically mean a scam, but a fully anonymous team raises the bar for skepticism.

3. Past Projects and Track Record

If the team has launched successful games or blockchain projects before, that's a strong indicator they can deliver again. Conversely, if you discover complaints about previous failed ventures or broken promises, proceed with caution. Past performance doesn't guarantee future success, but it can provide valuable context.

Community and Social Proof: The Power of a Thriving Player Base

A game is only as strong as its community. In P2E ecosystems, the player base's engagement, sentiment, and advocacy significantly affect demand for tokens, market liquidity, and the overall longevity of the project. A vibrant community can support the game during bear markets, provide useful feedback, and attract new players. On the other hand, a stagnant or toxic community might signal underlying problems.

1. Social Media Presence

Begin by examining the project's official Discord server, Telegram group, or Twitter account. What's the general tone?

- **Activity Levels:**

Are new messages and discussions frequent? A bustling server with player-generated content, guides, fan art, and strategy talk suggests a passionate user base.

- **Developer Responsiveness:**

Do team members appear in chats, answer questions, and share updates? Even if they can't reveal all details, active communication fosters trust.

- **Language and Accessibility:**

Does the community have multiple language channels or ambassadors? A global player base might indicate broad interest and growth potential.

2. Forums, Reddit, and Independent Reviews

Outside official channels, check third-party platforms:

- **Reddit and Quora:**

Players often share honest feedback or raise concerns here. If you find well-thought-out posts praising the game's mechanics and community events, that's positive. If you spot numerous unresolved complaints or accusations of rug pulls, think twice.

- **YouTube and Twitch Streams:**

Content creators who invest time in producing videos or streaming gameplay usually do so because they find the game engaging and profitable. Tutorials, let's plays, and eSports tournaments all reflect a healthy ecosystem.

3. Marketplaces and Secondary Markets

Look at the volume of NFT trades and token transactions. High liquidity and stable prices suggest robust interest. If everyone is trying to sell and no one is buying, the community may be losing faith. A balanced and active secondary market signals that players value the assets beyond just speculation; they might actually be using these assets in-game.

4. Community Governance and DAOs

Some P2E games implement decentralized governance via token-based voting. A thriving DAO, with regular proposals and constructive debate, shows that players care about the ecosystem's future. Governance participation indicates long-term commitment and could hint at more stable asset values.

Additional Considerations and Red Flags

Beyond the four main categories—game mechanics, tokenomics, team/roadmap, and community—there are other subtle factors and potential pitfalls to watch for.

1. Legal and Regulatory Compliance

As blockchain regulation evolves, projects that flout legal guidelines risk forced shutdowns, asset freezes, or investor lawsuits. While you may not be an expert in crypto law, look for signs that the game respects applicable regulations:

- **KYC Requirements:**

Some games or related exchanges may require identity verification. While not always popular, compliance measures can indicate a project taking legal requirements seriously.

- **Legal Disclaimers and Terms:**

Check if the website or whitepaper includes disclaimers about token usage, not being an investment product, or risk warnings. Proper legal framing suggests the team has consulted professionals.

2. Smart Contract Audits and Technical Security

Consider the game's technical backbone:

- **Smart Contract Audits:**

Reputable blockchain audit firms like CertiK, Quantstamp, or ConsenSys Diligence can lend credibility. If the project's token contracts and marketplace systems have undergone audits and made results public, that's a big plus.

- **Bug Bounties and Security Policies:**

Projects that encourage community security research and quickly patch vulnerabilities demonstrate responsibility. Security issues can devastate token prices overnight, so a proactive stance on security is vital.

3. Monetization Models and Fees

Assess how the developer team and ecosystem earn money:

- **Marketplace Fees:**

High transaction fees can eat into your profits. Is the game's marketplace fee structure transparent and fair?

- **Paywalls and Entry Costs:**

Some P2E games require purchasing expensive NFTs upfront. While this can be worthwhile if the NFT retains value, high barriers to entry raise your risk. Ensure the earning potential justifies the initial expense.

- **Subscription or Maintenance Costs:**

Are there ongoing costs to participate? If so, do the potential earnings outweigh them?

4. Innovations and Differentiation

In a crowded market, a game that offers innovative mechanics or unique intellectual property might stand out and attract long-term interest. Consider:

- **Original IP vs. Clones:**

Is the project a unique creation or a shameless clone of a popular title? Innovative concepts tend to retain player interest longer.

- **Multi-Chain Support and Interoperability:**

Games that integrate multiple blockchains, cross-chain NFTs, or interoperability with other ecosystems may have broader appeal and resilience against single-network issues.

5. Timing and Market Conditions

The broader crypto market can influence your decision. Launching into a bull market might make any project seem promising, but bear markets test a project's resilience and community loyalty. If possible, gauge how the game and its community have handled past market downturns.

Practical Steps to Narrow Your Choices

With so many factors, how do you practically pick the right P2E game?

1. Make a Shortlist

Start by listing a handful of games that catch your interest, either because of their genre, community buzz, or favorable reviews. Aim for variety—include a strategy game, a CCG, maybe a metaverse title.

2. Deep Dive Into Each Candidate

For each game on your shortlist:

- **Read the Whitepaper and Website Carefully:**

Understand tokenomics, roadmap, and gameplay.

- **Check the Team's Social Profiles:**

Look for LinkedIn pages, Twitter feeds, or Medium blogs.

- **Join Official Communities:**

Spend a few days lurking in Discord or Telegram channels. Note the atmosphere and quality of discussion.

3. Test the Gameplay If Possible

If the game offers a free trial, a testnet version, or a cheap starter pack, try it out:

- **User Interface and Experience:**

Is it intuitive or confusing? A frustrating interface might indicate poor development priorities.

- **Earning Mechanics in Practice:**

Is it easy to understand how to earn? Are you rewarded fairly for time invested?

4. Talk to Existing Players

Find veterans who've been active in the community. Ask about their experiences:

- **Earnings Over Time:**

Have their earnings increased or decreased? Why?

- **Developer Support and Updates:**

Is the team reliable and responsive to player feedback?

- **Market Stability:**

How stable are the token and NFT prices? Are there big price swings driven by hype or more consistent valuations?

5. Consider Your Budget and Time Horizon

Different P2E games require different levels of investment:

- **Initial Capital Outlay:**

If one game demands a $1,000 NFT upfront while another lets you start for $50, consider which aligns with your financial comfort level.

- **Time Commitment:**

A complex strategy game might require hours of engagement daily. A casual simulation might be playable in short bursts. Ensure the time commitment aligns with your lifestyle.

Case Studies: Applying the Criteria

Let's consider how these criteria come together by examining two hypothetical P2E games:

Game A: BattleLegends Tactics

- **Genre:** Turn-based strategy RPG with NFT heroes.
- **Tokenomics:** Detailed whitepaper shows two tokens—one governance, one utility. Heroes require in-game tokens to upgrade, creating a token sink. Rewards adjust based on player performance.
- **Roadmap:** Clear milestones (Closed beta Q1, Open beta Q2, Marketplace upgrade Q3). Team conducted two AMAs and released gameplay demos.
- **Team:** Lead developer worked at a known game studio, advisor is a reputable blockchain figure.
- **Community:** Active Discord with strategy guides, player tournaments sponsored by the team, YouTube channels covering tactics. High secondary market trade volume for rare heroes.
- **Verdict:** Solid tokenomics, strong team, engaged community. Seems like a good candidate.

Game B: CryptoFarm Frenzy

- **Genre:** Farming simulation with daily token rewards.
- **Tokenomics:** Unlimited token issuance with no sinks mentioned. Whitepaper vague on long-term plans.
- **Roadmap:** Promises metaverse integration and VR support but no concrete timelines. No working prototype yet.
- **Team:** Mostly anonymous. Little verifiable track record.

- **Community:** Telegram is full of price speculation, few gameplay discussions. Complaints about slow dev responses.
- **Verdict:** Risky. Vague tokenomics, no established track record, speculation-driven community. Likely to falter under market pressure.

By applying our framework, Game A looks more promising than Game B.

Long-Term Considerations: Beyond the Initial Choice

Selecting the right P2E game isn't just about day one. Conditions evolve over time, so think about the long-term trajectory:

1. Adaptability to Market Trends

Can the game adapt as new blockchain technologies emerge? A flexible development team that embraces Layer-2 solutions or cross-chain bridges can maintain competitiveness. A rigid team might struggle as player expectations shift.

2. Content Updates and New Features

A steady stream of new quests, events, expansions, or NFT drops can keep a game fresh. Players often remain loyal if they see the game evolving. Stagnation leads to declining interest and asset values.

3. Governance and Player Influence

If players have a say in how the game evolves, the ecosystem may align better with player interests long-term. Participating in governance can help you shape the environment, ensuring sustainability and fairness.

4. Educational Resources and Onboarding

As the player base grows, does the team invest in onboarding materials, tutorials, and user-friendly interfaces? The easier it is for new players to join, the more robust the ecosystem's growth.

Balancing Profit Motive with Fun and Ethics

While profit is a major draw in P2E, remember that these are still games, ideally enjoyable experiences. Consider the ethical dimension:

- **Is the Game Predatory?**

Some games might rely on pay-to-win mechanics, exploiting players who can't afford top-tier assets. A balanced ecosystem where skill and effort matter more than wallet size is healthier long-term.

- **Is the Community Welcoming?**

Toxic environments can wear you down, no matter how profitable the game might be. Supportive communities foster learning, collaboration, and shared successes.

- **Do You Truly Enjoy the Gameplay?**

Profit potential aside, if the game doesn't entertain you, you risk burnout. It's far easier to dedicate consistent time to something you genuinely like.

Preparing for the Future: Diversification and Exit Strategies

No matter how careful your choice, the crypto market can be volatile. Consider strategies to mitigate risk:

1. Diversify Your Gaming Portfolio

Just as you'd diversify investments, consider playing multiple P2E games. If one economy falters, another might remain stable. Different games may also excel in different market cycles.

2. Have an Exit Plan

Know how to liquidate your holdings if needed. Familiarize yourself with marketplaces, DEXs, and exchanges. Understand how quickly you can convert NFTs or tokens back to stablecoins or fiat.

3. Monitor the Project's Health Regularly

Set reminders to check the game's announcements, token price charts, community sentiment, and roadmap progress. If red flags appear—such as sudden team disappearances or failed milestones—be prepared to re-evaluate your involvement.

Conclusion

Choosing the right P2E game requires a balanced approach. Start by finding a genre and gameplay loop that resonates with you. Then, dive into the project's tokenomics, ensuring there are thoughtful measures to maintain long-term asset value. Investigate the team's credentials and the roadmap's realism to gauge whether they can deliver on promises. Finally, immerse yourself in the community to sense its vitality, stability, and supportiveness.

In a rapidly evolving sector like blockchain gaming, no set of criteria guarantees success. Still, a methodical approach can significantly increase your chances of selecting a P2E title that's both enjoyable and profitable. By treating your decision as a combination of entertainment preference and investment due diligence, you position yourself to thrive in these virtual economies—playing smarter, not just harder.

Over time, as you gain experience and confidence, you'll develop a keen sense for spotting promising titles early and avoiding pitfalls. You'll learn to navigate multiple projects, adapt to shifting market dynamics, and perhaps even influence the ecosystems you believe in by participating in governance. Ultimately, the right P2E game is the one that enriches you both financially and experientially, allowing you to savor the best of what this new era of interactive digital economies has to offer.

Chapter 6: Gameplay Strategies for Maximizing Earnings

The world of play-to-earn (P2E) gaming offers a blend of entertainment and financial opportunity that has become increasingly attractive to a wide range of players. In traditional video games, your time and effort result primarily in virtual achievements: new levels, defeated bosses, or bragging rights in a competitive lobby. However, in P2E environments, every battle you win, every quest you complete, and every strategic decision you make can translate into real-world value—usually in the form of cryptocurrencies or non-fungible tokens (NFTs).

Maximizing earnings in these digital economies demands more than just raw skill or grinding for hours on end. Players must understand the nuances of each game's tokenomics, adapt to changing metagames, and cultivate social connections that can enhance their efficiency and profitability. While the previous chapters explored how to choose the right P2E game and how to set up essential tools, this chapter focuses on the tactics and strategies within the game itself—how to get ahead early, how to keep up with meta shifts, and how to balance entertainment with financial gain in a healthy manner.

Although each title has its own ecosystem and gameplay loop, there are common patterns across P2E. Some players rely on intense "mining" or "farming" of in-game tokens, turning their gameplay into an equivalent of a digital job. Others become influential traders by flipping rare NFTs, and still others band together in guilds or alliances to leverage pooled resources.

Whatever your approach, developing a holistic understanding of gameplay strategies can help you earn more consistently and stay engaged for the long haul.

In this chapter, we'll delve into several key areas that can significantly boost your earning potential: leveraging early entry advantages, identifying and following meta strategies, striking a balance between fun and profit, and building or joining guilds and alliances. By the end of this chapter, you'll not only have a clearer understanding of how to maximize income in a specific P2E title, but you'll also have transferable skills and insights that apply to multiple blockchain gaming environments.

Early Entry Advantages

One of the most crucial lessons in the P2E space is that timing can dramatically impact your profitability. Like in cryptocurrency or NFT investment, getting in on a project at the right moment often means you can purchase assets at lower prices, farm higher yields, or secure unique collectibles that later become status symbols. Early movers sometimes see exponential growth in their holdings if the game gains traction.

Yet, being an early adopter also carries certain risks. Some projects fail to deliver on promises, fall victim to hacks, or lose community interest. Knowing how to evaluate early-stage opportunities with a level-headed approach can help you distinguish between potential gems and mere hype.

Below, we explore key areas in which being early can benefit you—and how you can mitigate the associated risks.

1. Pre-sales and Initial NFT Offerings

Many P2E games will offer pre-sales or initial NFT offerings (INO) before launching their core gameplay loops. These events let you purchase character skins, virtual land, or unique items at a discounted rate or at least at a fixed initial price. Once public demand surges (often after influencers or major media outlets spotlight the game), those NFTs might be worth significantly more.

- **Exclusive NFT Drops:** Some projects mint a limited batch of NFTs to raise funds or reward early supporters. Such NFTs often have special attributes—maybe they grant bonus in-game currency generation, better in-game stats, or exclusive access to closed beta tests. Owning these items can catapult you ahead of the competition once the game fully launches.
- **Founder Tokens or Genesis Items:** P2E projects frequently create "Genesis" or "Founder" editions of their assets. These items can have historical significance, extra functionalities, or unique appearance. Over time, these limited editions can become iconic within the community, leading to considerable price appreciation if the game becomes popular.
- **Risk and Reward:** Pre-sales carry an inherent risk: the game could fail to launch on time or at all. Alternatively, the project may overpromise, leading to disappointment. Before buying into any pre-sale, conduct thorough

research—look for a transparent team, a clear roadmap, and signs of real technical development or a working prototype.

2. Early Gameplay and Beta Phases

Some P2E games reward beta testers with special badges, tokens, or rare items. Participating in these trials not only helps you master the gameplay before the general public but also nets you exclusive digital rewards that can later sell at a premium. These "beta test" or "alpha test" assets function similarly to Founder NFTs in that they mark you as an early adopter.

- **Learning the Mechanics:** By playing an early version, you can experiment with different strategies, learn the best grinding spots, or discover hidden synergies in character builds. Once the game officially launches, you'll have a competitive edge over newcomers.
- **Contributing Feedback and Earning Rewards:** Many developers use beta phases to gather feedback. They may reward players who report bugs or suggest improvements. Beyond official incentives, you'll also build a rapport with the dev team and community, which could open future opportunities—like early invitations to expansions or whitelisting for subsequent asset drops.

4. Leveraging Price Appreciation

Suppose you acquire in-game tokens or NFTs during a pre-sale or immediately after a game's soft launch. If the game becomes wildly popular, market prices for those same assets may multiply. This price increase is partly speculation, but also driven by real demand as players join and need certain items to participate fully.

- **Identify Potential Secondary Markets:** Once you've bought into a project, keep an eye on secondary marketplaces. If you see prices surging beyond your comfort level, you might decide to sell and lock in profits, or hold if you believe in the project's long-term viability.
- **Balancing Sale Timing and Gameplay Needs:** Selling a powerful or rare NFT too early could rob you of future earning potential within the game. On the other hand, you might want to capitalize on hype. Striking that balance is a core skill in P2E.

5. Avoiding Hype Traps

While early entry can be lucrative, it's also where scams and overhyped vaporware projects proliferate. Be wary of overly polished marketing with no tangible product. Projects that promise unrealistic yields or lack transparency about their developers often fizzle out. Due diligence—like reading whitepapers, verifying audits, and checking the backgrounds of team members—is crucial.

Staying early in a project may yield significant advantages, but always balance it with caution. In the next section, we'll examine another powerful way to enhance your earnings: staying in tune with and capitalizing on the game's "meta" strategies.

Identifying Meta Strategies

In gaming, the term "meta" refers to the most effective strategies, character builds, or item combinations at a given time—often determined by the community's collective experiences, developer balance patches, and competitive trends. In P2E gaming, identifying the current meta isn't just about winning matches or expeditions; it's also about maximizing your token or NFT earnings. If a certain class of items or style of play is overpowered, those assets might fetch higher prices in the marketplace or let you grind tokens more efficiently.

Below, we discuss how to keep your finger on the pulse of a game's meta and use that knowledge to boost your in-game income.

1. Understanding the Meta Cycle

Games evolve constantly. What works today might be nerfed tomorrow. Developers regularly release patches to rebalance gameplay elements, especially if certain approaches dominate too heavily. As a result, the meta experiences a cyclical pattern:

- **Initial Discovery:** After a launch or major update, players experiment with new mechanics. Some "hidden gems" or synergies might not be immediately obvious. Early discoverers can earn big before everyone else catches on.

- **Peak Exploitation:** Once the broader community recognizes a powerful strategy, it becomes mainstream. Prices for relevant NFTs may spike, or the in-game economy shifts to favor those exploiting the approach.
- **Counter-Strategies or Developer Intervention:** Inevitably, either other players adapt to counter the strategy, or developers issue a patch that nerfs the exploit. This then reshapes the meta once again.

Staying ahead of these cycles can be highly profitable. Selling assets right before a nerf, or investing in upcoming counters, is akin to successful stock trading.

2. Tapping Into Player Forums and Social Media
One of the best ways to keep informed about the meta is by following community discussions:

- **Official Discord and Forums:** Large P2E projects often host official channels where players exchange tips. Watch for threads discussing specific builds or strategies that are performing exceptionally well. Pay attention to pinned community guides.
- **Independent Communities (Reddit, Twitter, Telegram):** Unofficial or community-run channels can be more candid. Players might share advanced tactics, talk about new item combos, or provide early warnings of planned developer changes.
- **Influencer Streams and Videos:** Some Twitch or YouTube personalities specialize in dissecting meta changes. They test new approaches live, giving you a chance to see them in action. While relying solely on

influencers can lead to groupthink, they can also highlight novel ideas that the broader community hasn't adopted yet.

3. Using Data Tools and Analytics

In many P2E games, especially competitive ones, third-party tools track match results or item usage. Websites or apps might compile data to rank which characters, decks, or strategies have the highest win rates:

- **Match-Tracking Services:** If a game's smart contracts are public, data analysts may create dashboards showing the most-used items in winning battles. You can glean crucial insights: for instance, if you see a surge in victories featuring a particular NFT type, that might indicate an emerging meta.
- **Earnings Analytics:** Some dedicated P2E analytics platforms detail the average earnings per day for different playstyles. This is especially relevant in games where you can choose multiple paths to earn tokens—combat, trading, land ownership, etc.
- **Blockchain Explorers:** For advanced users, scanning the blockchain directly can reveal transaction volume, which NFT categories are trading heavily, and how token flows are moving. This information can help you anticipate shifts before they become common knowledge.

4. Adapting to Meta Shifts Proactively

Awareness of meta changes is only half the battle. You also need to respond quickly:

- **Preemptive Investment:** If you sense that a certain class of items is about to become dominant, buying them while they're still cheap can yield strong returns. Alternatively, you might want to divest from items you suspect developers will nerf soon.
- **Skill Development:** If meta changes favor different classes or roles, pivot your gameplay. This might mean learning a new character archetype or retooling your deck. While there's a learning curve, you stay relevant in the competitive environment.
- **Political or Alliance Maneuvers:** In guild-based games, shifting alliances might become advantageous when the meta changes the strategic value of certain territories or resources.

No matter how quickly you adapt, it's inevitable that metas come and go. Instead of chasing every wave, focus on consistent improvement, keep multiple strategies in your arsenal, and remain flexible enough to pivot as needed.

Still, while chasing meta can improve earnings, an overemphasis on profit can lead to burnout or overshadow the joy of gaming. The next section explores how to balance fun and profit to create a sustainable, enjoyable gaming experience.

Balancing Fun and Profit

A common pitfall in P2E gaming is becoming so fixated on earnings that you forget why you started playing in the first place: for enjoyment. This tunnel vision not only risks mental fatigue but can also reduce your overall effectiveness. Players who dislike the game might not have the motivation to keep up with evolving mechanics or maintain the discipline for daily quests. Balancing profit-seeking with genuine engagement is key to building a long-term presence in P2E worlds.

1. The Dangers of "Grinding Syndrome"
The grind is a reality in many P2E games. You might have daily tasks or quests that yield tokens, or you might be expected to farm resources to upgrade your NFTs. If the process feels too much like a second job, the game's charm can fade:

- **Emotional Exhaustion:** Constantly clocking in hours just for incremental token gains can lead to burnout. Over time, you may resent the game, miss out on creative or social experiences, and exit the ecosystem prematurely.
- **Declining Efficiency:** When gaming becomes drudgery, you're less likely to experiment with new tactics, interact with the community, or stay updated on meta changes—eventually harming your earnings.

A better approach is to pace yourself, focusing on tasks you genuinely find rewarding or interesting. By tailoring your activities to your personality—be it PvP arenas or crafting in a virtual environment—you maintain enthusiasm, which often translates to better overall performance.

2. Setting Realistic Goals and Time Management

Another key to balancing fun and profit is establishing a sustainable schedule:

- **Daily or Weekly Targets:** Decide how many hours per day or tokens per day you aim to earn. These goals should fit around your life responsibilities (work, school, family) rather than dominating them.
- **Milestones for Big Achievements:** If you're working toward a significant in-game asset—like a legendary NFT or control of a strategic area—break that goal into smaller milestones. Each step's completion becomes a mini-celebration, maintaining motivation.
- **Prioritizing High-Value Activities:** Not all in-game tasks yield equal rewards. Identify the most profitable quests or gameplay modes and focus on them first. If time remains, explore other parts of the game purely for fun.

3. Enjoying the Community and Social Aspects

Many P2E games emphasize community interaction, from guild raids to land ownership cooperatives. Participating in these social elements can reinvigorate your passion:

- **Social Bonds:** Teaming up with friends or like-minded players fosters a sense of camaraderie. Working together toward mutual goals—defeating a tough boss, building a guild hall, or defending territory—can be far more engaging than solo grinding.
- **Collaborative Learning:** You don't have to discover every meta shift on your own. Pool your intelligence and

resources with allies. Share strategies, gear, or NFT rentals. These social dynamics often lead to deeper satisfaction than purely individual achievements.

- **Community Events:** Many games host special in-game festivals, tournaments, or building contests. Even if these events aren't the highest earners, they inject variety, fun, and a sense of belonging.

6. Avoiding Overinvestment

It can be tempting to pour significant capital into a game— buying expensive NFTs, premium tokens, or upgrades— believing it will amplify your earnings. While strategic investments are often necessary, overspending can lead to high stress if the game's market fluctuates. Spread out your risk across multiple games or even non-gaming crypto assets to avoid tying your entire portfolio to a single ecosystem.

By structuring your playtime around realistic goals, mixing profitable tasks with enjoyable ones, and embracing the social aspects, you turn P2E from a potential grind into a sustainable hobby (or side gig) that enriches multiple facets of your life. Next, we'll explore how building or joining guilds and alliances can multiply your earning potential and deepen your immersion in P2E worlds.

Building Guilds and Alliances

Collaboration stands at the heart of many successful P2E communities. Rather than going it alone, players can form or join guilds (also known as clans or alliances), pooling resources, strategic know-how, and manpower to achieve collective goals. This collaborative approach can greatly increase individual earning potential while also making gameplay more exciting and dynamic.

1. Why Guilds Matter in P2E

In some blockchain games, the concept of guilds is embedded into the very core of the gameplay. For example, you may need a group to tackle high-level bosses that drop rare NFT loot, or controlling territory might require multiple players working in harmony.

- **Resource Sharing:** Guild members often share resources, from in-game currencies to crafting materials. If a guild collectively invests in an expensive piece of virtual land, each member can benefit from the land's yields, generating more reliable income than a solo player could manage.
- **Pooled Investment:** Beyond in-game items, some guilds pool real funds to buy early NFT assets or large swaths of land during pre-sales. This approach lowers individual risk while opening access to high-value investments.
- **Structured Education:** Established guilds typically have internal training resources, guides, or mentors that help newbies get up to speed quickly. This structured

knowledge-sharing fosters a supportive environment that accelerates everyone's earning curve.

3. Types of Guilds

Different P2E games give rise to various guild archetypes:

- **Competitive PvP Guilds:** These guilds focus on high-stakes tournaments, ranked matches, or territory wars. They recruit top talent, often awarding performance-based shares of token earnings. If you relish competitive gameplay, joining such a guild can propel you to the top brackets.
- **Farming or Resource Guilds:** In games that revolve around resource extraction—be it mining precious stones or cultivating farmland—guilds may coordinate large-scale "farming operations." Members pool time and gear, then split the profits.
- **Social and Casual Guilds:** Not every guild aims for top-tier competition. Some groups prioritize a relaxed environment, focusing on mutual cooperation, in-game friendship, and moderate earnings. Casual guilds can still be profitable if they organize events or trade knowledge effectively.
- **Hybrid or Multi-Game Guilds:** Some well-established guilds extend their presence across multiple P2E titles. This diversification benefits players who want to spread their risk. The guild brand might hold significant clout, securing valuable partnerships or early access to new games.

4. Forming Your Own Guild

If no existing guild meets your goals or standards, consider founding one yourself. This approach requires organizational skill and a willingness to lead:

- **Establish a Core Mission:** Are you aiming to dominate PvP or simply create a welcoming community for new players? Clarifying your guild's purpose helps attract the right members.
- **Set Clear Rules and Profit-Sharing Structures:** How will you handle loot distribution or sharing token earnings? Transparent, fair rules encourage trust. For example, you might set a "guild treasury" that takes a small cut of all earnings to invest in shared resources.
- **Recruitment and Onboarding:** Active recruitment on official forums or Discord can attract like-minded players. Offer a simple onboarding process—like a short Google Form or voice chat interview—to gauge each applicant's commitment and skill level.
- **Leadership and Administration:** Successful guilds often have roles like officers or co-leaders, each overseeing different aspects (like training newbies, managing finances, or coordinating large-scale raids). Delegate tasks, communicate regularly, and keep morale high.

5. Maximizing Guild Benefits

Once you join or form a guild, how do you leverage it for maximal gain?

- **Specialized Roles and Team Composition:** Divide tasks according to player skill sets. Some might excel at resource gathering, while others are top-notch fighters or savvy traders who manage the guild's marketplace transactions.
- **Coordinated In-Game Events:** Plan group raids, resource runs, or tournaments. Collaboration reduces the chance of failure and often yields greater loot or tokens per person than solo attempts.
- **Profit-Sharing Models:** If your guild invests in expensive NFTs or land, implement a transparent system for dividing earnings. Some guilds distribute rewards proportionally based on individual contributions. Others reinvest part of the earnings in more assets to grow the guild's "portfolio."
- **Cross-Promotion and Networking:** Strong guilds often forge alliances with other guilds or even partner with the game's developers to organize major community events. This networking amplifies your guild's visibility and influence, indirectly boosting potential earnings.

5.   Avoiding   Guild   Drama   and   Pitfalls
Guild dynamics can be complex. Conflicts arise if members feel profit distribution is unfair, or if leadership is unresponsive to concerns:

- **Transparent Communication:** Use clear channels— like a dedicated Discord server—to keep everyone updated on important decisions, financial records, and upcoming events. Transparency defuses suspicions or rumors.

- **Conflict Resolution Mechanisms:** Sometimes, players clash over strategy or resource allocation. Having a neutral mediator or an established voting system can keep disputes from escalating.
- **Exit Options:** Members leave guilds for various reasons—time constraints, shifting interests, or personal disagreements. Make it easy for them to exit gracefully, ensuring they receive any outstanding share of joint profits fairly.

By embracing guilds and alliances, you can transform an individual gaming experience into a collaborative venture that benefits from pooled knowledge, resources, and capital. This synergy often translates to higher earnings than any single player could achieve alone.

Advanced Tactics to Further Boost Earnings

While early entry, meta awareness, a balanced mindset, and guild alliances form the core pillars of successful P2E participation, there are additional advanced tactics that can give you an extra edge. Below, we delve into strategies that require deeper understanding or greater risk tolerance but can yield considerable rewards if executed well.

1. Cross-Game Arbitrage

Some players specialize in finding price discrepancies between different marketplaces or even between different blockchain games. For instance, if a popular weapon NFT is cheaper on one platform but sells for more on another, you can buy low, sell high, and pocket the difference. This approach demands:

- **Constant Market Monitoring:** Tools like NFT aggregators or price trackers can help you spot opportunities.
- **Blockchain Familiarity:** You must be proficient in bridging assets across blockchains or dealing with different token standards.
- **Timely Execution:** Price gaps can vanish quickly once other arbitrageurs jump in.

While cross-game arbitrage can be lucrative, it's also labor-intensive and fraught with potential pitfalls—such as network congestion or bridging delays.

2. Token Staking and Yield Farming
Many P2E games integrate decentralized finance (DeFi) elements, allowing you to stake your in-game tokens or pool them to earn passive rewards. For example, you might provide liquidity to a decentralized exchange (DEX) pair featuring the game's native token. In return, you receive a share of trading fees or additional tokens. This approach can boost your overall earnings, but it also introduces risks:

- **Impermanent Loss:** If the token's price fluctuates significantly while you're providing liquidity, you might lose some value compared to simply holding the tokens.

- **Smart Contract Risk:** Malicious exploits, rug pulls, or code vulnerabilities could lead to lost funds. Verify that the staking platform or liquidity pool has reputable audits.
- **Lock-Up Periods:** Some staking programs lock your tokens for a set duration. If you anticipate a market crash or urgent need for liquidity, being locked can be problematic.

2. Scholarship Programs

Some established players or guilds run scholarship programs, lending their NFTs or accounts to newcomers in exchange for a cut of the earnings. As a scholar, you can access high-level assets without paying upfront. As a lender, you earn passive income while focusing on other activities. If you have surplus NFTs, setting up a scholarship program can be a strategic way to monetize idle assets.

4. Community Leadership and Content Creation
Another overlooked way to maximize earnings is to become an authority within the game's community:

- **Guide Authors and Streamers:** If you produce high-quality content—like video tutorials, written guides, or daily Twitch streams—you can generate ad revenue, sponsorship deals, or direct tips from the community.
- **Influencer Collaborations:** Popular P2E titles often partner with established content creators, providing them with exclusive NFTs to promote. You might secure

early access to new expansions, giving you an edge in acquiring and selling rare items.

- **Moderator or Ambassador Roles:** Some games pay or reward active community leaders in tokens or NFTs. Stepping into these roles can give you insider knowledge about upcoming changes or events that might affect the meta.

5. Diversification Within the Game

Instead of focusing on a single activity—like only fighting bosses or only farming resources—many advanced players diversify within the same game:

- **Trading + PvE/PvP:** Earn tokens by playing normally, then reinvest those tokens into the in-game marketplace, flipping undervalued assets for profit.
- **Owning Land and Operating Businesses:** In metaverse-style titles, you might run a virtual store or event venue that charges fees to visitors. This approach merges gameplay with entrepreneurial endeavors, creating multiple revenue streams.
- **Multi-Character or Multi-Account Strategies:** Some P2E games allow players to run multiple accounts (if permitted by the terms of service). While it takes more effort, managing multiple avatars or teams can multiply your token income. However, ensure this is legal within the game's rules to avoid bans.

These advanced tactics require more knowledge, capital, or time investment but can elevate your earning potential significantly. For players who treat P2E as both a hobby and a business, exploring these avenues might prove highly rewarding.

Common Pitfalls and How to Avoid Them

Maximizing earnings in P2E is not just about adopting winning strategies; it's also about recognizing and sidestepping pitfalls that can undermine your gains. Below are some of the most frequent mistakes players make, along with tips on how to steer clear of them:

1. Overextending Financially Spending more money than you can afford to lose—chasing rare NFTs or large swaths of virtual land—can backfire if the game's economy falters. Always treat P2E investments with the same caution you would any volatile asset.

2. Ignoring Patch Notes or Updates

Developers often release patch notes that detail nerfs, buffs, or new features. Skipping these updates is a surefire way to miss important shifts in the meta. Prioritize reading official announcements to stay well-informed.

3. Neglecting Security

As covered in earlier chapters, your digital assets are at risk if you fail to secure your wallet or fall for phishing scams. Always double-check URLs, store seed phrases offline, and be wary of unsolicited offers or suspicious links.

4. Failing to Diversify Within and Across Games

Relying entirely on one game or one specific strategy leaves you vulnerable to abrupt changes. Diversifying your approach—both in a single game (e.g., playing PvP and running a resource farm) and across multiple P2E titles—helps cushion against unexpected shifts.

5. Underestimating Time Commitments

Some P2E strategies are time-intensive, requiring daily log-ins to remain competitive. If you can't commit the necessary hours, you might underperform or miss key events. Set realistic expectations about how much time you can consistently invest.

Case Studies: Putting Strategies into Practice

To solidify the concepts discussed, let's examine two hypothetical players and how they implement the strategies outlined in this chapter.

Case Study 1: Maria, the Early Adopter

- **Approach to Early Entry:** Maria hears about a new fantasy-based P2E game launching soon. She attends the AMA sessions, checks the founding team's credibility, and decides to participate in the pre-sale of limited-edition character NFTs. Because these NFTs are sold at a fixed rate, she secures a powerful wizard character at a relatively low price.

- **Building the Meta Advantage:** Upon launch, Maria uses the wizard's unique abilities to climb the game's PvP ranks. She records data on which spells have the highest win rate. Soon after, she notices the developers mention an upcoming patch that might nerf wizards. She trades the wizard NFT at a high market price shortly before the nerf hits.
- **Balancing Fun and Profit:** Even though she sold her wizard NFT, Maria still enjoys the game and switches to a warrior class, which she finds entertaining. She invests her profits into staking the in-game token, earning passive income while continuing to battle casually.
- **Guild Collaboration:** Maria joins a mid-sized guild. They coordinate resource gathering and share knowledge on the best farming routes. She occasionally leads raids due to her extensive PvP experience, helping newbies level up faster.

Result: By leveraging early access NFTs and actively tracking meta changes, Maria consistently profits without sacrificing the fun of exploring new classes and social interactions.

Case Study 2: Devante, the Guild Leader

- **Approach to Guild Formation:** Devante is an experienced gamer who sees a major opportunity in a sci-fi P2E title. He forms a guild called "Starlight Syndicate," focusing on controlling resource-rich asteroids. He recruits members who each bring specific skills—some are experts in spaceship combat, others excel at mining or marketplace trading.

- **Identifying Meta Strategies Together:** The guild sets up a shared Discord channel where members post combat logs, successful mining runs, and item crafting data. Over time, they discover that a certain mining laser, combined with a stealth-based ship, yields the highest resource returns. Starlight Syndicate invests heavily in these ship modules before they become widely popular. When the price of modules quadruples, some members sell to fund more advanced ships.
- **Balancing Workload:** Devante implements a schedule so no single member burns out. They rotate mining shifts, combat patrols, and exploration. This structured approach allows the guild to dominate multiple resource asteroids while members still enjoy real-life balance.
- **Profit-Sharing and Long-Term Vision:** The guild's treasury receives 10% of all resource sales. This pooled fund buys additional land parcels on newly discovered planets. Over time, the value of these assets rises, boosting each member's share of passive income.

Result: Devante's guild-based strategy combines advanced knowledge, resource-sharing, and systematic scheduling to multiply earnings for all. The cooperative environment also fosters strong camaraderie and consistent engagement.

Conclusion

Within the realm of play-to-earn gaming, success hinges on more than just raw reflexes or luck. It requires strategic thinking, an understanding of economic principles, and a willingness to adapt to constant change. This chapter explored four major areas—early entry advantages, identifying meta strategies, balancing fun and profit, and building alliances or guilds—that can transform a casual player into a savvy participant in the emerging digital economies.

1. **Early Entry Advantages** can help you secure rare assets before the masses arrive, but require careful due diligence to avoid scams.
2. **Identifying Meta Strategies** allows you to stay ahead of the curve and maximize efficiency, whether that involves power-leveling a favored character class or flipping undervalued items in NFT marketplaces.
3. **Balancing Fun and Profit** is crucial for preventing burnout; a schedule that merges worthwhile in-game tasks with genuine enjoyment keeps you engaged over the long haul.
4. **Building Guilds and Alliances** taps into the collective power of community, where pooled resources, shared knowledge, and strategic cooperation amplify earnings.

To push your expertise further, you can adopt advanced tactics like cross-game arbitrage, yield farming with in-game tokens, or even participating in scholarship programs. Ultimately, the most consistent earners in P2E are those who combine curiosity, risk management, skill development, and social engagement. They treat every gameplay session as both entertainment and an opportunity to learn, refine strategies, and discover new ways to thrive in these vibrant virtual worlds.

In the chapters ahead, we'll continue exploring how to evaluate game tokens and digital assets, understand broader metaverse economies, and incorporate decentralized finance mechanisms into your gaming strategies. For now, armed with the principles and techniques in this chapter, you're well on your way to maximizing your earnings—while keeping the spirit of gaming alive and well.

PART III: EVALUATING GAME TOKENS AND DIGITAL ASSETS

Chapter 7: Tokenomics 101

The emergence of blockchain-based play-to-earn (P2E) gaming has brought with it a new layer of complexity and opportunity: tokenomics. While traditional games revolve primarily around gameplay mechanics, narrative, and monetization through expansion packs or microtransactions, P2E titles rely on intricate economic systems that fuse gaming, finance, and community governance. Tokens lie at the heart of these ecosystems, functioning as both digital currencies and assets that hold real-world value.

However, the success of a P2E project is not guaranteed merely by issuing a token. Designing sustainable tokenomics requires balancing many moving parts—such as supply and demand, deflationary or inflationary pressures, reward distribution, utility, governance, and community trust. Mistakes in any of these areas can lead to economic instability, price crashes, or player attrition. On the other hand, well-structured tokenomics can help build vibrant economies, attract long-term players, and foster robust communities.

This chapter provides a broad foundation for understanding how tokenomics works in P2E games. We'll begin by exploring the critical interplay of supply and demand dynamics, then delve into the intricacies of token distribution and vesting. Finally, we'll examine the difference between governance tokens and utility tokens, highlighting how each plays a unique role in shaping player incentives and the overall health of a P2E ecosystem. By the end, you'll have a deeper appreciation for the subtle economic mechanisms that underpin token-based gaming platforms, and you'll be better equipped to evaluate projects' viability before investing time or money.

Supply and Demand Dynamics

At the most fundamental level, the value of a P2E token emerges from the interplay of supply and demand. While this concept applies to virtually all markets—from commodities to stocks and even collectible trading cards—it has unique implications in blockchain gaming. The number of tokens available (supply) and players' desire or need for them (demand) form a delicate equilibrium that drives the token's price. If developers fail to manage this balance, a game's economy can collapse under rampant inflation or stagnate due to insufficient liquidity.

Below, we delve into key factors that influence supply and demand dynamics, along with the strategies that P2E designers deploy to maintain economic stability.

1. **Token Supply Models**

   Different P2E games adopt different supply models for their tokens, each with its pros and cons. Let's look at the three most common approaches:

- **Fixed Supply (Deflationary)**: Some projects start with a maximum cap on tokens that will ever exist (e.g., 100 million tokens). No new tokens are minted beyond that cap. Bitcoin is the most famous example of a fixed-supply currency. In a gaming context, a fixed-supply model may appeal to players who expect scarcity to drive up the token's value over time. However, if demand surges and no new tokens can be created, prices might become prohibitively high for new entrants, potentially inhibiting user growth.
- **Unlimited Supply (Inflationary)**:
- Other P2E titles issue tokens continuously as rewards for gameplay activities—battles, quests, or resource harvesting. This can encourage player engagement but also risks inflation if the issuance rate outpaces demand. Developers must carefully calibrate the rate at which new tokens enter circulation, or else players may see their holdings' value diminish over time. High inflation can lead to short-term speculation and subsequent crashes if utility does not keep pace.
- **Elastic or Algorithmic Supply**: A third model adjusts the token supply algorithmically to stabilize its value. If demand rises, the algorithm mints more tokens to keep prices within a target range; if demand falls, it burns or locks tokens to prevent a crash. While this approach can smooth out price volatility, it's relatively complex to implement. Additionally, players may find it

harder to grasp how these automatic adjustments affect their long-term holdings.

Each model can succeed or fail based on the game's design, player behavior, and broader market sentiment. More important than the raw supply model is how well it integrates with the overall gameplay and economy.

2. **Demand Drivers: Utility, Speculation, and Community**

On the demand side, three key drivers typically apply in P2E contexts:

- **Utility**: Players need the token for in-game purchases, crafting, breeding new characters, staking for additional rewards, or participating in governance. The more real use cases a token has, the higher the baseline demand. For instance, a P2E farming game might require tokens to upgrade virtual land. If upgrades significantly boost yields or provide access to rare items, players actively seek tokens, creating robust demand.
- **Speculation**: Some players buy tokens hoping to sell them later at a higher price. This can create rapid price appreciation if the game is trending, though it also introduces volatility. Speculative bubbles can inflate token prices beyond sustainable levels, leading to sharp corrections when enthusiasm wanes.

o **Community Engagement**: A passionate, growing community often translates into organic demand for the token. People want to participate in a beloved game or support its development. Moreover, strong community sentiment can cushion the token's price against market downturns, as loyal players hold rather than panic sell.

Balancing utility-driven demand with speculative fervor is a constant challenge. Games that offer genuine, recurring reasons for using and holding tokens stand a better chance of sustaining demand beyond short-lived hype cycles.

3. **Token Sinks and Deflationary Mechanics**

If new tokens continually flood the market without control, the result is inflation—each token's value may drop over time. To counteract this, many P2E designs incorporate "sink" mechanisms, which remove tokens from circulation:

o **Burning**: A portion of tokens spent on fees or in-game upgrades is permanently destroyed (removed from the total supply). This deflationary practice can bolster token value, as fewer tokens are available over time.

o **Spending on Consumables**: Certain in-game items might be "consumed" (and thus vanish) when used, with players required to pay tokens repeatedly for them. This continuous outflow of tokens acts as a natural sink. Examples include potions, ammo, or energy refills in RPG settings.

- **Fee Structures**: If the game's marketplace charges fees in the native token, those tokens could be partially burned or locked in a treasury. Over time, such fees can act as a steady deflationary force, assuming a consistent level of marketplace activity.

Without these token sinks, inflationary pressures can run rampant, diminishing player earnings in real terms. However, setting sinks too high can stifle participation by making the game expensive or discouraging transactions. Striking a healthy balance is key.

4. **Real-World Economic Factors**

While P2E games can feel like self-contained worlds, broader economic and crypto market trends also shape token price. During bull markets, investors look for new opportunities, often driving up P2E token prices. Conversely, bear markets dampen enthusiasm and shrink liquidity. Macroeconomic factors—like interest rates, inflation fears, or regulatory shifts—may also ripple into the crypto space, influencing P2E token values.

Developers have limited control over these external forces, but they can mitigate the impact by ensuring their token has genuine utility, fostering strong community loyalty, and avoiding overly speculative narratives.

5. **Measuring Supply and Demand Health**

Some metrics can help both developers and players gauge whether a token's supply and demand are balanced:

- o **Circulating Supply Growth Rate**: If tokens are minted faster than they're used or burned, inflation could become problematic.
- o **Active Player Growth vs. Token Price**: Ideally, as more players join, demand for tokens increases. If player numbers plateau but token issuance remains high, oversupply might occur.
- o **Marketplace Liquidity**: Are enough buy and sell orders present so that players can trade tokens easily? Low liquidity can cause dramatic price swings.

Effective tokenomic models continuously monitor these metrics, adjusting rewards or sinks as needed to keep the economy robust. This dynamic approach fosters long-term viability, ensuring that the game remains attractive for both new and existing players.

Understanding supply and demand dynamics is a vital starting point for analyzing any P2E token. Next, we'll examine how tokens are typically distributed among different stakeholders and how vesting schedules can protect against sudden market dumps.

Distribution and Vesting

The way tokens are allocated and released into circulation can have a tremendous impact on a P2E project's trajectory. If a small group of early backers holds the majority of tokens—able to sell them at any time—this concentration of power can create massive price volatility. Alternatively, if distribution is too fragmented and no single entity has enough stake to fund or guide long-term development, the project might lack direction.

Below, we'll dissect how distribution works, explore vesting schedules that protect token value, and highlight the importance of transparency in these arrangements.

1. **Initial Token Allocation**

   Before a game's official launch, the project's team decides how to split the total token supply among various stakeholders. Common allocations include:

   o **Founders and Team**: Developers and core contributors are often rewarded with tokens for their work. The key question is how large this slice is. If founders hold too much, it raises fears they might dump tokens. However, they should also be incentivized to continue improving the game.

- **Private Investors / VCs**: Many blockchain projects secure seed funding from venture capital or angel investors who receive tokens at a discount. This capital can accelerate development, but it also means these investors might eventually sell large chunks of tokens for profit.
- **Public Sale / Crowdsale**: Some projects conduct an Initial Coin Offering (ICO), Initial DEX Offering (IDO), or other public fundraising method. The public can buy tokens at a set price, injecting liquidity early. However, poorly structured sales can lead to hype-driven speculation.
- **Community / Airdrops**: Some portion of tokens may be reserved for airdrops, marketing events, or distribution to early supporters. This can build goodwill but must be executed carefully to avoid a quick sell-off.

The more balanced and transparent this allocation is, the less likely the project suffers from big price dumps or concerns over centralization. Players should always review published token allocation charts, which often appear in the project's whitepaper or website.

2. **Vesting Schedules: Preventing Sudden Dumps**

Vesting schedules lock allocated tokens for a certain period, releasing them gradually rather than all at once. This mechanism ensures that early stakeholders—

founders, team members, private investors—cannot immediately flood the market with their tokens and tank the price.

- ○ **Linear Vesting**: Tokens release evenly over time, say 25% every 6 months for two years. This approach gives everyone clarity on when unlocking events occur, reducing speculation.
- ○ **Cliff Vesting**: Some portion of tokens remains fully locked until a specific date (the "cliff"), then begins releasing. For example, a founder might receive no tokens for the first 6 months, followed by steady release thereafter.
- ○ **Performance-Based Vesting**: In some P2E games, a portion of team or investor tokens may vest only upon hitting key milestones—like reaching 100,000 monthly active players or launching a new game mode. This aligns stakeholder incentives with ongoing success.

Strong vesting schedules reassure the community that major holders share a long-term vision. Conversely, short or non-existent vesting signals that a project might be a cash grab—where insiders can dump tokens on the public at inflated prices. Checking the vesting schedule is thus a crucial part of due diligence when evaluating a P2E ecosystem.

3. **Ecosystem Reserves and Treasury**

Beyond these allocations, many P2E games maintain an "ecosystem reserve" or treasury fund. This pool of tokens serves multiple purposes:

- o **Future Development**: Funding expansions, technical upgrades, and new features, ensuring the game evolves.
- o **Marketing and Partnerships**: Incentivizing collaborations, influencer promotions, or strategic alliances with other crypto projects.
- o **Rewards for Events and Tournaments**: Hosting eSports competitions or in-game celebrations can generate buzz and attract top-tier players. The treasury often bankrolls prize pools.

Community governance mechanisms—discussed later in this chapter—can oversee how treasury funds are deployed. This transparency fosters trust, as players know tokens won't be misused by a single, centralized authority.

4. **Distribution to Players: Rewards and Emission Rates**

Once the game launches, tokens typically flow to players through in-game activities. The rate at which tokens are "minted" and distributed (often called the "emission rate") has a direct bearing on inflation. Many P2E projects design emissions to be higher in the early stages—attracting new players and bootstrapping liquidity—and then taper off over time to prevent excess inflation.

- o **Milestone-based Reductions**: A game might reduce token rewards by a fixed percentage every year, akin to Bitcoin's halving. This fosters a sense of scarcity over time, motivating early adoption.
- o **Dynamic Adjustments**: Some advanced systems dynamically adjust token rewards depending on on-chain metrics like active user count, marketplace volume, or token price stability. This approach tries to keep inflation in check automatically.

Observing how a project plans to reduce or manage token rewards can reveal much about its commitment to long-term viability.

5. **Transparency: The Key to Trust**

Because distribution and vesting heavily influence token prices, transparency is paramount. Reputable P2E projects:

- o **Publish a Token Distribution Chart**: Showing exact percentages allocated to each category (team, investors, public sale, treasury, etc.).
- o **Provide Vesting Schedules**: Stating when locks end, how many tokens will be released, and over what period.

- o **Offer Real-Time Tracking**: Some projects use specialized dashboards or block explorers to show exactly how many tokens are vested or unlocked at any given time.

By scrutinizing these details, players can gauge whether big unlocks are imminent—potentially causing price dips—and whether the overall structure is fair and balanced. Now that we've unpacked how tokens are distributed and managed over time, let's turn to the types of tokens themselves—specifically, governance tokens versus utility tokens.

Governance Tokens vs. Utility Tokens

As P2E gaming evolves, so do the roles tokens play within these ecosystems. Two broad categories have emerged to describe their primary functions: governance tokens and utility tokens. While both can hold real-world value, they differ in how they engage players, influence game development, and shape the token's overarching purpose. Some projects even combine these categories, offering "hybrid" tokens that serve dual roles.

1. **Governance Tokens**

   A governance token grants holders a say in the project's direction. By owning such tokens, players, investors, and stakeholders can vote on major decisions—from economic policies and treasury allocations to feature rollouts and partnership deals.

- o **On-Chain Voting**: Typically, governance tokens enable on-chain voting through smart contracts. The more tokens you hold, the greater your voting power. Proposals can cover everything from adjusting token emission rates to funding community initiatives.
- o **DAOs (Decentralized Autonomous Organizations)**: Many P2E games host their governance tokens within a DAO structure, where decisions are collectively made. The DAO might allocate treasury funds for marketing, developer grants, or eSports tournaments.
- o **Incentivizing Long-Term Participation**: Governance tokens can encourage players to hold rather than flip. If the community expects game expansions, new partnerships, or other price-boosting developments, they'll want to keep their tokens to maintain influence—and potentially benefit from future appreciation.

However, governance tokens can also introduce complexities:

- o **Voting Fatigue**: If every minor decision goes to a vote, participants may tire of constant proposals. Real-world experience shows many governance participants quickly become apathetic or only vote on the largest issues.

- **Concentration of Power**: Wealthy whales who hold large amounts of governance tokens can dominate votes, sometimes pursuing self-serving agendas contrary to the broader community's interests. Mechanisms like quadratic voting or delegated voting can mitigate this problem but introduce added complexity.
- **Regulatory Risks**: In some jurisdictions, governance tokens may be seen as akin to securities if they confer significant control or a share of profits. This legal uncertainty can shape how projects structure and promote governance.

Despite these challenges, governance tokens remain an appealing way to decentralize decision-making, align incentives, and empower the player community.

2. Utility Tokens

In contrast to governance tokens, utility tokens serve functional purposes within the game's ecosystem. Players must spend or earn these tokens to unlock game features, craft items, pay fees, or access special content.

- **In-Game Currency**: Often, a utility token acts like a local currency for item purchases, upgrades, breeding mechanisms, or tournament entry fees. This ensures that the token is in constant circulation, ideally matching the game's growth.
- **Burning and Staking**: Utility tokens may be burned for one-time uses (e.g., breeding a new

NFT hero), or staked to earn rewards. Both features help regulate supply, combating inflation.

- ○ **Reward Mechanism**: Players earn utility tokens through quests, battles, or resource gathering. These tokens have inherent value if they enable more efficient gameplay, yield generation, or the acquisition of high-level NFTs.

Utility tokens can suffer if insufficient demand exists for the in-game functions they facilitate. A classic pitfall is a token with "no real use case," sustained temporarily by speculation but eventually collapsing. Hence, robust utility tokenomics often revolve around meaningful, recurring demand loops.

3. **Hybrid Tokens**

Some P2E projects combine governance and utility into a single token. For instance, a game might call its token "XYZ," which not only grants voting rights but also serves as the in-game currency for purchases and upgrades.

- ○ **Advantages**: Streamlines the ecosystem, preventing confusion from multiple tokens. Can lead to broader holder engagement if everyone who uses the token also wants a say in governance.
- ○ **Challenges**: If the token's supply must cater to in-game usage, balancing it with governance

demands can be tricky. Additionally, players who only want to buy items might not care about governance, while large governance holders might not be active players.

A well-designed hybrid system can be powerful, aligning incentives across multiple roles within the community. However, missteps in balancing these dual functions can produce the worst of both worlds—tokens that are neither effective as currency nor successful as governance assets.

4. **Evaluating Token Types Before Investing**

As a player or investor, consider the following questions when you encounter a new P2E token:

- o **Does the token offer meaningful utility that enhances gameplay?** If it's just slapped onto the project with no real use, the token's staying power may be weak.
- o **What kind of governance (if any) does the token enable?** Are important decisions truly community-driven, or is governance a superficial feature?
- o **Is the community engaged with governance or do only whales vote?** This can affect the fairness and direction of the project.
- o **Are there multiple tokens in the ecosystem, and how do they interact?** Some

P2E projects employ a dual-token system—one for governance, one for utility—to avoid conflicts.

Understanding a token's designated function in the ecosystem—be it governance, utility, or both—goes a long way toward predicting its demand patterns and long-term viability.

Beyond the Basics: Advanced Considerations in Tokenomics

While supply-and-demand, distribution, and token function provide the core framework for analyzing a P2E project's economics, some advanced topics round out a deeper understanding of tokenomics. These include the interplay of NFTs with token systems, multi-chain considerations, yield farming, and regulatory impacts. Let's explore each briefly.

1. **NFT Integration**

   Non-fungible tokens (NFTs) often coexist alongside a project's fungible tokens. NFTs represent unique characters, land plots, items, or cosmetics. The synergy between NFTs and tokens can define the project's revenue model:

   o **NFT Minting with Utility Tokens**: Players might need to spend utility tokens to mint or breed new NFTs. This continuously drives token demand.

- o **NFT Ownership and Governance**: In certain DAOs, NFT holders gain special voting privileges. For instance, each NFT might represent a seat on a "council," creating a parallel governance track.
- o **NFT DeFi Collateral**: Some advanced ecosystems allow NFT owners to stake or collateralize their assets in return for more tokens or stablecoins, blending gaming and decentralized finance.

A balanced relationship between tokens and NFTs can be a powerful lever, but it also adds complexity. Overreliance on NFT sales to fund development may overshadow token-driven gameplay loops, or vice versa.

2. **Multi-Chain and Cross-Chain Economics**

As blockchain technology advances, many P2E games opt to launch on multiple networks or use sidechains to reduce fees and improve scalability. This multi-chain approach can expand the player base but complicate tokenomics:

- o **Bridging Tokens**: If a token exists on multiple chains (e.g., Ethereum, Binance Smart Chain, Polygon), bridging solutions must lock tokens on one network and mint them on another. Mismanagement of bridges can lead to double-spending or supply inflation.

- Liquidity Fragmentation: Having tokens across different networks can dilute liquidity, making it harder to maintain stable prices. Project teams often rely on liquidity incentives or bridging alliances to unify markets.
- Chain-Specific Features: Some networks offer unique DeFi integrations or governance tooling. If the P2E game tries to replicate them on multiple chains, design inconsistencies or imbalances may arise.

Multi-chain deployment can increase a project's reach but requires careful coordination of token supply, bridging mechanics, and community governance across platforms.

3. Yield Farming and DeFi Elements

Another emerging trend is the integration of yield farming and DeFi protocols within a P2E title. For instance, the game's native token might be paired with a stablecoin on a decentralized exchange (DEX), and the project offers additional token rewards (like a liquidity mining program) for providing liquidity. This approach can rapidly bootstrap liquidity for new tokens but also invites speculative capital:

- High APYs and Risks: While initial yield programs may advertise impressive annual percentage yields (APYs), these can plummet once the initial hype fades. Additionally, impermanent loss can affect liquidity providers.

- o **Complex Contracts**: Smart contract exploits or hacks in DeFi pools can lead to major losses for participants. Thorough audits and proven code libraries are essential.
- o **Ecosystem Synergy**: If done right, yield farming can encourage players to hold tokens and generate stable markets, enhancing the game's long-term viability. However, it must integrate smoothly with gameplay loops.

4. **Regulatory Environment**

The legal status of P2E tokens varies by jurisdiction. Some regulators view certain token structures as securities, especially if investors expect profit from the efforts of others. Issues can also arise around anti-money laundering (AML) laws, know-your-customer (KYC) requirements, and gambling regulations:

- o **Location-Based Restrictions**: Some P2E titles bar residents from specific countries, or certain functionalities (like prize pools) may be locked based on IP geolocation.
- o **Tax Implications**: Earning tokens in-game might be taxable income in some countries, and selling tokens could incur capital gains taxes. Players must track transactions carefully.
- o **Evolving Frameworks**: Because laws change frequently, game developers must stay updated and adapt tokenomic models to avoid regulatory

crackdowns. This uncertainty can affect token value, especially if large user bases are cut off.

While these advanced considerations may not be top of mind for casual players, they critically shape a project's future. Serious P2E investors and avid gamers benefit from at least a basic awareness of these issues.

Real-World Examples and Case Studies

To illustrate the principles covered in this chapter, let's look at a few well-known P2E projects and how they handle tokenomics.

1. **Axie Infinity**
    - **Two-Token Model**: Axie Infinity uses Axie Infinity Shards (AXS) as a governance token, while Smooth Love Potion (SLP) functions as a utility token for breeding Axies. This bifurcated system helps ensure each token has a distinct role—AXS for staking and voting, SLP for in-game mechanics.
    - **Supply Management**: SLP is minted by players as rewards for winning battles, but breeding Axies requires spending SLP, effectively burning it. This creates a cyclical sink. AXS has a capped supply and is often locked in staking contracts.
    - **Evolving Economy**: A surge in Axie Infinity's player base in mid-2021 sparked runaway growth

in SLP prices, eventually leading to speculation and inflation concerns. Developer interventions—like adjusting SLP rewards—highlight how P2E economies require continual calibration.

2. **The Sandbox**

   ○ **Multiple Utilities**: The SAND token is used to buy virtual land, pay for avatar upgrades, and stake for yield. This wide range of in-game utilities forms a strong demand base, reinforced by frequent land sales.

   ○ **Community-Centric Governance**: SAND holders can vote on asset creation guidelines or new features. The Sandbox has also allocated tokens to a foundation that supports user-generated content, fueling game expansions.

   ○ **Layer-2 Integrations**: High gas fees on Ethereum led The Sandbox to explore Layer-2 solutions (like Polygon) to ensure microtransactions remain feasible. This demonstrates adaptability in tokenomics strategy.

3. **Decentraland**

   ○ **MANA Token**: Decentraland's token, MANA, is burned whenever users buy land parcels or certain in-world items. This deflationary mechanism counters new tokens introduced via the marketplace.

   ○ **Decentralized Governance**: Decentraland uses a DAO for major decisions, with MANA token holders able to propose and vote on changes. Over time, the community has influenced land policies, event subsidies, and more.

- ○ **Challenges**: MANA's price can fluctuate strongly based on overall crypto market sentiments. The community also debates how best to incentivize content creation so that land remains valuable.

Each case underscores the need to balance supply, demand, distribution, and governance in a dynamic environment. Despite differences in design, the core tokenomic principles we've explored remain highly relevant.

Practical Steps for Evaluating a P2E Token's Viability

Given the breadth and complexity of tokenomics, how can you, as a prospective player or investor, quickly gauge whether a project's economy is stable and promising? Below is a concise checklist:

1. **Read the Whitepaper Thoroughly**

   Look for details on:

   - ○ **Total Supply and Emission Rate**: Is the supply capped, inflationary, or algorithmic? How fast are new tokens issued to players?

- o **Token Sinks**: Are there robust burning or spending mechanisms that offset minting?
- o **Utility**: Are tokens essential for meaningful in-game actions, or are they merely a speculative asset?

2. **Examine Distribution and Vesting**
   - o **Allocation Percentages**: How much goes to founders, private investors, public sales, and community rewards?
   - o **Vesting Schedules**: Are big unlock events looming that might flood the market with tokens?

3. **Assess Community and Governance**
   - o **Governance Model**: Does the token offer real voting power, or is governance superficial?
   - o **Decentralization**: How evenly distributed are tokens among holders? Do whales dominate?

4. **Check Marketplace Activity**
   - o **Liquidity and Trading Volume**: Is the token widely traded, or is volume thin and easily manipulated?
   - o **NFT or Asset Turnover**: Are the game's NFTs selling regularly, or is the market stagnant?

5. **Monitor Ongoing Development and Updates**
   - o **Roadmap Progress**: Has the team delivered on promised features, or are updates perpetually delayed?
   - o **Response to Economic Fluctuations**: Do developers actively recalibrate reward rates or add new sinks when inflation appears, or do they ignore economic warnings?

6. **Watch the Broader Crypto Market**
   - ○ **Risk Tolerance**: If the overall crypto market is bearish, even solid P2E projects can see token prices dip.
   - ○ **Project Branding**: In bull runs, hype can overshadow fundamentals; in bear cycles, only projects with strong use cases tend to survive.

By applying these steps consistently, you protect yourself against poorly designed economies and identify the projects that have real staying power.

The Future of P2E Tokenomics

As P2E gaming continues to mature, tokenomics will remain a vital area of experimentation and evolution. Here are some future-oriented trends and possibilities:

1. **Dynamic, Adaptive Economies**

   We may see more games implement automatic, algorithmic adjustments to token supply or rewards. If the player base grows significantly, the system could scale token issuance accordingly, and vice versa. AI-driven analytics might even identify potential exploits or surpluses in real time, adjusting parameters to maintain equilibrium.

2. **Greater Emphasis on Interoperability**

Imagine tokens that are not only useful in a single game but also in multiple titles within a shared metaverse. Projects might form alliances, enabling cross-game item transfers, combined staking pools, or joint governance initiatives. This expanded utility would bolster token demand and potentially reduce volatility.

3. **Real-World Partnerships**

Some P2E economies may integrate with real-world brands or offline experiences. A governance token could grant access to special events, digital-physical crossover merchandise, or brand-sponsored tournaments. Such collaborations would broaden the token's appeal beyond crypto natives, driving mainstream adoption.

4. **Regulatory Clarity and Compliance**

As governments refine crypto regulations, P2E tokens that comply with consumer protection and financial disclosure rules may find it easier to operate globally. This might involve implementing KYC processes or restricting certain features in specific regions. While adding friction, it also paves the way for larger institutional partnerships.

5. **Evolving Role of Community Governance**

Current DAO structures may not be the final word in decentralized governance. Future models could refine voting power distribution, incorporate off-chain data, or delegate specialized roles for different aspects of the game (e.g., storyline development vs. treasury management).

Ultimately, tokenomics will remain a blend of art and science. Developers who strike the right balance of scarcity, utility, equitable distribution, and community empowerment will likely build thriving, long-lived games. Players who understand these dynamics gain an edge, both in identifying promising projects early and in optimizing their in-game strategies.

Conclusion

Tokenomics forms the backbone of any successful play-to-earn ecosystem. By deftly managing supply and demand, ensuring fair and transparent distribution, and designing tokens with meaningful utility or governance functions, project teams can foster robust virtual economies that benefit all participants— from casual gamers to professional traders. Conversely, projects that neglect these fundamentals risk becoming cautionary tales of inflationary collapse, concentrated wealth, or fleeting hype.

For players and investors alike, comprehending tokenomic principles can transform your journey through P2E worlds. You'll better judge whether a game's in-game currency is likely to appreciate, remain stable, or tumble in value. You'll also recognize the importance of governance as a tool for community self-determination, potentially shaping the features and policies that guide an entire metaverse.

As blockchain-based gaming continues to expand, tokenomics will undergo further experimentation, refinement, and evolution. The winners will be those who continually adapt to changing market conditions, community feedback, and technological innovations. In this exciting, uncharted landscape, knowledge is power. Understanding the nuances of supply and demand, distribution, and governance arms you with the insight to spot genuine opportunities—while steering clear of economic pitfalls.

By applying the lessons in this chapter, you can make more informed decisions about which P2E games to engage with, how to navigate token drops and reward systems, and how to evaluate projects' potential for long-term sustainability. Ultimately, tokenomics is about forging a virtuous cycle of engagement, value creation, and community empowerment—a synergy that lies at the heart of the play-to-earn revolution.

Chapter 8: Identifying Valuable NFTs

Non-fungible tokens (NFTs) have become a defining feature of the play-to-earn (P2E) landscape. As blockchain-based gaming evolves, NFTs represent unique characters, items, land parcels, and other digital properties that can be traded and owned with genuine scarcity. While early interest in NFTs once centered on collectible art or simple profile pictures, the gaming world has embraced NFTs for far more robust and practical reasons. In a play-to-earn environment, NFTs can confer in-game advantages, generate revenue streams, and serve as status symbols. Whether you are a casual gamer exploring P2E for fun or a strategic investor looking to build a diversified portfolio, the ability to identify valuable NFTs is a critical skill.

Yet, determining the value of any particular NFT is no simple task. While some tokens skyrocket in price and cultural relevance, others languish, never finding a significant audience or demand. What differentiates a hyped, fleeting success from a truly valuable digital asset? How can you spot NFTs that hold both intrinsic and speculative worth, or at least have the potential to do so over time?

This chapter delves into the essential factors that underpin an NFT's value in the context of play-to-earn gaming: scarcity and provable ownership, in-game utility, branding and lore, and secondary market considerations. You'll learn how to evaluate a collection's supply and rarity structure, how to assess whether an NFT's functionality can drive demand, why brand partnerships or a compelling narrative matter, and how liquidity and trading volumes affect your exit strategy. By exploring these core pillars, you'll be better equipped to make informed decisions about which NFTs might truly prove valuable, rather than chasing short-term hype or misleading marketing.

We'll start with the basics: scarcity and provable ownership. In blockchain gaming, as in any market, items that are legitimately scarce often garner premium prices. Yet scarcity alone is not enough; the blockchain's role in verifiable scarcity also shapes the reliability and authenticity of an NFT's supply. From there, we'll examine how genuine in-game utility can elevate an NFT from a speculative curiosity to a must-have digital asset. We'll then explore how storytelling, brand affiliations, and cultural resonance can transform an otherwise ordinary NFT into a social and economic phenomenon. Finally, we'll investigate the role of secondary markets—where the true test of demand and liquidity emerges—and why analyzing volumes and user sentiment is indispensable for making savvy acquisitions (or timely sales).

By the end of this chapter, you'll understand that "value" in NFTs is multifaceted. It's not just about having a rare piece of code on a blockchain but also about how that code interacts with the game's ecosystem, cultural cachet, and marketplace. Whether your goal is to collect, profit, or simply play effectively, a solid grasp of these principles will position you to navigate the ever-expanding universe of NFT-driven gaming with confidence and insight.

Scarcity and Provable Ownership

Scarcity is one of the foundational drivers of value in virtually every kind of collectible market, whether physical or digital. In the world of NFTs, scarcity takes on a new level of significance because it is mathematically verifiable on the blockchain. Each NFT is represented by a unique token ID, and reliable smart contracts ensure that no duplicates can be minted (unless explicitly authorized). But not all scarcity is created equal. For an NFT to hold or appreciate in value, it needs to be part of a collection or system where the supply is both credible and relevant to the game's ecosystem.

Below, we'll explore why scarcity matters, how to gauge whether an NFT is truly rare, and what role provable ownership plays in assuring collectors that they have something authentically unique in an ocean of digital assets.

1. **The Psychology of Scarcity**

   The principle of scarcity is deeply rooted in psychology and economics. People tend to attribute higher value to things that are in limited supply. When a P2E game releases only 10 "Legendary Dragons" or 500 "Special Edition Mechs," collectors and gamers alike see these items as more prestigious and possibly more powerful in-game. The fewer there are, the higher the price individuals are often willing to pay—especially if these items are perceived as "best in class" or hold status symbolism.

This phenomenon is akin to physical collectibles, such as trading cards or limited-run sneakers. Part of the value comes from the exclusivity—owning something that few others can have. However, in the digital realm, trust in scarcity was historically difficult to establish; anyone could copy a digital file. Enter the blockchain, which ensures that each digital asset can be tracked and verified across an open ledger, making duplication effectively impossible (unless contractually permitted). This cryptographic guarantee empowers the psychological power of scarcity with the reliability of transparent supply.

2. **Understanding Total Supply and Collection Structure**

When evaluating an NFT project, especially in gaming, a crucial step is to examine the total supply of the collection:

- o **Finite vs. Infinite Supply**: Some NFT series specify a strict cap (e.g., "There will only ever be 5,000 of these heroes"), while others are open-ended. If supply can keep expanding without clear limits, any single NFT could be diluted in value over time. A finite series, however, might maintain scarcity, assuming the game remains popular.
- o **Tiered Rarity**: Often, collections break down into tiers (common, rare, epic, legendary) or unique 1-of-1 items. Understanding how the

supply is distributed across these tiers is key. A game might have 10,000 total NFTs, but only 100 "Legendary" items. That ratio shapes your assessment of a particular NFT's potential worth.

- o **Seasonal or Time-Based Releases**: Some games introduce new NFTs periodically, tying them to "seasons" or "epochs." Early-season NFTs might hold special significance, as they represent the original release. Over time, if the player base grows, those early items could become more coveted for both nostalgic and scarcity-related reasons.

By understanding the structural and temporal aspects of supply, you gain insight into whether your potential NFT purchase might remain unique or face an onslaught of new variants, thus eroding rarity.

3. **Provable Ownership and Authenticity**

Blockchain technology's primary breakthrough for digital collectibles is the capacity to provide verifiable ownership. In older gaming systems, items existed purely on centralized servers; if the publisher shut down or changed the database, your "rare" item could be duplicated or invalidated. With NFTs, your ownership is recorded on a decentralized ledger. No single entity can unilaterally erase or counterfeit your asset.

- o **On-Chain Metadata**: Ideally, an NFT's metadata—its unique traits, appearance, stats—

should be stored or at least hashed on-chain. If metadata is kept off-chain, there's a slight risk that external servers could alter it. While storing large files on-chain is expensive, critical identifying information can still be written to the blockchain, bolstering authenticity.

o **Smart Contract Verification**: You can confirm the authenticity of an NFT by examining the smart contract address and token ID. Reputable projects typically verify their contracts on blockchain explorers like Etherscan or Polygonscan, giving you confidence that you're buying an official NFT rather than a knockoff.

o **Immutable Ownership History (Provenance)**: Blockchain records every transfer of the NFT from wallet to wallet, forming an unalterable chain of custody. This provenance can enhance value for certain items, similar to how collectors appreciate the documented history of a famous painting. If an NFT was once owned by a well-known player or minted under special conditions, the item's lore may grow, further increasing its worth.

4. **Supply vs. Demand: The Real Equation**

Of course, scarcity is only half the equation. An NFT can be extremely rare but still worthless if nobody desires it. Real demand arises from multiple factors, including a project's community, gameplay mechanics, brand associations, or alignment with current cultural trends.

Before buying an NFT purely because "there are only 50 in existence," ask yourself, "Will enough people want this to sustain or grow its value?"

In some gaming contexts, scarcity aligns with utility. If only 10 specialized spaceships exist and they dominate high-level PvP matches, serious competitors might pay a premium. However, if those ships are simply cosmetic, the demand may hinge on collector interest rather than competitive advantage.

5. **Marketplaces and Data Tools**

To gauge scarcity effectively, you can leverage various blockchain-based tools:

   o **NFT Marketplaces**: Platforms like OpenSea, Blur, or Magic Eden (depending on the blockchain) often list total supply and how many items are currently on sale. They also break down rarity rankings if the project metadata supports it.
   o **Analytics Sites**: Websites like NFTGO, CryptoSlam, or specialized dashboards may provide deeper metrics—such as distribution of rarities, floor price changes over time, or the top holders of a particular NFT series.

These resources help you determine whether a given NFT is "rare" but also in demand. If the floor price for a "Legendary" tier keeps climbing, it's a sign of strong market interest. If it's stagnant or declining, either the game's player base is dropping, or new supply has overshadowed the old.

6. **Red Flags of Artificial Scarcity**

Some unscrupulous projects use "artificial scarcity" as a marketing tactic. They might claim a low supply while quietly preparing to release additional "special editions" or "expansion sets." Alternatively, they might inflate the notion of scarcity by setting high minting prices but not actually capping supply. Always verify the actual contract terms and talk to the community to ensure the project is truly limited in a sustainable way.

Another red flag is if the game's developers frequently "rebrand" items or introduce near-identical assets under new sets, effectively cannibalizing the original collection. This approach might be a short-term cash grab at the expense of early supporters, so be alert if you see repeated expansions that undermine the value of previously rare NFTs.

In sum, scarcity underpinned by verifiable ownership is a powerful value-driver for NFTs in play-to-earn gaming. However, scarcity alone doesn't guarantee you'll strike digital gold. The item must also intersect with meaningful demand— whether competitive, social, or cultural. In the next section, we'll move from scarcity to utility, exploring how functional advantages or capabilities can dramatically boost an NFT's worth in a P2E environment.

In-Game Utility

While rarity and unique ownership can spark initial interest, long-term value in a P2E setting often hinges on in-game utility. An NFT that grants tangible benefits—like improved combat abilities, access to exclusive areas, or the ability to generate passive income—holds intrinsic worth. Even during market downturns, utility-driven NFTs may retain demand because players actually need them to participate fully in the game.

In this section, we'll dissect the multiple forms of in-game utility NFTs can provide, why utility is crucial for sustaining value, and what factors to consider when evaluating whether a particular NFT's functionality will remain relevant over time.

1. **Functional vs. Cosmetic Value**

    P2E gaming NFTs fall into two broad categories:

    o **Functional NFTs:** Provide gameplay advantages or additional features. These might be powerful weapons, characters with unique skill sets, land parcels generating resources, or specialized tools that speed up certain in-game tasks. Functional NFTs directly influence your effectiveness or earning potential in the game.

    o **Purely Cosmetic NFTs:** Offer visual flair— special skins, outfits, or animations—without altering gameplay mechanics. While cosmetics can still be highly valuable if they're rare or culturally iconic (think of limited-edition Fortnite skins), they lack the immediate, tangible use cases that functional NFTs provide. Their value leans more on aesthetic appeal, brand recognition, or collector demand.

If your goal is to maximize earnings or in-game performance, functional NFTs often yield a more stable or predictable value. However, cosmetic NFTs can still achieve significant worth if they become culturally significant or if the developer fosters strong brand and community attachments.

2. **Resource Generation and Yield Farming**

One of the most popular forms of NFT utility is the capacity to generate tokens or resources:

- o **Land Ownership**: Many metaverse-style or strategy P2E games sell virtual plots. Owners can "rent out" land to other players for resource production, host events that generate fees, or collect taxes in a game's token. In these scenarios, land NFTs may produce passive income, making them particularly attractive to both gamers and investors.
- o **Production Buildings**: Some NFTs might act as digital factories, forging items that are necessary for broader gameplay. If the items are crucial and the game population is large, these NFTs become revenue generators.

- Staking Mechanisms: Certain NFTs can be staked in a protocol to earn yield—possibly in the game's native token or a governance token. This blends decentralized finance (DeFi) with gaming. If the yields remain competitive, the NFTs that enable staking can appreciate significantly.

The downside is that if a game's economic model proves unsustainable, the yield can drop swiftly, or the token might lose value. Therefore, you must assess whether the developer's approach to reward distribution is balanced and consistent with the game's growth potential.

3. **Access to Exclusive Game Modes or Content**

Another form of utility revolves around gating content:

- Unique Quests or Dungeons: An NFT might grant entry to challenging missions that drop rare loot or large amounts of in-game currency. Players who own such NFTs can earn more, fueling consistent demand if the returns are lucrative.
- Beta Testing and VIP Passes: Some projects allow NFT holders to test expansions early, giving them a head start on new items or mechanics. Others might give NFT owners VIP perks—like skip-the-line benefits in queue-based events.
- Community Hubs or Social Spaces: In virtual worlds, an NFT might function as a "key" to an exclusive district or server. Within these

hubs, you might network with influential players, form alliances, or trade high-value goods more easily.

The allure here is exclusivity and potential advantage. However, if the game's gating mechanisms are too restrictive, the broader player base may revolt or simply lose interest. Striking a healthy balance between open accessibility and gated benefits is essential for any sustainable P2E ecosystem.

4. **Character Progression and Breeding**

In games that feature collectible characters—like monsters, heroes, or pets—an NFT might serve as your protagonist or a key piece of your team. Unique genes or traits could define combat performance, synergy with other characters, or cosmetic flair. Some P2E titles also introduce "breeding" systems, where two NFTs can produce offspring with genetic traits inherited from the parents. This breeding mechanic can be a powerful driver of demand:

- **Rarity of Traits**: If certain attributes are extremely rare or synergistic, NFTs that carry them become valuable breeding stock.
- **Breeding Fees**: Typically, breeding requires spending tokens, which also burns or locks those tokens in the process. If the game's population grows, demand for breeding climbs, potentially elevating the price of parent NFTs.

- **Generational Rarity**: Early generation NFTs might hold special statuses. For instance, "Generation 1" characters could have distinct attributes or a collectible aura that later generations lack. This can lead to consistent price appreciation if the game stands the test of time.

Of course, breeding-based economies can become oversaturated if new NFTs flood the market, so it's crucial to confirm that developers implement effective controls, like limiting how often an NFT can breed or requiring substantial fees.

5. **Longevity and Updates**

A key question: Will the NFT's utility remain relevant in future updates or expansions? Some P2E games may rotate "meta" or introduce power creep, where newly released NFTs overshadow older ones. To maintain or grow an NFT's worth, developers might:

- **Buff and Nerf Cycles**: Regularly rebalance characters or items. While this keeps gameplay fresh, it can tank the value of an NFT that gets nerfed, or conversely, skyrocket one that's buffed.
- **Cross-Game Compatibility**: In some forward-looking projects, NFTs can be ported or recognized across multiple titles. This "interoperability" can preserve value even if one game version sunsets or transforms.

- **Community-Focused Changes**: Developers might poll NFT holders on how expansions or rebalances should proceed. If a core group invests heavily in certain NFTs, they may push for their continued relevance, reinforcing confidence in the asset's durability.

Always analyze the roadmap and developer communications to see if they have a thoughtful strategy for preserving or evolving NFT utility over time. A single patch can drastically reshape the game's economy, so an NFT that's all-powerful today might not be so tomorrow, unless the dev team has a stable plan.

6. **Assessing Potential Utility Before You Buy**

Here are some practical tips:

- **Read the Whitepaper or Game Documentation**: Look for explicit explanations of how the NFT fits into game systems, whether it's integral or merely decorative.
- **Talk to the Community**: Players with experience often know which NFTs are "must-haves" or "meh." Engaging in Discord or Reddit can yield honest feedback.
- **Observe Gameplay Streams**: If the game is live, watch Twitch or YouTube streams to see how top players use these NFTs in practice. Is the item essential or just a novelty?

- Check Future Plans: Does the roadmap feature expansions that might upgrade the NFT's capabilities? Or are existing assets possibly overshadowed by upcoming releases?

Focusing on genuine functionality can protect you from purely speculative hype. While purely cosmetic NFTs can yield profits if they achieve cultural cachet, those with robust in-game utility often enjoy more stable demand and price floors—particularly in player communities that value performance and efficiency. But even a powerful in-game NFT can falter if it lacks broader appeal, branding, or narrative depth, which brings us to our next major factor: the role of storytelling, partnerships, and cultural resonance.

Branding, Partnerships, and Lore

NFTs that boast strong narrative elements, connections to established brands, or endorsement by popular influencers often enjoy sustained demand—sometimes even overshadowing purely functional considerations. In the gaming sphere, items that tie into a beloved story, a blockbuster IP, or an iconic figure can spark emotional attachment and collector fervor. Moreover, brand partnerships can reassure players and investors about a project's legitimacy, fueling longer-term interest.

Below, we dive into how branding, strategic alliances, and lore can transform an otherwise ordinary NFT into a must-have digital artifact.

1. **The Power of Narrative and Storytelling**

Humans connect deeply with stories. A sword is just a sword—unless it's the legendary "Blade of Aeons," wielded by a fabled warrior who saved the kingdom in the game's lore. By weaving in detailed backstories, developers can elevate an NFT's status beyond mere pixels and code:

- **In-Game Quests and Lore**: Players who embark on epic quests to earn or discover an NFT are more likely to see it as a symbol of personal achievement or narrative immersion.
- **Collectible Journals or Artifacts**: Some games design NFTs that represent pieces of the world's history—like ancient artifacts or diaries from legendary heroes. These items can become cornerstones for lore-centric collectors.
- **Fan Communities and Cosplay**: Lore-rich games often inspire fan art, cosplay, and roleplaying communities, all of which reinforce the cultural value of key NFTs. If your NFT is recognized as part of the official canon, fans might pay a premium to acquire it.

This storytelling aspect is reminiscent of how physical collectibles linked to famous movies or comic universes can fetch high prices. The difference in P2E is that you also get interactive utility, a bigger draw for players who want to live out the story while earning.

2. Brand Collaborations and Licensing

Partnerships with major brands can significantly boost an NFT project's credibility:

- **Renowned IPs and Franchises**: If a P2E game partners with a film studio, anime series, or a well-known gaming franchise, the NFTs can inherit a built-in audience. Fans of that IP might flock to the new venture, quickly driving up demand.
- **Sports and Celebrity Tie-Ins**: Some games partner with popular athletes, musicians, or celebrities who release signature NFTs or in-game avatars. These collaborations tap into fan bases that might not otherwise be into crypto or gaming.
- **Cross-Promotion**: Co-branded events (e.g., a seasonal event featuring characters from a famous manga) can generate massive buzz, especially if exclusive, limited-edition NFTs drop during that period. The association alone can catapult an NFT's value.

Of course, not every brand partnership guarantees success. Some can be seen as cash grabs if there's no meaningful integration into the actual gameplay or community. Players can sense authenticity versus shallow endorsements, so evaluate how the brand's identity meshes with the game's core themes.

3. **Influencer and E-Sports Endorsements**

In the P2E space, top streamers, e-sports pros, or crypto influencers can wield significant sway. If a major figure publicly praises an NFT or uses it as their in-game persona, the market often takes note:

- **E-Sports Teams**: Competitive gaming teams that adopt certain NFTs as official skins or gear can raise the profile of those assets. If the team performs well, the NFT's perceived prestige might climb accordingly.
- **Content Creators**: YouTube guides or Twitch streams that consistently feature a specific NFT or brand can rally followers to want the same item. Over time, this can feed into rising prices.
- **Celebrity Endorsements**: While high-profile endorsements can spark short-term hype, they need to be consistent and credible to sustain interest. An abrupt exit or negative publicity from an influencer can just as easily deflate prices.

Always investigate whether an influencer is genuinely enthusiastic or merely doing a one-time sponsored post. Long-term brand ambassadorship typically has more impact on market confidence.

4. **Cultural Moments and Memes**

It's not just official lore or big-name partnerships that matter; sometimes, community-driven memes or viral moments give an NFT its cultural weight. For instance, if a certain in-game pet becomes the subject of hilarious viral memes, that pet might see a surge in value, no matter how common it is. This phenomenon is unpredictable but can lead to enormous spikes in demand:

- o **Inside Jokes or Easter Eggs**: NFTs containing Easter eggs that reference a popular meme or developer in-joke might gain "cult" status.
- o **Community-Driven Artwork**: Players may create derivative art or fan fiction, turning an NFT into a broader phenomenon that transcends the game itself.
- o **Social Media Virality**: A tweet or clip about a bizarre or incredible NFT gameplay moment can go viral, elevating that NFT's profile overnight.

While meme-driven interest can be explosive, it can also be fleeting. Without underlying utility or consistent cultural interest, prices may retreat as quickly as they rose. Still, in the unpredictable world of P2E, cultural resonance can spark huge opportunities for savvy observers.

5. **Long-Term Commitment by the Developer**

If a studio invests significantly in world-building—releasing comics, animated shorts, or expansions that expand on the game's universe—NFTs from that universe can become anchor points in the franchise's lore. The more the developer invests in fleshing out the story and forging external partnerships (e.g., with merchandise or streaming platforms), the more likely the NFTs become iconic rather than ephemeral.

As a prospective buyer, gauge whether the developers mention lore, brand integration, or storyline expansions in their roadmap. Are they producing short stories, cinematics, or crossovers that highlight these NFTs? Do they host recurring lore events, encouraging players to learn about and collect items that connect to the narrative? Such activities can be strong indicators that the project has a robust cultural heartbeat, potentially supporting higher and more stable valuations.

In essence, branding, partnerships, and lore inject a deeper layer of emotional or cultural meaning into an NFT. While "purely functional" NFTs can command strong prices, those that also resonate with fans on a personal or narrative level often outshine the rest—particularly if they become emblematic of the game's identity or a broader cultural moment. Yet even the best lore or brand synergy may fail to translate into profits if secondary market dynamics are weak, which leads us to the final section: understanding liquidity, volume, and trading behaviors in NFT marketplaces.

Secondary Market Considerations

No matter how rare, functional, or well-branded an NFT is, its actual trade value depends on its liquidity and demand within secondary markets. Liquidity—the ease with which you can buy or sell without drastically affecting price—matters greatly to both collectors and players. An NFT may be theoretically worth a fortune, but if only a handful of buyers are interested and no trades occur, you might struggle to realize that value.

In this concluding section, we delve into how secondary markets operate, key metrics to watch, strategies for listing and pricing your NFT, and how to read market sentiment for timely decisions.

1. **Liquidity and Trading Volume**

   Trading volume is often the first indicator potential buyers or sellers consult to gauge an NFT's health. Volume reveals how many transactions took place over a certain period (24 hours, 7 days, 30 days, etc.) and the total amount of cryptocurrency spent:

   - **High Volume**: Signals strong demand and a stable stream of buyers and sellers. It's easier to enter or exit a position without steep discounts or markups.
   - **Low Volume**: Suggests a smaller, possibly more niche market. While niche items can yield large profits if you find the right buyer, it can take weeks or months to complete a sale.

   Liquidity is closely tied to volume. In a highly liquid market, your NFT can be sold relatively quickly at near the going rate. In an illiquid market, a single big order can push prices up or down substantially, creating volatility or stuck listings.

2. **Floor Price and Rarity Premiums**

NFT marketplaces typically display a "floor price," the lowest price at which an NFT from a given collection is listed. Floor price is a quick metric for how the market collectively values the most common or entry-level assets in that collection. Meanwhile, rarer or more special NFTs command a premium over the floor.

- **Floor Price Trends**: A rising floor price over weeks or months can indicate growing demand. A rapidly dropping floor price might warn of waning interest or oversupply.
- **Rarity Multipliers**: If an NFT is in the top 5% of the rarity scale, it might list at several times the floor price. Check if recent sales actually support that multiplier. Sometimes sellers overprice rare items that never move.
- **Market Depth**: Are there a large number of listings around the floor price, or does the price jump quickly after a few tokens? A shallow market can lead to fast price swings.

Observing how quickly rare NFTs sell at their premium can help you determine if the collection's top end is healthy or inflated.

3. **Historical Sales Data**

Studying historical transaction records offers insights into a collection's volatility, cyclical trends, and potential triggers:

- **All-Time High (ATH)**: Identifies the collection's peak price and how far current prices stand from that mark. If prices are near ATH amid strong fundamentals, it may signal momentum; if they're far below ATH, you must evaluate whether the project has lost popularity or is simply in a down cycle.
- **Sales Frequency**: How many NFTs from this collection sell on a daily or weekly basis? If consistent, that suggests an active and engaged market. A near-dead sales chart can indicate you'll struggle to find buyers.
- **Seasonality or Update-Driven Spikes**: Do prices surge after major patches, tournaments, or expansions? Understanding these patterns can help you time purchases or sales to capitalize on hype or content drops.

Blockchain explorers or NFT analytics websites let you filter and analyze transactions, checking average sale prices, number of unique owners, and the time intervals between major price shifts. This data is vital for making an informed decision.

4. **Platform Choice**

Different NFT marketplaces have varying user bases, fee structures, and reputations. Some are specialized in gaming, while others handle a broader range of collectibles and digital art. To get maximum exposure for your NFT:

- o **Identify the Main Hub**: Usually, each P2E project has a recommended or official marketplace—be it OpenSea (Ethereum-based), Magic Eden (Solana-based), or a proprietary in-game marketplace. That's where you're likely to find the most relevant traffic.
- o **Compare Fees**: Transaction fees, listing fees, and royalties to the creator can erode your profit margin. If fees are extremely high, it might push buyers away. Some marketplaces also offer lower fees for early adopters or stakers of their platform token.
- o **Look for Verified Collections**: Many marketplaces verify official collections. Listing a "fake" NFT or falling for a counterfeit listing is a risk in unverified corners of the market.

If a game's user base is mostly active on a particular platform, listing your NFT elsewhere might result in fewer eyeballs. Conversely, cross-listing can reach broader audiences if you're willing to pay multiple listing fees and carefully manage orders.

5. **Timing Your Buy or Sell**

Timing in NFT markets can be crucial for maximizing returns or securing good deals:

- o **Buying Into Dips**: When markets correct, you might acquire NFTs at discounted prices if you still believe in the game's fundamentals. FUD (fear, uncertainty, doubt) can push weak hands to sell.
- o **Selling at Hype Peaks**: Major expansions, influencer endorsements, or e-sports championships can temporarily spike demand. Listing your NFT during these windows may yield premium offers.
- o **Diamond Hands vs. Quick Flips**: Decide if you're a long-term collector or aiming for shorter-term profit. Quick flippers constantly search for hype cycles, while diamond-hand collectors bank on future expansions, brand growth, or stable game ecosystems.

Remember, day-to-day fluctuations can be noisy. If you truly believe in a project's long-term viability, you may ignore minor dips. However, if you see fundamental cracks—diminishing player counts, developer scandals—consider offloading sooner rather than later.

6. **Community Sentiment and Future Potential**

Liquidity in NFT markets is also correlated with how the community feels about a game or collection. Negative news—like exploit hacks or abrupt rule changes—can spook holders, drying up demand. Conversely, a well-received patch or high-profile partnership can reenergize trading.

Always stay plugged into the game's official channels, developer updates, and fan discussions to sense whether morale is high, cautious, or outright skeptical. If an upcoming expansion is rumored to make existing NFTs more valuable, that speculation can drive a wave of purchases. If a new wave of supply might overshadow old collections, sellers might rush to liquidate.

Ultimately, secondary market success for any NFT lies in synergy among scarcity, utility, brand narrative, and robust buyer interest. Even the most interesting or well-promoted NFT can fail in an inert or negative marketplace, so weigh all these factors before making big moves.

Conclusion

The emergence of NFTs in play-to-earn gaming has forever changed how players engage with digital assets. No longer are items locked in a developer's database, intangible and at risk of disappearing if a server shuts down. Instead, NFTs deliver genuine ownership: you can verify provenance, track rarity, and sell or trade your assets openly on decentralized marketplaces. But with the freedom of ownership comes the need for careful discernment. Not every NFT will prove valuable in the long run. Many collections vanish into obscurity, overshadowed by more innovative games or overshadowed by new expansions within the same ecosystem.

By understanding the four core pillars explored in this chapter, you can significantly improve your ability to pick NFTs with enduring appeal:

1. **Scarcity and Provable Ownership**: Verify that supply is truly finite and that the project's smart contract and metadata confirm genuine scarcity. Watch out for artificial or unbounded supply expansions that dilute value.

2. **In-Game Utility**: Seek items that do more than look pretty. Whether it's land generating passive income, characters yielding in-game tokens, or gear granting competitive advantages, utility often underpins real, consistent demand.

3. **Branding, Partnerships, and Lore**: Cultural resonance can elevate an NFT from a functional tool to a coveted collectible. Look for reputable collaborations, compelling storylines, and strong developer commitment to the game's lore and identity.

4. **Secondary Market Considerations**: Ultimately, liquidity matters. Investigate trading volumes, floor price trends, and how the community responds to market fluctuations. A high-value NFT is only as good as its liquidity—can you readily sell it or find enough bidders at the price you want?

Knowledge in these areas helps you avoid the pitfalls of hype-driven cycles and focus on assets with actual staying power.

Still, success in NFT collecting or investing remains partly an art. Gaming communities can be unpredictable, memes can propel a seemingly irrelevant NFT to stardom, and developer decisions can change the course of an entire ecosystem overnight. Stay adaptable, do your due diligence, and engage with fellow players to remain updated on emergent trends.

Above all, remember that value can also be deeply personal. You might choose an NFT because you love its artwork, relish the story behind it, or find joy in using it in daily play. That subjective dimension of "fun" and "attachment" can be as important as any calculation of supply, demand, or brand synergy. If your NFT also happens to appreciate in market price, that's an additional benefit.

As you proceed in your P2E journey, continue refining your approach. Keep tabs on new game releases, expansions, and shifts in NFT technology. With each transaction or community discussion, your instincts for spotting legitimate value—rather than fleeting hype—will sharpen. Armed with the insights from this chapter, you'll be better prepared to navigate the dynamic interplay of rarity, utility, cultural cachet, and liquidity, ultimately identifying NFTs that both enrich your gaming experience and offer meaningful long-term prospects in the flourishing world of play-to-earn blockchain gaming.

PART IV: UNDERSTANDING THE BROADER VIRTUAL ECONOMIES

Chapter 9: The Metaverse and Interoperability

The concept of the metaverse has expanded from the realm of speculative science fiction into a tangible cornerstone of emerging digital economies. Once an abstract vision conjured by futurists, the metaverse is rapidly becoming the next frontier in online interaction, entertainment, and commerce. Driven by the convergence of blockchain gaming, social media, and decentralized virtual worlds, this new digital sphere promises to offer immersive experiences where identity, ownership, and creativity flow freely across multiple platforms.

In previous chapters, we examined the foundations of play-to-earn (P2E) gaming, the intricacies of tokenomics, and the nuances of NFTs. All of these developments converge in the metaverse, where they unlock a realm of interoperable assets, persistent digital identities, and boundless creative expression. Interoperability—an ability to move seamlessly between different virtual environments without losing your achievements, inventory, or personal status—lies at the heart of what makes the metaverse so compelling. It transforms isolated games and apps into interconnected experiences, forming an expansive tapestry of opportunities for players and creators alike.

Yet, the metaverse is also fraught with challenges, from technical hurdles around data portability and blockchain scalability to ethical questions about digital identity and privacy. As major tech companies, indie studios, and decentralized communities race to define and build their own versions of the metaverse, the landscape can look simultaneously chaotic and exhilarating. This chapter explores how the metaverse is defined, the potential of cross-game assets, and the significance of persistent digital avatars. By understanding these core concepts, you'll see why the metaverse is more than a buzzword—it's a profound shift in how we interact, transact, and represent ourselves online.

Defining the Metaverse

Although the term "metaverse" has gained mainstream attention, there is no single, universally agreed-upon definition. Broadly, the metaverse refers to a collective, persistent virtual space that incorporates aspects of social media, gaming, augmented reality (AR), virtual reality (VR), and blockchain-based economies. Unlike traditional games or online platforms that exist as discrete, siloed entities, the metaverse is envisioned as an interconnected network of digital worlds where users can seamlessly move their identities, assets, and social connections.

1. Origins and Evolution

The word "metaverse" first gained prominence in Neal Stephenson's 1992 science fiction novel *Snow Crash*, where it described a shared virtual reality realm accessible via the internet. Early virtual worlds like *Second Life* and MMORPGs such as *World of Warcraft* laid some groundwork by enabling millions of users to coexist online, but these ecosystems remained closed and under the control of centralized operators. With the advent of blockchain and decentralized networks, the possibility of player-owned assets, decentralized governance, and cross-world migration has rekindled the dream of a truly open metaverse.

2. Shared Persistent Spaces

The metaverse is persistent, meaning it continues to exist and evolve even when you're offline. Your actions in one session can have lasting implications, from changing the virtual landscape (buying real estate, building structures, affecting local economies) to forging relationships that persist across multiple games or social platforms. This persistence contrasts with traditional single-player or even multiplayer games where states reset or remain inaccessible once you leave a particular server.

3. Real-Time Interactivity and Social Presence

A core pillar of the metaverse is real-time, synchronous interaction. Think of thousands or millions of users coexisting in a space, each represented by an avatar, conversing, building, trading, playing mini-games, or attending virtual concerts and conferences together. This social dynamism fosters community, collaboration, and cultural phenomena that can rival those in the physical world.

4. Player-Centric and User-Generated

Many visions of the metaverse place players at the center. Instead of passively consuming pre-packaged content, participants actively shape the environment—designing avatars, crafting games, selling digital art, organizing events, or launching decentralized businesses. User-generated content (UGC) is a key driver of creativity and innovation. In a well-designed metaverse, players can monetize their creations via NFTs or tokens, aligning incentives to fuel a self-sustaining economy of creation and trade.

5. Integration of Diverse Technologies

The metaverse is inherently cross-disciplinary. It incorporates elements of VR and AR to enhance immersion, AI for smart NPCs and procedural generation, social media for communication, and blockchain for ownership and finance. Over time, these technologies may become more interoperable, offering experiences that fluidly transition from a VR headset to a mobile phone or an AR overlay, each interface connecting you to the same persistent reality.

6. Decentralized Ownership and Governance

Underpinning many metaverse projects is the premise of decentralization. Users truly own their digital items and identities, and they may participate in governance decisions about world-building or economic policies through token-based voting systems (DAOs). This dynamic fosters a sense of communal stewardship and can engender powerful loyalty, as people are invested not just as players but as co-owners.

7. Fragmented Yet Interconnected

It's important to note that there is unlikely to be "one metaverse to rule them all." Instead, multiple platforms—each focusing on different niches, aesthetics, or game styles—will interconnect to form a collective metaverse. Some might emphasize competitive gaming, others social experiences or art galleries. The key is ensuring that a user's identity, assets, and achievements can transfer across these different virtual domains—a technological feat still in development.

By understanding these foundational elements, we see that the metaverse is not merely an advanced version of an online game but a new digital layer of human interaction. And while the ultimate shape of the metaverse remains up for grabs, cross-game assets stand as a defining aspect of its promise—an idea we'll explore in depth next.

Cross-Game Assets

One of the major breakthroughs blockchain technology brings to gaming is the concept of cross-game assets. Traditionally, each title maintains its own closed economy: items you acquire in *Game A* are non-transferable and non-usable in *Game B*. If you stop playing *Game A*, your investment of time and money effectively disappears. Interoperability flips this script by allowing a single NFT or digital token to have utility, or at least recognized existence, in multiple virtual environments. The ramifications are profound:

1. **What Are Cross-Game Assets?**

A cross-game asset is any digital property—most commonly an NFT—that can be recognized, displayed, or utilized in more than one game or platform. For instance, you might own a "Sword of Titans" in a medieval fantasy RPG. Because it's an NFT minted on a blockchain, another sci-fi-themed platform could choose to interpret that same NFT as a high-tech laser blade—different look, same underlying token. Or a VR art gallery might display this sword in a 3D glass case as part of a user's curated items.

2. **Expanded Utility and Value**

The central advantage here is that each new game or platform that supports the asset adds to its utility. Instead of a single-app use case, your sword or avatar skin can "travel" with you. This multiplicative effect significantly increases the value proposition for collectors and investors. The more cross-compatibility an NFT enjoys, the more robust and stable its demand can become. It's akin to a piece of clothing you can wear to any event or environment, rather than having to purchase a new wardrobe for each occasion.

3. Bridging and Data Standards

Achieving true interoperability, however, requires more than conceptual alignment—it needs technical frameworks. Different games might operate on different blockchains or use different NFT standards (like Ethereum's ERC-721, ERC-1155, or alternate protocols on Solana, Polygon, etc.). "Bridging" solutions are software mechanisms that lock tokens on one chain while minting a corresponding asset on another, allowing an NFT to exist effectively across networks. Metadata standards also matter: for a sword NFT to be recognized across five different games, those games must parse the same metadata fields—like item name, type, and stats—and reinterpret them within their unique aesthetics.

4. Collaborations and Partnerships

Many cross-game endeavors occur through official partnerships. Suppose two P2E titles sign an agreement that each will honor the other's items. They might create special attributes for imported NFTs or provide bonus quests to players carrying cross-game gear. These collaborations can be marketing gold: fans of each game become curious about the partner's universe, fostering broader community growth. The more alliances an NFT can form, the more cross-pollination and synergy happens, spurring an interconnected web of gameplay experiences.

5. Monetizing Cross-Game Assets

Beyond gameplay convenience, cross-game assets open up creative ways to earn:

- **Rentals**: Maybe you own a rare wizard staff that grants powerful spells in multiple games. You can rent it out to other players who want a temporary advantage or to appear stylish in a social VR setting.
- **Collectible Hubs**: An NFT can be showcased in a digital museum or marketplace visited by thousands. If it gains fame across multiple titles, it can appreciate in resale value.
- **Brand and E-Sports Integrations**: E-sports teams might sponsor an NFT, allowing the same "team-branded" weapon or avatar skin to be recognized in many different competitive arenas. Players could buy, sell, or trade these team-themed NFTs, forging deeper loyalty.

6. Potential Challenges

Of course, cross-game assets face technical and design challenges. Balancing is a prime concern—if an item is too powerful in one game, translating it directly to another might break that game's internal balance. Some games may choose to interpret cross-game gear in purely cosmetic ways. Another barrier is a lack of universal standards, leading to fragmented approaches to metadata, bridging, and ownership tracking. And from a business perspective, not all studios are comfortable letting external assets into their carefully crafted ecosystems. They risk losing control over their in-game economy or brand cohesion.

7. Future Outlook

Despite these hurdles, cross-game assets represent a defining future trend in the metaverse. As more developers see the competitive edge in cooperating and offering players expanded utility, interoperability is poised to become a major selling point. Gamers increasingly demand that the time and money they invest in digital goods transcend single-game boundaries. Over time, we may witness interconnected networks of games that share entire item libraries, user reputation scores, and even narrative crossovers—a phenomenon that was almost unimaginable a few years ago.

The notion of cross-game assets lays the foundation for a truly immersive metaverse, one in which the lines between separate games blur. Yet beyond items and equipment, there's another layer to this concept: the very identities and avatars we wear as we traverse these virtual worlds.

Digital Identity and Avatars

A persistent, blockchain-verified digital identity is arguably the linchpin of the metaverse. Rather than being forced to create a new login and avatar each time you download a game, you carry a cohesive digital persona across different environments. This unification of identity, achievements, and ownership can drastically improve user experience, fostering a stronger sense of continuity and personal investment. In this section, we'll dissect how digital identity and avatars function in the metaverse, and why they're crucial to unlocking its full potential.

1. **What Is a Digital Identity?**

A digital identity in the metaverse context refers to a core representation of "you" that persists across various platforms. This identity could encompass:

- o **Username or Handle**: A unique name that identifies you, recognized by multiple apps or games.
- o **Avatar Aesthetics**: Visual representation, from realistic VR models to stylized 2D avatars or humanoid creatures, that you can maintain consistently or modify at will.
- o **Ownership Records**: A record of the NFTs, tokens, or achievements tied to your account.
- o **Social Graph**: Lists of friends, guild affiliations, or community memberships that carry across different titles.

Typically, blockchain-based identities rely on cryptographic wallets or addresses that prove you're the rightful owner of certain NFTs or tokens. This wallet-based approach ensures you can log in to a new platform, connect your wallet, and instantly show your assets or avatar customization without duplicating sign-up steps.

2. Advantages of Unified Identity

Having a persistent identity across multiple environments yields several benefits:

- **Seamless Transition**: Jump from a fantasy RPG to a virtual nightclub to a digital art gallery, keeping your avatar's outfit, username, and relevant items.
- **Reputation and Trust**: Positive behavior or achievements in one community can translate into credibility in another. Alternatively, toxic behavior or cheating can tarnish your reputation across platforms, incentivizing better conduct.
- **Personal Branding**: Influencers, e-sports players, or digital entrepreneurs can cultivate a consistent brand, rather than fracturing their fanbase across different games with different user profiles.
- **Simplified Asset Management**: All your NFTs, tokens, and in-world currencies are tied to your single identity, making it straightforward to track or trade them, or to showcase them in multiple contexts.

3. Avatar Customization and Expression

Avatars in the metaverse can take countless forms, from hyper-realistic virtual humans scanned from your physical likeness to fantastical creatures or even abstract geometric shapes. Your avatar becomes an extension of your self-expression—just as clothing or tattoos might in the real world. Thanks to NFTs, you can collect and mix various avatar skins, accessories, or animations from multiple sources:

- ○ **Cosmetic Interoperability**: A pair of NFT sneakers purchased in one game might appear on your avatar in another game, adapted to that game's graphics engine. This cross-platform wardrobe is a major draw for those who see digital fashion as a means of identity.
- ○ **Functional Upgrades**: Avatars might gain stats or special abilities in certain ecosystems. For instance, a "Neon Ninja" outfit NFT might boost stealth in a cyberpunk action game while offering a luminescent glow in a VR chat lounge.
- ○ **Metaverse Marketplaces**: Entire digital shopping malls or marketplace worlds could emerge, dedicated to avatar accessories, from hairstyles to backpacks to facial expressions. Users can test items in real time, see how they'd look in various games, and then purchase them on the spot.

4. **Proof of Skill and Experience**

Another emerging concept is that your avatar can display badges, trophies, or stats verifying your achievements across games. If you're a champion at a competitive MOBA, other players can see that record in an FPS or open-world MMO. This persistent skill portfolio can become an asset if you apply for a digital job—like e-sports coaching, streaming partnerships, or even community moderation.

- **Credentialing**: Some platforms experiment with awarding "on-chain credentials" for completing tutorials, proving creativity in building mini-games, or being an early beta tester. These badges may unlock exclusive content or job postings.
- **Reputation Tokens**: In more socially oriented metaverse spaces, you might accrue reputation points if you've helped moderate a forum, created popular UGC, or resolved conflicts. These intangible achievements become part of your avatar's social capital.

5. Privacy and Identity Control

Alongside these gains, persistent digital identity poses privacy concerns. If too much personal data is linked to one wallet or username, malicious actors might track your entire online history across different worlds. Conversely, advanced privacy tools on blockchain can allow you to prove certain credentials (like "I am over 18" or "I own 50 tokens") without revealing your entire identity or wallet content. Striking the right balance between identity continuity and selective anonymity is a key challenge, especially as the metaverse becomes more mainstream.

6. Challenges to Uniform Avatars

Despite the promise, unifying avatars across multiple games is no trivial task. Different engines have different polygon counts, animation rigs, color palettes, and file formats. A hyper-realistic face scan for a VR environment might not translate well into a voxel-based survival game. Developers must find ways to "convert" or interpret an avatar's base data to their unique style. Alternatively, users might maintain multiple versions of their avatar, each adapted for a particular environment but cryptographically tied to the same underlying identity.

7. Sovereignty Over Identity

Because your avatar can store so much value—both emotional and financial—maintaining sovereignty is crucial. The last thing a user wants is for a developer or platform to ban them, effectively seizing their identity or assets. A blockchain-based identity with no single point of control reduces this risk, though platforms still have the right to block users or disallow specific NFTs. The interplay between user autonomy and platform governance becomes a central ethical question in the metaverse space.

By fostering persistent, customizable avatars tied to a single blockchain-verified identity, the metaverse aspires to offer continuity of self across digital experiences, bridging everything from fantasy battles to corporate conferences. This vision, while ambitious, is increasingly within reach, thanks to advancing technology and the growing appetite for connected virtual life.

Expanding the Metaverse: Additional Dimensions of Interoperability

While cross-game assets and digital identities form the backbone of interoperability, the concept extends far beyond item sharing or avatar continuity. The metaverse envisions a tapestry of interconnected experiences, bridging gameplay, social interaction, work, education, and commerce. Below, we dive into further dimensions that broaden interoperability's scope.

1. Financial Interoperability

Beyond in-game assets, cryptocurrencies and tokens themselves can flow across platforms. For instance, if you earn native tokens by playing a fantasy RPG, you might spend them in a VR art gallery or swap them for stablecoins on a decentralized exchange. This cross-platform economic scaffolding allows a new wave of "meta-entrepreneurs" who run businesses entirely within virtual worlds. They might rent out NFT-based storefronts, hire other players using tokens, and even pay taxes or fees to game-specific DAOs. Over time, multi-chain bridging and improved DeFi integration will likely streamline these cross-environment financial transactions.

2. Communication Protocols and Social Graphs

Apart from items, your social relationships also need to be interoperable. Imagine a scenario in which your friend list from one MMO is automatically recognized in a different game, letting you message them or form a guild instantly. Achieving this requires standardized communication protocols and possibly decentralized "social graphs" stored on blockchain or distributed databases. Some projects, like Lens Protocol, aim to create universal social graphs that any app can read or update, letting users and devs maintain consistent social networks across apps.

3. Creative Collaboration Spaces

The metaverse is poised to empower real-time creative collaboration—artists, musicians, coders, or architects can collectively design a virtual environment or craft an in-game item, each contributing from their unique vantage point. Interoperable platforms might share asset libraries or building tools, letting a 3D modeler create a house in a VR design tool, then export it to a puzzle adventure game and a digital festival venue. Such synergy can drastically accelerate content creation, attracting even more players who crave fresh experiences.

4. Distributed Governance and Multi-World DAOs

Many P2E titles adopt decentralized autonomous organizations (DAOs) to govern tokenomic parameters, community events, or code updates. Interoperability might see the rise of multi-world DAOs that oversee not just one game but a network of related experiences. For instance, a "Metaverse Racing League DAO" might coordinate tournaments across multiple racing games, unify leaderboards, and distribute winnings in a shared token. This layering of decentralized governance across connected platforms could scale to entire "meta-federations" representing tens or hundreds of titles.

5. Cross-Domain Identity for Work and Learning

Expanding beyond entertainment, the metaverse can also host remote workspaces or educational hubs. Imagine attending a virtual university campus that recognizes your gaming achievements as well as your professional credentials stored on-chain. Collaborative workplaces might let you access specialized tools if you own certain NFT licenses. This blending of professional, recreational, and educational domains underscores how interoperability can unify all aspects of digital life, not just gaming.

6. Hardware Compatibility and Device Spanning

True metaverse interoperability must also span different devices—PC, console, mobile, VR headsets, or AR glasses. A user might explore an open-world environment in VR, switch to a phone-based chat in transit, then resume the same environment on a home console with advanced graphics. Ensuring a persistent experience across disparate hardware poses enormous UX and technical challenges.

Standardizing input methods, display capabilities, and user interfaces is key to preventing fragmentation.

7. **Personal Data Portability**

Beyond avatars and assets, personal data such as preference settings, customized UI layouts, and accessibility tools could also be "interoperable." A user who requires large font sizes or colorblind-friendly interfaces shouldn't have to reconfigure these settings in every new environment. In the metaverse, storing your preferences in a personal "data vault" could let each game auto-adapt, significantly improving quality of life for players with specific needs.

Challenges and Limitations

The ideals of an interconnected metaverse brimming with cross-game assets and persistent digital identities are undoubtedly alluring. Yet, significant roadblocks remain:

1. **Technical Complexity**

Bridging blockchains, interpreting different metadata standards, and ensuring real-time updates for millions of concurrent users is a monumental technical feat. Layer-2 solutions, sidechains, or advanced off-chain scaling are necessary, but each brings new complexities and potential vulnerabilities.

2. **Intellectual Property and Licensing**

For cross-game assets to work, each developer must grant permission to use or reinterpret the item. This touches on deep-seated IP concerns: studios fear losing brand control or allowing "foreign" assets that don't match their lore or aesthetic. Even in decentralized environments, forging official crossovers might require legal and licensing frameworks that have yet to be fully defined.

3. Balancing Gameplay and Economics

A primary challenge is how to maintain balanced, fair gameplay when outside assets come into a different ecosystem. If a user imports an overpowered NFT from another game, it may ruin the local economy or competitiveness. Developers might reduce the item's power or limit it to cosmetic functions, which can disappoint owners expecting full interoperability.

4. Centralization vs. Decentralization

Even if assets are minted on a public blockchain, a game's server logic often remains centralized. A developer could theoretically block or ban an NFT from use if they see it as exploitative or contradictory to the game's design. Realizing a fully decentralized metaverse would require user-run servers and open protocols, which remain in early stages.

5. Regulatory and Legal Gray Zones

The metaverse's economic potential invites scrutiny from governments worldwide. Questions about securities law, tax obligations for digital earnings, money transmitter licenses, and even digital zoning could emerge. Gaming companies unprepared for regulatory shifts could face fines or forced closures that disrupt entire cross-game ecosystems.

6. User Experience Friction

Not all players are comfortable with crypto wallets, bridging processes, or comprehending how to display their cross-game NFTs in different engines. Tools and interfaces must simplify these workflows for mass adoption. Achieving frictionless interoperability remains an ongoing design challenge.

7. Potential for Hyper-Corporatization

As big tech corporations move into the metaverse, they may push walled garden approaches—creating partial "metaverses" that only pretend to support interoperability while locking users into proprietary ecosystems. If these giants dominate, the open, decentralized ideal could be overshadowed by corporatized versions with limited cross-platform freedom.

Despite these hurdles, the momentum behind the metaverse remains robust. Entrepreneurs, developers, and communities are tackling each limitation with creative solutions, forging a path toward richer digital worlds that transcend traditional boundaries.

Cultural and Social Implications

Beyond the technical and economic aspects, a metaverse where assets, identities, and experiences intertwine raises profound cultural and social ramifications:

1. **Blurred Real-World and Virtual Boundaries**

With more lifelike VR, advanced avatars, and realistic social interactions, the line between virtual existence and everyday life blurs further. Some worry about "depopulation" of physical spaces or excessive escapism, while others see it as a new frontier for human creativity and connectivity.

2. **Identity Fluidity and Expression**

The metaverse can empower individuals to explore multiple identities—male, female, non-binary, anthropomorphic, or fluid forms—across various worlds. This flexibility can promote self-discovery, but it can also complicate social norms about trust, accountability, and personal representation.

3. **Digital Class Systems**

Just as in the physical world, disparities in resources and access can lead to digital hierarchies. Owners of expensive NFT assets or those with capital to invest in rare cross-game items may gain advantages. Without careful design, the metaverse could replicate or even exacerbate existing social inequalities.

4. Ownership vs. Open Sharing

Blockchain-based ownership fosters strong user agency but also introduces "private property" concepts into digital realms. Some communities might prefer more open, communal models. Striking a balance between user ownership and communal collaboration is an ongoing debate, reminiscent of real-world economic philosophies.

5. Global Community, Fragmented Cultures

The metaverse has no inherent geographic limits, allowing people worldwide to gather. This can foster cross-cultural exchange, but it may also create echo chambers as like-minded groups retreat into specialized micro-worlds. Governance tensions could arise when conflicting cultural values or laws collide in a single digital domain.

6. New Art, Media, and Storytelling

On a more optimistic note, the metaverse serves as a canvas for new forms of interactive art, media, and storytelling. Creators can stage transmedia experiences—perhaps starting with a webcomic, continuing in a VR puzzle game, culminating in a live concert inside a fantasy city. The synergy of real-time collaboration, user-generated content, and cross-platform synergy paves the way for genuinely novel cultural phenomena.

The Road Ahead: Future Outlook

The path to a fully realized metaverse is neither linear nor guaranteed. Yet, the convergence of blockchain technology, NFTs, advanced graphics, VR/AR, and decentralized financial models pushes the industry to reimagine how digital spaces function. Here are some developments to watch:

1. Widening Developer Adoption

As more studios experiment with NFT integration and open-world design, cross-game collaborations will become more common. Indie devs, lacking big budgets, can stand out by offering strong interoperability with existing popular titles or forming alliances with other creative teams.

2. E-Sports Metaverse

Competitive gaming could anchor the early stages of the metaverse, with players carrying their e-sports achievements, sponsor-branded gear, and personal followings across tournaments in different titles. In this scenario, "stadium" worlds host multi-game events, letting fans hop from one match to another seamlessly.

3. Bridging Traditional Media

Music, film, and literature creators may expand their IPs into the metaverse, letting fans immerse themselves in shared story universes. Exclusive NFT launches, live watch parties, or interactive spin-offs can create revenue streams beyond conventional entertainment.

4. UGC-Driven Worlds

Platforms like Roblox demonstrate the power of UGC, where millions of user-created "micro-games" flourish. A blockchain-backed alternative could combine robust user creation tools with real asset ownership, letting players monetize their worlds and expansions. Over time, these micro-worlds might connect to form a broader metaverse fabric.

5. Enterprise and Education

Businesses and universities might adopt metaverse principles for remote collaboration, training simulations, or global summits. If these 3D spaces interoperate with gaming realms, we could see cross-pollination of professional and entertainment ecosystems. A user's professional NFT-based credentials might also unlock special content in a historical simulation game, for instance.

6. Environmental and Ethical Considerations

As digital worlds scale, questions about energy consumption, e-waste (VR hardware), and responsible AI usage for in-world governance and content moderation will loom larger. Expect solutions like proof-of-stake blockchains, hardware recycling programs, and ethical guidelines on how AI interacts with user-generated content.

7. Regulatory Frameworks and Consumer Protection

Governments may impose rules for NFT exchanges, consumer protections against fraud, or guidelines for age-restricted content. Some might even attempt to shape the "metaverse public domain," ensuring certain standards of accessibility and fairness across the digital realm. The outcome will significantly shape how free or restricted cross-world travel and ownership can become.

In many ways, we stand at an inflection point analogous to the early internet: a nascent technology realm brimming with possibilities, controversies, and collaborative opportunities. The winners of the metaverse era will likely be those who embrace openness, empower users with genuine ownership, and design experiences that transcend the boundaries of a single brand or platform.

Conclusion

The metaverse heralds a new epoch in how we experience digital life. Rather than isolated games or apps, we are entering a connected tapestry of virtual environments where identity, items, and social relationships can flow freely—fueled by blockchain-based ownership, decentralized governance, and cross-platform collaboration. For gamers, this shift promises unparalleled freedom: items you earn or buy in one realm don't become worthless if you switch games; instead, they maintain or even expand their utility. For developers and entrepreneurs, it opens up new market opportunities for interoperability solutions, cross-IP partnerships, and user-generated expansions that collectively enrich the digital ecosystem.

Yet, the realization of this grand vision remains a work in progress. Technical standards are still evolving, bridging solutions can be clunky, and debates about balancing corporate interests with open access loom large. Moreover, the concept of a unified digital identity raises intricate questions of privacy, control, and social norms. One user's dream of a cohesive, permanent self might be another's nightmare of lacking anonymity or data exposure. The metaverse is as much a societal experiment as it is a technological one.

Nonetheless, the trajectory seems clear: an increasingly interconnected online world that transcends single-game boundaries. P2E gaming, with its emphasis on genuine asset ownership and token-based economies, sits at the forefront of this metamorphosis. Whether you're a casual player eager to carry your favorite avatar across different titles or an investor looking to back promising cross-world technologies, the metaverse extends an invitation to be part of a digital renaissance.

Just as the internet reshaped commerce, communication, and culture, the metaverse stands poised to reshape how we define reality, identity, and value. It won't happen overnight, but step by step—through cross-game items, blockchain-verified avatars, multi-chain bridging, and user-driven governance—the walls between virtual worlds will dissolve. We'll no longer just game or work or socialize online; we'll inhabit a vast mosaic of experiences that merges digital life with day-to-day reality, forging a new dimension of human society. And at the heart of it all stands the user's capacity to choose, connect, and create—

empowered by interoperability and the boundless imagination of a globally networked community.

Chapter 10: Virtual Real Estate, Land Sales, and Renting Models

The rapidly expanding metaverse offers unprecedented opportunities for digital asset ownership and monetization. Among the most compelling and tangible of these opportunities is virtual real estate, where parcels of land in online worlds can become profitable and socially vibrant spaces. No longer confined to speculative investments or mere gameplay cosmetics, virtual land can generate passive income, host immersive experiences, and serve as the backbone of entire virtual economies. From blockchain-based platforms like Decentraland and The Sandbox to more traditional virtual spaces such as Second Life, digital real estate is transforming into a legitimate asset class that mirrors many of the same economic forces as physical property.

Yet, virtual real estate is not merely an echo of the "real world." It encompasses novel forms of ownership, complex tokenization strategies, and collaborative investment models that redefine our understanding of property rights. Through smart contracts, fractional ownership solutions, and decentralized governance, even average players can become landlords, event hosts, or creative directors of online communities. Moreover, the line between commercial, residential, and entertainment districts in virtual worlds blurs, as these digital spaces incorporate anything from e-sports arenas and VR art galleries to sprawling shopping malls and immersive concert venues.

In this chapter, we'll examine the fundamentals of virtual land ownership, explore various approaches to leasing and fractional investment, and survey the wide array of commercialization opportunities that are emerging in these digital domains. Whether you're an aspiring "metaverse mogul," a casual player curious about the potential to earn passive income, or an investor looking to diversify into new forms of digital property, understanding the mechanics and economics of virtual real estate is crucial. By the end, you'll see how virtual land is not just a gimmick or a passing fad but a transformative part of the broader play-to-earn ecosystem—one that offers robust earning potential and shapes how we socialize, create, and do business in these persistent online worlds.

Land Ownership in Virtual Worlds

Although the idea of owning virtual land dates back to early experiments like Second Life in the mid-2000s, the concept has evolved considerably, propelled by blockchain technology and new game designs. Virtual worlds now offer land parcels as non-fungible tokens (NFTs), granting owners verifiable, transferable property rights. This shift has elevated the stakes: instead of ephemeral in-game territory subject to developer revocation, virtual land can be openly traded, rented, or built upon, much like traditional real estate.

Below, we explore why virtual real estate can be so valuable, how different platforms manage their land markets, and which factors influence land prices.

1. **Why People Value Virtual Land**
Virtual land's appeal transcends simple speculation:
   o **Passive Income**: By renting space to other users, hosting events, or running advertisements, landowners can generate revenue streams within the platform's native token or other cryptocurrencies.
   o **Creative Freedom**: Many platforms let owners create customized experiences—building shops, obstacle courses, interactive stories, or entire minigames. This fosters both artistic expression and commercial possibilities.
   o **Social Capital**: Land can become a hub for social gatherings, concerts, conferences, or gamer meetups. Owning a parcel in a bustling area can enhance your status and deepen community ties, which, in turn, can further boost foot traffic and profits.
   o **Limited Supply and Scarcity**: Most blockchain-based virtual worlds limit the amount of land available. Rarity can drive up demand, especially if the platform gains mainstream popularity. Much like real-world land, location matters: parcels near popular attractions or spawn points command higher prices.

2. **How Land Sales Typically Work**
While each virtual world handles land sales differently, certain common patterns emerge:

- ○ **Initial Land Offering**: Platforms usually hold an initial sale of parcels, often at a set price or through an auction system. Early participants may secure prime locations at relatively low costs. Over time, once the platform's popularity grows, resales can fetch significantly higher sums.
- ○ **Secondary Market**: After the initial sale, land is traded on NFT marketplaces or within the platform's internal marketplace. Using smart contracts, these transactions are trustless and transparent—ownership is proven via the public ledger.
- ○ **Land Terraforming or Development**: Some platforms let owners alter terrain, add buildings, or script unique activities on their parcels. Others keep the environment more uniform, restricting user modifications to simpler forms of content creation.
- ○ **Maintenance Fees or Taxes**: Certain virtual worlds impose monthly fees for holding land to encourage active use. The logic is similar to property taxes, discouraging squatting and promoting development.

3. Location Desirability and Traffic

One of the most direct parallels with real-world real estate is location-based pricing. Parcels near major "teleport hubs," spawn areas, or top attractions are at a premium. Why? Because foot traffic—i.e., the number of avatars passing by or visiting your property—drives business opportunities. A digital café in a well-traveled district might see considerably more visitors than one in a remote corner of the map. Platforms like Decentraland even emulate "district" concepts, where theme-based regions (art districts, fashion streets, gaming zones) cluster together, further concentrating traffic around popular niches.

4. Speculation vs. Utility

While plenty of land buyers have purely speculative motives—holding parcels with the hope that a future wave of users will inflate prices—others aim for long-term utility. Land hosting e-sports events, educational seminars, or NFT galleries can yield consistent returns as these experiences bring in paying visitors or sponsorships. Balancing speculation and actual utility is crucial; a healthy virtual land market typically sees robust development and user engagement rather than just hoarding.

5. Tech Considerations: Scalability and User Experience

For virtual land to remain valuable, the platform must handle large user bases and supply user-friendly creation tools. If a platform becomes too congested, with lag or high fees, land can lose its allure. Similarly, if building on your land requires complex programming skills, mainstream users might feel discouraged. Projects that streamline this process often attract a broader pool of potential landowners.

6. **Risk Factors**

Despite the upside, land ownership in virtual worlds is not without risks:

- o **Platform Survival**: If the developer abandons the project, the land's value could plummet. Even on decentralized platforms, a dwindling user base undermines the reason for owning land in the first place.
- o **Regulatory Uncertainty**: Some governments could impose taxation or classify digital land as a form of security, complicating things for owners.
- o **Technological Obsolescence**: Emerging virtual worlds might outcompete older ones with better graphics, features, or IP partnerships. The land you own in a fading platform might become akin to real-world property in a town with a shrinking population.

Still, for those who do their due diligence—examining a project's roadmap, community engagement, and technical underpinnings—virtual land can offer an appealing intersection of creativity, community, and profit. Owning a piece of the metaverse becomes a tangible experience, heightened by the knowledge that you can monetize your corner of cyberspace in myriad ways. Next, we'll examine how renting and fractionalized ownership models expand access to virtual land and can help owners further capitalize on their digital holdings.

Leasing and Fractional Ownership

Not everyone who wants to participate in virtual real estate has the capital or desire to purchase an entire parcel. Meanwhile, some landowners may lack the time or skill to develop and manage their property to its full potential. Leasing and fractional ownership solutions bridge these gaps, offering flexible ways to invest, earn, or use digital land. These arrangements also mimic real-world real estate markets, where subletting or forming investment groups is common.

1. **Renting Virtual Land**
   2. The simplest arrangement is a direct lease: one party owns the land, and another pays a fee to use it for a set period. This model can be lucrative for both sides:
      - **Benefits for Landowners**: Owners earn passive income without needing to personally develop or operate the space. They can also form revenue-sharing deals with talented builders or event organizers.
      - **Benefits for Renters**: Renters access prime locations without massive upfront costs. For instance, an indie game studio might rent a stage area in a high-traffic zone to showcase its new NFT game during a major conference.
      - **Duration and Payment Terms**: Smart contracts typically govern the lease, specifying monthly rent in the platform's native token or a stablecoin. Some deals might incorporate profit-sharing if the renter's venture is commercial (e.g., a store or event with paid tickets).

- **Security and Dispute Resolution**: Because these transactions happen on the blockchain, if a tenant stops paying rent, the contract can automatically revoke building permissions or revert control. Landlords can also track real-time usage data to ensure renters aren't violating platform guidelines.

3. **Sub-Leasing and Syndicate-Led Projects**

It's possible for a renter to further sub-lease sections of the land if the contract permits it. For instance, a user who rents a large plot might subdivide it into small stalls for digital merchants, each paying micro-rent. Additionally, some communities form cooperative "guild towns," pooling resources to rent or buy large parcels collectively. These emergent social structures can spark robust micro-economies, akin to bustling markets or business parks, where multiple ventures flourish side by side.

4. **Fractional Ownership**

Fractional ownership takes a different approach: rather than a single individual owning a parcel, multiple investors co-own it, each holding a "fraction" token that represents part of the property. Here's how it often works:

- **Tokenization of Land**: The land NFT is locked in a smart contract. The contract mints "fraction tokens"—ERC-20 or similar—that correspond to partial ownership stakes. Investors can buy or sell these fractions on decentralized exchanges, enjoying liquidity akin to a stock or real estate investment trust.

- **Decision-Making**: Major decisions (e.g., who rents the land, how it's developed) can be voted on proportionally by fraction holders. If 100 tokens exist, each representing 1% ownership, a user with 10 tokens has a 10% vote.

- **Profit Sharing**: Any rental income or event revenue is distributed among fraction holders in proportion to their stake. This approach allows small investors to earn from prime virtual locations that would otherwise be cost-prohibitive to purchase outright.

- **Advantages and Risks**: Fractional ownership improves accessibility and can diversify risk. However, complexities arise in coordinating many stakeholders, especially if consensus is required for critical development choices. Low liquidity or internal disputes can hamper the project's progress.

5. **DAO-Governed Real Estate**

A more decentralized approach emerges when a Decentralized Autonomous Organization (DAO) fully controls a land asset. DAO members hold governance tokens, and the DAO itself owns the land NFT. Proposals for how to develop or monetize the property are posted on a governance platform, and token holders vote. If the community decides to host a music festival, the DAO can allocate funds to hire developers or event organizers.

Revenues from ticket sales or sponsor fees go back to the DAO treasury, and token holders may receive distributions or see token value appreciation.

6. Combining Renting and Fractionalization

These models can coexist. A group of fractional owners might collectively rent their land to a single business or a set of tenants. Alternatively, they could hire a professional "metaverse management" group to handle daily operations, from maintaining content to collecting rent. This layering of new job roles—digital architects, events managers, real estate brokers—reflects the evolving labor market of the metaverse.

7. Practical Applications

- **Short-Term Event Rentals**: A brand wanting to hold a week-long product launch in a high-traffic district can rent land from an owner or DAO. The ephemeral nature of such events parallels real-world trade shows.
- **Pop-Up Stores**: Virtual "pop-up shops" are increasingly popular, letting artists or NFT projects temporarily occupy land to showcase special items, then vacate it once the campaign ends.

- **Testing Ground for Devs**: Some owners partner with smaller studios who experiment with new mini-games or interactive experiences on the property, paying rent or a revenue share for the privilege.

8. Potential Pitfalls

While renting and fractional ownership models increase liquidity and spread risk, challenges persist:

- **Scams or Mismanagement**: In a less regulated environment, unscrupulous individuals might pose as land managers, collect rent, and disappear. Verifying trust is crucial.
- **Legal Complexity**: If fractional tokens are deemed securities by certain jurisdictions, regulation might hamper open trading or impose heavy compliance requirements.
- **Exit Strategies**: Dissolving a fractional arrangement or closing out a lease can be messy, especially if some stakeholders want to sell while others resist. Smart contracts aim to streamline these issues but can't always account for real-world complexities.

In short, renting and fractional ownership illustrate that virtual property markets are not monolithic. They're fluid, inventive, and open to the same complexities that shape real estate in the physical world—but with added flexibility, thanks to blockchain's programmable nature. Owners, renters, investors, and communities each play interlocking roles, creating a vibrant, multi-layered economy. Next, we'll see how advanced commercialization strategies are transforming virtual land from a novelty into a bustling arena for concerts, sports, shopping, and professional workspaces.

Commercialization Opportunities

Arguably the most exciting aspect of virtual land is its capacity to host profitable ventures that blur traditional boundaries between gaming, retail, entertainment, and professional activities. In the metaverse, an "empty lot" can become an e-sports arena, a multi-story fashion hub, or a VR nightclub. By leveraging NFTs, tokens, and interactive design tools, landowners can foster robust ecosystems that rival real-world malls or event venues in terms of foot traffic, revenue generation, and cultural impact.

1. **Virtual Malls and Retail Districts**

Just as physical malls rent storefronts to various businesses, virtual malls aggregate vendors under one roof. Visitors can browse a mix of products—digital assets such as NFT fashion, limited-edition avatar skins, or even real-world goods represented by tokenized inventory. Why malls?

- **Concentrated Traffic**: Shoppers come for the variety. Multiple brands in one location mean higher foot traffic for everyone, fueling synergy.
- **Immersive Merchandising**: In VR or 3D environments, stores can incorporate interactive displays, special effects, or augmented reality

"try-on" features for avatar clothing. The novelty can enhance sales compared to flat 2D webshops.

- o **Events and Promotions**: Seasonal sales, brand collaborations, influencer meet-and-greets— these replicate the real-world mall culture, but with global reach. If a brand wants to release a new NFT sneaker, they can hold a live unveiling in the mall, complete with a digital queue and a minted collectible pass.

2. **Concerts and Music Festivals**

Virtual concerts gained mainstream attention during the COVID-19 pandemic, with platforms like Fortnite hosting massive in-game shows featuring major artists. Now, metaverse-focused worlds offer dedicated concert venues where landowners can:

- o **Sell Tickets as NFTs**: Grant exclusive access to an event, potentially with limited-edition digital merchandise or backstage passes.
- o **Partner with Musicians**: Split revenue from ticket sales, brand sponsorships, or merchandise. This can be lucrative if the artist has a strong fan base eager to experience an immersive show.
- o **VIP Zones**: The venue might have premium seats or private rooms that cost extra. Some fans will pay for a front-row VR seat with the best vantage point.
- o **After-Parties and Social Spaces**: Attendees can mingle in lounges or clubs after the main event, further monetizing the experience with

custom drinks, NFT party accessories, or performance-based mini-games.

3. Exhibition Centers and Museums

Art galleries and cultural institutions are increasingly exploring virtual land to exhibit digital art or tokenized versions of real-world masterpieces. The synergy with NFTs is natural: each displayed artwork can be an NFT for sale or for demonstration. Some landowners devote entire complexes to curated digital exhibitions:

- **Public vs. Private Collections**: Users might pay an entry fee to view exclusive pieces, or the exhibit could be free, relying on donations, sales commissions, or sponsorship.
- **Interactive Education**: Museums can integrate quizzes, holographic docents, or gamified experiences, turning a standard art show into an immersive learning journey.
- **Cross-Promotions**: Partnerships with well-known artists or real-world museums can drive large spikes in attendance. The digital gallery experience might also offer unique vantage points impossible in physical spaces, like a rotating 360° sculpture at massive scale.

4. Esports Arenas and Competitive Hubs

Competitive gaming is a huge draw, attracting millions of viewers and participants. Virtual land can serve as the foundation for e-sports stadiums or training centers:

- **High-Stakes Tournaments**: Sponsors pay to brand the arena, while ticket sales, merch, and streaming rights create revenue.
- **Team Training Facilities**: Some organizations might rent or build dedicated spaces for their players to practice, host fan meet-and-greets, or review game tactics with interactive replays.
- **Crossover Events**: Esports aren't restricted to one title; an arena could cycle through tournaments in different P2E games, bridging communities and driving consistent foot traffic.
- **Betting Systems**: In jurisdictions that allow it, owners could integrate decentralized betting platforms, letting spectators place bets with tokens. This can be profitable but also raises regulatory questions.

5. **Professional Hubs and Virtual Offices**
6. As remote work rises, some companies are experimenting with metaverse-based offices. Landowners could build coworking spaces or specialized corporate hubs:
   - **Office Rental**: Offer furnished "virtual offices" or large auditoriums for company meetings, conferences, or product launches.
   - **Networking Events**: Host job fairs, business expos, or developer summits. By charging sponsors or participating companies, landowners generate revenue while facilitating professional interactions.

- Cross-Integration with Productivity Tools: The next wave of VR collaboration software might integrate with Slack, Trello, or Google Drive, making the virtual environment a seamless extension of corporate workflows.

7. **Mixed-Use Districts**

The lines between these categories often blur. A single development might feature commercial floors, gaming arenas, and social clubs. This synergy can be beneficial— visitors who come for an e-sports match may wander into a gallery or buy collectibles in a mall. Creating well-designed, thematically coherent areas can spark organic cross-traffic and engagement, an advantage that typical real-world zoning can't match as fluidly.

8. **Role of Professional Services**

With so many commercial opportunities, specialized service providers are emerging:

- **Metaverse Event Planners**: They handle logistics for large-scale gatherings, from designing the environment to setting up NFT ticketing.
- **Digital Architects and Designers**: Skilled creators craft custom buildings, interactive exhibits, or brand-themed spaces.
- **Advertising Agencies**: Craft ad campaigns or sponsor integrations that appear in the

environment, mindful not to disrupt user immersion.

- o **Data Analysts and Marketers**: Evaluate traffic patterns, user demographics, and ROI on virtual land projects.

9. **Financial Metrics for Commercial Ventures**
As digital real estate matures, landowners rely on analytics to measure success:

- o **Visitor Count**: The total number of unique and repeat visits.
- o **Engagement Duration**: How long users stay at a venue, indicating the stickiness of the experience.
- o **Sales Conversion**: For shops, the ratio of visitors who make a purchase.
- o **Return on Investment (ROI)**: Compares the cost of acquiring and developing the land to the revenue from ticket sales, rent, or brand sponsorship.
- o **Community Feedback**: Reviews, social media mentions, or forum discussions that gauge public sentiment.

10. **Emerging   Ecosystems**
As more metaverse platforms expand, the opportunities continue to multiply:

- o **Themed Neighborhoods**: Entire zones dedicated to sci-fi fans, anime lovers, or historical reenactments. Land in these themed regions can command niche premiums.

- Travel and Tourism: Virtual "travel agencies" organize tours across different worlds, each with unique attractions. Landowners can pay commissions to get featured stops on these tours.
- Gambling and Casinos: Legal issues aside, some owners open virtual casinos or lotteries, drawing parallels to real-world gambling revenue, but with blockchain-based transparency (and sometimes unregulated pitfalls).

Indeed, the commercialization of virtual land reshapes our perception of "jobs" and "professions." Traditional roles like event coordinator or shopkeeper become viable inside a digital sphere. Aspiring entrepreneurs can conceive entire companies that operate exclusively in the metaverse—perhaps hosting events, creating 3D merchandise, or renting stadium seats. By fusing creative freedom, global reach, and tokenized transactions, these projects showcase the transformative potential of P2E ecosystems.

Broader Implications and Future Outlook

Owning, renting, or commercializing virtual land goes beyond personal profit or novelty. It reflects a profound evolution in how we value and engage with digital spaces. As the metaverse matures, communities worldwide are likely to treat these spaces with the same level of seriousness and emotional investment as physical locations. Here are some key emerging narratives:

1. **Shifts in Urban Design and Architecture**

Architects and urban planners may become just as concerned with designing functional, aesthetically pleasing digital habitats. Entire new disciplines might emerge around user flow, traffic heatmaps, or VR comfort in large-scale digital urban planning.

2. Digital Culture and Tourism

Tourists in the future could plan "digital vacations," visiting multiple high-profile virtual worlds to experience unique landmarks, interactive museums, or historical reconstructions. Landowners hosting these attractions become the digital equivalents of national parks or heritage sites, with all the associated responsibilities for preserving and showcasing the environment.

3. Educational Institutions

Schools and universities could purchase land to conduct immersive lessons in science, history, or art. Picture a geography lesson in VR, where students literally walk through a simulated Grand Canyon or planetary surface. This approach might revolutionize remote learning, especially if it's cost-effective relative to building real-world facilities.

4. Extended Real-World Integration

An intriguing frontier is linking digital real estate to physical properties—for instance, owning a virtual replica of a real building. This can serve as a marketing tool (virtual tours of an upcoming construction project) or an entirely new revenue model (someone rents a VR version of your store to cross-promote goods). The boundary between digital and physical property might become increasingly fluid, inviting novel forms of hybrid commerce.

5. Ecosystem Fragmentation and Dominant Platforms

While decentralization is a core ethos for many projects, some major players (like Meta/Facebook, Microsoft, or large gaming corporations) might build closed or semi-closed ecosystems. Users might have to balance their desire for open interoperability with the draw of big-budget offerings. The future could see multiple competing "megaverses," each claiming to be the definitive environment for social, commercial, or creative endeavors.

6. Financial Innovation

Traditional real estate is a cornerstone of modern finance, often serving as collateral for loans or as a stable investment. Similarly, virtual property could become collateral in decentralized finance (DeFi) applications, allowing owners to borrow against their land's tokenized value. We may see mortgage-like systems for digital property or REIT-style funds that package sets of land parcels. While this invites new investment, it also raises questions about speculation, bubble risks, and the vulnerability of these assets to market sentiment swings.

7. Cultural Conflicts and Legal Boundaries

As more people stake claims and earn incomes in virtual worlds, controversies will arise. Who sets the zoning laws if a landowner builds a chaotic or adult-themed environment next to a family-friendly district? How do trademark laws apply if someone builds a mock-up of a copyrighted brand store without permission? Jurisdiction is murky, as these digital realms often operate outside traditional national boundaries. The emergence of "metaverse law" is a real possibility, dealing with IP rights, property disputes, and financial compliance on a global scale.

8. Sustainability and Environmental Impact

While virtual property avoids physical land development, the underlying servers and blockchains consume energy. Some critics question the ecological footprint of large-scale NFT transactions and persistent VR experiences. Solutions like proof-of-stake blockchains, green data centers, or carbon offsets might become standard for conscientious projects, appealing to environmentally conscious investors.

9. Community Governance

Because many metaverse platforms embrace decentralized governance, land policies could be shaped by player votes. Proposals might revolve around land expansions, new building regulations, or revenue-sharing models. This democratization fosters a sense of shared ownership but can also stall progress if consensus is hard to achieve.

Strategies for Prospective Virtual Land Investors and Creators

If you're considering diving into virtual real estate—whether buying, renting, or building large-scale projects—here are strategic pointers:

1. **Platform Research and Due Diligence**
   - **User Base**: Check active player counts, retention rates, and developer engagement. A platform with steady growth and vibrant community has stronger long-term prospects.
   - **Roadmap**: Assess whether the development team has a clear vision for future expansions, marketing, or tech updates. Vaporware or missed deadlines may signal trouble.
   - **Blockchain Metrics**: Confirm which chain or layer-2 solution the platform uses, transaction fees, and cross-compatibility with major NFT marketplaces.
2. **Location, Location, Location**
   - **Identify High-Traffic Spots**: Being near central "portals," recognized districts, or famous attractions can exponentially boost foot traffic.
   - **Thematic Alignment**: If you plan to open a digital art gallery, situate it in an arts or cultural district—synergy with local communities yields better organic traffic.
3. **Diversify Holdings**

- **Spread Your Bets**: Invest in multiple platforms or different districts within the same platform to reduce risk.
- **Balance Speculation and Utility**: A mix of prime, expensive parcels for potential capital gains plus more affordable ones you can develop yourself can provide a balanced portfolio.

4. **Engage and Develop**
   - **Active Community Member**: Host events, sponsor giveaways, or run collaborative projects. The more you contribute, the more you attract repeat visitors who in turn might rent or buy from you.
   - **Quality Builds**: Hire skilled digital architects or use advanced creation tools. Memorable or user-friendly designs keep visitors returning and sharing experiences on social media.

5. **Leasing and Partnerships**
   - **Offer Flexible Terms**: Long-term tenants might prefer stable monthly rates, while short-term event organizers often pay a premium for shorter, high-demand windows.
   - **Revenue-Sharing Models**: Instead of a flat rent, propose splitting profit from ticket sales or merchandise. This aligns incentives for both landlord and tenant to build successful projects.

6. **Consider DAO or Fractional Models**
   - **Liquidity**: Selling fractional shares of your land can help you recoup initial costs or fund further

development without fully relinquishing ownership.

- o **Community Governance**: If you prefer distributed decision-making, forming or joining a DAO can ensure that multiple voices guide land usage.

7. **Marketing and PR**
   - o **Collaborate with Influencers**: Hosting well-known streamers or personalities can yield a significant attendance boost.
   - o **Cross-Promotions**: Engage in cross-world or cross-title events. For example, if you own land in The Sandbox, partner with a Decentraland event for a "dual-venue" experience, linking user bases.

8. **Stay Aware of Market Cycles**
   - o **Bull and Bear Phases**: Crypto markets can be volatile. Land prices often follow broader sentiment, spiking in bull runs and deflating in bear markets. Keep a reserve of funds for build-outs or expansions.
   - o **Regulatory Shifts**: Monitor headlines about new rulings or platform-level changes. Even small policy updates can significantly impact land values.

By approaching virtual land investments and developments with a strategic mindset, you can navigate the complexities of an emerging market. While not every parcel or platform will become a goldmine, the potential for creative expression, community building, and financial reward is substantial—

especially for those willing to adapt and innovate within the metaverse.

Conclusion

Virtual real estate stands at the heart of the metaverse revolution, transforming digital landscapes into bustling centers of commerce, entertainment, creativity, and community. Land ownership in virtual worlds no longer represents just an intriguing curiosity; it has become a tangible extension of the global shift toward decentralization, tokenized assets, and immersive social experiences. Players-turned-landlords, entrepreneurs, and digital architects are pioneering new frontiers, discovering that the value of a pixelated plot can rival, or even surpass, physical property under the right conditions.

By focusing on location, scarcity, community engagement, and consistent innovation, landowners can yield significant returns—ranging from passive rental income to high-profile brand sponsorships. Leasing and fractional ownership models democratize access to these opportunities, enabling more people to join the digital property boom without bearing the full cost or risk alone. Meanwhile, a diverse array of commercialization avenues—from virtual malls and e-sports arenas to museums and office complexes—highlight the boundless imagination fueling this space. As technology evolves, so does the potential for bridging the physical-digital divide, with advanced hardware, global user bases, and decentralized governance ensuring that virtual properties remain vibrant hubs of economic and social activity.

Still, success in virtual land is not guaranteed. Pitfalls such as platform instability, regulatory obstacles, competitive saturation, and over-speculation must be navigated. Forward-thinking investors, developers, and community members who embrace the fluid, experimental nature of the metaverse stand the best chance of sustaining long-term benefits. Indeed, the interplay between creativity, economic incentives, and community-driven governance can yield digital realms more responsive, inclusive, and dynamic than any physical location. The metaverse thus becomes both an escapist dream and a real economic proposition, a playground and a marketplace woven into one tapestry.

With virtual land, we see how play-to-earn gaming transcends the boundaries of a mere pastime to become a transformative platform for new ways of living, working, and socializing online. By controlling and innovating within your slice of digital real estate, you can shape the metaverse's cultural fabric, leading experiences that blur the lines between players, content creators, and entrepreneurs. In the chapters that follow, we'll continue exploring these newly emerging roles and best practices, delving deeper into advanced topics such as decentralized finance integration, advanced governance models, and the ethical dimensions of a world where pixels carry both emotional weight and material value.

Chapter 11: DeFi, Staking, and Yield Farming Within Games

The emergence of blockchain technology has ushered in radical shifts across various industries, but few have been so profoundly reshaped as finance and gaming. Once parallel spheres—one concerned with numerical models and markets, the other with interactive entertainment—these two sectors are increasingly converging into a hybrid space often called "GameFi." In particular, the integration of decentralized finance (DeFi) mechanics into blockchain-based play-to-earn (P2E) titles has expanded the ways players can generate income, invest, or leverage their digital assets. Instead of merely earning tokens by playing, they can stake those tokens for interest, provide liquidity in yield farms, or even use rare in-game items as collateral for loans. This chapter explores how DeFi protocols and P2E gaming intersect, the opportunities they create, and the risks that come with this frontier of innovation.

At its core, DeFi aims to replicate traditional financial services—lending, borrowing, trading, interest-earning accounts, and more—on public blockchains without centralized intermediaries. In a parallel trend, blockchain gaming uses tokenization to grant players genuine ownership of in-game items and currencies. Conjoining the two, developers can create environments that are not just about gameplay but about real-world economics, blending quest-based achievements with yield strategies or liquidity pools. In these new ecosystems, you can farm tokens while you're battling monsters, stake NFTs for an additional yield, or even mortgage a legendary sword as collateral to fund expansions in another game. The result is a dizzying array of financial possibilities—alongside equally weighty risks of hacks, market volatility, and complicated user experiences.

But for many enthusiasts, the lure of *earning real returns* from their in-game exploits makes these risks worthwhile. Not only can you earn tokens by completing quests or competing in PvP tournaments, but you can also invest those tokens in staking contracts, governance protocols, or cross-chain liquidity pools to generate passive income. Meanwhile, the lines between gaming and work blur, creating a new digital economy that draws participants from around the globe. Individuals who once dismissed gaming as a leisure activity can now see it as a legitimate source of income, investment, and entrepreneurial opportunity—provided they navigate the technical and economic complexities responsibly.

In this extensive chapter, we'll address three main areas:

1. **Merging Gaming and DeFi**: The variety of ways developers weave decentralized financial mechanisms into P2E environments, from simple token staking to more sophisticated yield farming loops.
2. **Game Tokens as Collateral**: How in-game tokens and NFTs can evolve into genuine financial instruments, used in lending or margin trading scenarios, and what that implies for players seeking liquidity.
3. **Risks and Rewards**: While DeFi integration can amplify gains, it introduces its own spectrum of threats,

from code exploits to liquidity crises, highlighting the importance of caution and robust design.

By the end, you'll grasp not only how DeFi shapes new gameplay structures but also how it fosters entire ecosystems of economic collaboration, competition, and governance. This confluence of finance and gaming marks one of the most intriguing frontiers in the blockchain revolution, transforming casual entertainment into a rich tapestry of earning opportunities for those prepared to adapt.

Merging Gaming and DeFi

Initially, the term "play-to-earn" focused on the premise that players could accumulate tokens or NFTs simply by engaging with a blockchain game. However, as the technology matured, creators realized that the financial dimension could extend far beyond basic token rewards. DeFi offered an entire toolkit of yield-farming methods, lending protocols, automated market makers, and more. By embedding these elements, a P2E title could transform its economy from a closed loop into an interconnected network of financial possibilities. This heightened complexity not only made games more appealing for crypto-savvy investors but also demanded that developers maintain balanced economies that appeal to both casual gamers and "DeFi degens" alike.

1. **From Basic Rewards to Complex Economic Loops**

In the earliest blockchain games, the concept of "earn" was straightforward: you'd collect some tokens, then either spend them on in-game items or exchange them on an external marketplace. Examples included simple collectible card games or idle mining clones. While groundbreaking in proving the viability of real digital ownership, these systems still resembled typical microtransaction models, merely with the addition of token trading.

DeFi changed the game by introducing composable financial services on-chain. Projects like Uniswap, MakerDAO, and Compound illustrated how individuals could earn interest, swap assets in automated liquidity pools, or borrow/lend against collateral, all without centralized gatekeepers. Within a P2E title, each of these DeFi functions could be integrated into the fabric of gameplay. Instead of awarding tokens that players then manually trade off-site, the game itself can embed the infrastructure for staking, yield farming, or liquidity incentives. One might deposit a portion of their daily token winnings into a "treasury" feature, generating interest that can be used to upgrade character stats or minted as new NFTs.

Result: Players no longer exit the game world to participate in DeFi protocols. Instead, they remain within the game ecosystem to invest or earn additional rewards, creating a more holistic and sticky user experience.

2. In-Game Banks, Liquidity Pools, and DEX Integrations

The notion of an in-game bank or liquidity pool is perhaps the most direct translation of DeFi concepts into gaming. A typical scenario might look like this:

- **Player Earnings**: Each day, players earn a utility token (e.g., ALCHEM or BATTLE) from completing quests or winning matches.
- **Voluntary Deposits**: Players can visit the in-game bank, where they deposit these tokens into a staking pool. The bank or pool might also accept stablecoins or cross-game assets.
- **Yield Generation**: On the back end, the game's smart contracts route these deposits into a decentralized exchange (DEX) or yield aggregator. A portion of trading fees, governance token rewards, or interest from lending protocols flows back to depositors.
- **Game-Specific Rewards**: Beyond the standard yield, the game might layer additional incentives, such as exclusive NFTs, stat boosts, or governance tokens that let depositors vote on game policies.

In some advanced setups, the game's internal marketplace is effectively a DEX: players trade items, potions, or materials using the native token, with a portion of each trade fee directed to stakers. This is a far cry from legacy games where transaction fees simply disappear into the developer's coffers. Instead, the game fosters a sense of co-ownership, as participants collectively earn from the platform's success.

3. **NFT Staking and Layered Interactions**

Another prime DeFi-gaming crossover is NFT staking. NFTs—unique digital assets representing characters, weapons, lands, or cosmetics—can themselves become "productive" once staked. For example:

- **Character NFTs**: Staking a warrior or mage in a "training camp" contract might yield a secondary token used for advanced gear or breeding new avatars. This design encourages players not only to collect rare characters but also to hold them long-term, as they generate passive benefits.
- **Land Parcels**: Virtual real estate, often minted as NFTs, can be staked in a contract that periodically pays out tokens or resources based on territory location, resource extraction rates, or user traffic. Owners who invest time in developing or promoting their land might see higher yields.
- **Guild or Team NFTs**: Some games let you stake sets of NFTs from a particular guild or faction, opening unique quests or collaborative yield farming events. The synergy between collection building and game-based yield fosters both speculation and dedicated play.

In these models, deciding whether to keep your NFT "active" in actual gameplay or stake it for financial returns can be a strategic dilemma. A powerful sword might yield valuable tokens when staked in a forging pool, but you lose its in-game advantage during that time. This interplay of short-term gameplay strength versus long-term monetary gain adds tactical depth.

4. **Liquidity Mining and Reward Distribution**

Many DeFi protocols popularized the concept of "liquidity mining," where users deposit assets into a pool and receive extra token rewards, often minted by the protocol itself. Within gaming:

- o **Dual-Token Economies**: A game might have a utility token (for daily transactions) and a governance token (for voting rights and profit-sharing). Players who add both tokens to a liquidity pool can receive governance token rewards on top of typical trading fees.
- o **Quest Integration**: The game could gamify the liquidity provision. For instance, a daily quest might require players to "stake 100 utility tokens and 1 governance token" in the official liquidity pool to claim a unique badge or NFT. The synergy between quest-based engagement and DeFi encourages the broad user base to actively reinforce the token's liquidity.
- o **Seasonal Campaigns**: Some P2E games run time-limited events (like "Harvest Season" or "Crypto Summer Festival"), offering elevated APYs or rare item drops to liquidity miners. This

can spark a surge of activity, but also carry the risk of a "farm and dump" scenario if the rewards are too high or poorly balanced.

5. **Governance Tokens and Player Empowerment**

DeFi often revolves around governance tokens that let holders shape a protocol's future. Translating that to gaming, a governance token might let players vote on:

- **Token Emission Schedules**: Determining how many tokens are minted daily, or whether to halve issuance after certain block intervals.
- **Gameplay Changes**: Proposing new dungeons, balancing heroes, or introducing expansions. If the community is deeply invested, this fosters strong loyalty and a sense of co-creation.
- **Platform Partnerships**: Deciding which external DeFi protocols or bridging solutions the game should integrate, or choosing which NFT collections to partner with.

This democratic approach resonates with players who crave more agency in how a game evolves. However, it also demands an educated user base—if voters lack knowledge of game design or economics, they might pass detrimental proposals. Whale dominance can further complicate the notion of fair governance. Balancing inclusive decision-making with developer oversight or multi-tier voting systems remains an unresolved tension.

6. **Real-World Onramps and Offramps**

While many P2E games operate in a self-contained environment, the integration of DeFi can make "offramping" to fiat or stablecoins more seamless. If a game token is listed on a widely used DEX or aggregator, a player can swap it for stablecoins and eventually withdraw to a bank account within minutes. Conversely, bridging stablecoins into the game can allow frictionless purchases of items or land. This fluidity cements the notion that gaming wealth can transform into real-world capital, which can be transformative in regions with limited job opportunities or entrenched economic inequities.

In sum, merging gaming with DeFi drastically extends the economic lifeblood of a P2E title. By weaving in liquidity mining, NFT staking, governance, or innovative yield structures, developers can cultivate an ecosystem that simultaneously rewards gameplay, fosters robust secondary markets, and entices external capital. Yet the next evolutionary step is even bolder: using game tokens and NFTs as actual collateral for loans or margin trading, bridging the gap between fantasy and "serious" finance.

Game Tokens as Collateral

The concept of pledging your digital weapon or in-game currency to secure a loan was once purely speculative. Yet, in the new era of cross-pollination between gaming and finance, this idea is gaining tangible momentum. Collateralization transforms in-game assets from ephemeral collectibles into real financial instruments. By locking them in a lending protocol, players can unlock liquidity without selling their prized possessions, fueling expansions, speculative ventures, or real-world needs.

1. **Why Collateralize Game Assets?**

   Traditional borrowers pledge houses or stocks. But for a hardcore gamer, a "Legendary Dragon NFT" might be just as valuable—especially if the market for these items is liquid, with consistent buyers at predictable price points. Collateralizing game tokens or NFTs:

   o **Retains Upside**: You don't have to sell the asset, so if its value rises, you still benefit.
   o **Generates Liquidity**: Borrow stablecoins or other crypto to fund new investments, pay bills, or farm yields, all without relinquishing your item's ownership.
   o **Supports Diversification**: By using your in-game asset as collateral, you can branch into other projects or tokens, hedging risk.

   This strategy requires healthy confidence in the item's price stability. If your NFT's value nosedives, lenders might forcibly liquidate the collateral, depriving you of the item altogether.

2. **NFT Lending Platforms and Protocols**

A growing number of specialized protocols cater to NFT-backed loans. Typically, one of two models applies:

- **Peer-to-Peer (P2P)**: Borrowers list their NFT, specifying desired loan amount, duration, and interest rate. Potential lenders browse listings, decide which NFTs to back, and if a match is found, the NFT is locked in escrow. If repayment fails, the NFT transfers to the lender.
- **Peer-to-Pool (P2Pool)**: A protocol aggregates multiple lenders' capital into a pool. Borrowers deposit an NFT, and an algorithmic oracle assigns a value or loan-to-value ratio. If accepted, the user can borrow a certain amount automatically. While more streamlined, it demands robust oracle systems to appraise NFT rarity and market trends accurately.

Both approaches require reliable market data: the protocol or lenders need to trust that the game item is indeed worth the borrowing amount. If your in-game token trades on major DEXs with consistent volume, or if your NFT collection has a track record of stable price floors, the risk is lower for lenders. Conversely, illiquid or obscure assets might fetch minimal lending offers.

3. **Collateralizing Fungible Game Tokens**

Beyond NFTs, many P2E ecosystems revolve around fungible tokens like AXS or SLP in Axie Infinity. If these tokens have gained enough traction to be listed on DeFi lending platforms (e.g., Aave, Venus, or Kava), you can deposit them to draw stablecoins. The protocol sets a collateral ratio based on token liquidity, volatility, and reliability. For instance, if the ratio is 50%, depositing $1,000 worth of game tokens might yield a $500 loan.

Key advantage: Players keep their in-game tokens. If the token appreciates, they still benefit. Should the token crash below a threshold, the protocol auto-liquidates enough collateral to repay the loan, incurring a penalty or liquidation fee. This scenario can be nerve-racking if you strongly believe in the token's future but face short-term volatility.

4. **Fractionalizing High-Value NFTs for Collateral**

Some NFTs—like extremely rare in-game land parcels or unique mythical creatures—can be worth tens or hundreds of thousands of dollars. Fractional ownership frameworks (explained in earlier chapters) allow multiple parties to co-own the NFT through share tokens. If these share tokens are recognized as valid collateral by a DeFi platform, co-owners can collectively leverage the NFT's value. For instance, if the land is worth $100,000, the DAO or group controlling it can borrow $50,000 against it to finance in-game developments, expansions, or yield-farming strategies. Meanwhile, the group members retain partial ownership and the chance for future appreciation, albeit sharing risk and responsibility.

5. Innovations in Insurance and Hedging

As the collateralization of game assets grows more common, new categories of insurance and hedging instruments are emerging. Players might purchase coverage against smart contract hacks or catastrophic market drops. Alternatively, a specialized insurer might cover an NFT in case a game's developer closes shop or the NFT's utility is significantly undermined. Though these products are in early stages, they signal how the financialization of game economies is sparking secondary services reminiscent of real-world finance.

For instance, imagine you deposit your "Epic Sword NFT" and borrow stablecoins. You also pay a small premium to an insurance pool that promises partial reimbursement if the sword's Oracle-based floor price collapses beyond a certain threshold. This arrangement, while complex, reduces the fear of abrupt liquidation, encouraging more players to explore collateral-based strategies.

6. Economic Impact on Games

Permitting tokens or NFTs to be widely used as collateral changes the in-game economy's character. Items that double as financial instruments can become scarce if many holders lock them up in lending contracts, potentially raising prices. Or, if a wave of panic selling hits, many borrowers may face liquidation simultaneously, flooding the market with forcibly sold assets and crashing prices. This volatility can affect actual gameplay, especially if these assets are also needed for in-game progression. Balancing financialization with stable gameplay loops is a delicate dance.

7. **Benefits and Drawbacks for Players**
   - **Pros**:
     - Unlock liquidity from valuable items without losing them.
     - Access capital for expansions, yield farming, or real-life expenses.
     - Retain potential price upside and emotional satisfaction of "owning" the asset.
   - **Cons**:
     - Risk of liquidation if prices fall.
     - Complexity: many players may not fully understand collateral ratios or liquidation mechanics.
     - Additional transaction fees, interest costs, or insurance premiums that erode profits.

Overall, using game tokens or NFTs as collateral exemplifies how the gaming sector can integrate with broader financial markets, intensifying the synergy between entertainment and money. Yet, as with any advanced technique, it introduces its own complexities. The final piece of the puzzle is to weigh the potential for profit against the real, and sometimes unpredictable, risks of merging decentralized finance with game-based economies.

Risks and Rewards

DeFi-based gaming can deliver eye-catching yields, skyrocketing token prices, and the chance for players to become digital entrepreneurs. But it also amplifies vulnerabilities that come from both the gaming and crypto spheres. From smart contract exploits and market whipsaws to developer rug pulls and user error, these pitfalls are real and sometimes severe. However, there are also prudent ways to navigate the space, gleaning substantial rewards if one proceeds with due diligence and a firm grasp of best practices.

1. **Smart Contract Exploits and Hacks**

   DeFi protocols typically revolve around code that automates deposits, withdrawals, or yield distribution. A single bug can open the door to catastrophic losses. For instance:

   - **Re-entrancy Attacks**: A malicious contract exploits repetitive calls to drain funds.
   - **Oracle Manipulation**: If a game's price feed or NFT valuation oracle is compromised, attackers can artificially inflate or deflate asset prices, seizing advantage in lending or yield scenarios.
   - **Infinite Mint Exploits**: Careless logic might let someone mint an unlimited supply of in-game tokens, collapsing the economy.

Mitigation: Thorough audits, bug bounty programs, multi-signature (multi-sig) upgrade systems, time-locked contract changes, and community vetting. Players should check audit reports from reputable firms and remain alert to potential patch announcements or red flags.

2. **Market Volatility, Liquidity Crises, and Impermanent Loss**

DeFi's hallmark is that markets can move swiftly—often in ways that even experienced traders fail to predict. If you stake your tokens in a liquidity pool, you become exposed to "impermanent loss," where shifts in token prices can reduce your overall position compared to just holding them. Meanwhile, if you lock assets as collateral, a sudden crash might trigger forced liquidations. In gaming contexts, these events can be doubly impactful since in-game tokens typically lack the mature infrastructure or stable demand found with top crypto assets like ETH or BTC. A big content update could spike prices, while developer controversies or rumors of an exploit can tank them.

Mitigation: Diversify across multiple tokens or ecosystems, avoid over-leveraging, keep track of how the game's roadmap or player sentiment might influence token supply/demand, and use stablecoins or hedging instruments where possible.

3. **Regulatory and Legal Hurdles**

As GameFi merges real money with entertainment, regulators may question whether certain tokens are unregistered securities or if the "gaming" aspect crosses into gambling territory. Specific jurisdictions might clamp down on yield-bearing tokens or NFT-based financial instruments, causing delistings from major exchanges or forcing compliance burdens on developers. Although decentralized structures can resist direct censorship, players in regulated regions could be barred from participation.

Mitigation: Projects with established legal counsel and open communication about compliance are generally safer. For players, researching local regulations and staying abreast of news can help preempt any abrupt enforcement or region locks.

4. **Rug Pulls and Malicious Dev Teams**

The gaming veneer may lull some participants into a false sense of security. But opportunistic or unethical teams still exist. If the project's tokens are concentrated in dev wallets with no vesting, they can dump on the market, or they might siphon liquidity from staking pools under the guise of "maintenance." Overhyping a release or forging partnerships can be part of a bigger scheme to attract deposits.

Mitigation: Inspect token distributions, vesting schedules, and developer track records. Seek projects with multi-sig treasury controls, transparent governance, and an engaged community. If a project's marketing efforts focus solely on short-term APYs, approach with skepticism.

5. **User Error and Phishing Attacks**

   A key difference between conventional gaming and blockchain-based P2E is that there is no "account recovery" if you lose your private keys or approve the wrong contract. Phishing websites that mimic the official game or malicious dApps that request unlimited spending approvals can drain your wallet in seconds. This risk magnifies if you juggle multiple yield farms or bridging solutions.

   Mitigation: Rigorously verify URLs, use hardware wallets for large holdings, keep seed phrases offline, and periodically revoke token approvals through blockchain explorers. Educate yourself about common scams, remain cautious with random links or airdrop offers, and never share private keys or seed phrases with anyone.

6. **Complexity Overload**

   The interplay of gaming and DeFi can be exhilarating for advanced users but alienating for newcomers. Complex staking interfaces, multi-step bridging, or complicated yield-farming recipes may deter broad adoption. Even robust user interfaces can't fully mask the inherent intricacies of DeFi. This complexity can reduce potential player bases or create a two-tier system where only expert players realize the highest gains, while casual participants remain on the sidelines.

Mitigation: Developers can adopt incremental tutorials, layered complexity, or "casual-friendly" modes that let beginners dip their toes in simpler yield mechanics. Meanwhile, players should treat the learning process like an investment in financial literacy: read reputable guides, watch tutorials, or join guilds that help novices climb the learning curve.

7. **Potential Rewards: Summarizing the Upside**

Despite the minefield of hazards, the synergy of DeFi and gaming can be profoundly rewarding:

- **Passively Earn Beyond Basic Gameplay**: Instead of just selling items or tokens, you can stake, farm, or lend them for steady yields.
- **Asset Appreciation**: If a game's user base grows, demand for its tokens or NFTs often surges, boosting both gameplay and investment returns.
- **Active Governance**: You're not merely a customer but a stakeholder. You can vote on how the game evolves, shaping expansions or tokenomics.
- **Real-World Financial Inclusion**: For users in regions with few banking options, blockchain-based DeFi can democratize access to credit, savings, or stable value storage. A P2E game

might serve as their gateway to broader financial empowerment.

Given this spectrum of possible outcomes, participants must weigh personal risk tolerance, liquidity needs, and gameplay interests. Mastering a P2E title's DeFi features can accelerate your earnings and amplify fun, but it also demands vigilance, self-education, and a willingness to adapt to an ever-shifting environment.

Expanding Horizons: Future Trends in GameFi and DeFi Integration

Although the present synergy between gaming and DeFi is already rich, the story is far from over. The next wave of GameFi is poised to push boundaries further, unlocking new mechanics, bridging multiple gaming universes, and making DeFi interactions more intuitive. Below are several trends and possibilities that could reshape this landscape in the years to come:

1. **Hyper-Casual Games with Embedded DeFi**

   Today, many DeFi-oriented games lean toward mid-core or hardcore audiences. But millions of users prefer quick puzzle games, idle clickers, or social sim titles. As user onboarding improves, these casual gaming categories may incorporate micro-staking or yield elements. Imagine a FarmVille-style game where each crop is a token that accrues interest if left unharvested, or a Candy Crush clone that rewards matching certain tiles with bonus tokens. Streamlined wallets and zero-knowledge rollups can further reduce friction, fostering mainstream acceptance.

2. **Metaverse-Wide Financial Ecosystems**

With the vision of an all-encompassing metaverse, numerous virtual worlds—each with distinct aesthetics and gameplay styles—could interconnect. Cross-world liquidity pools might let you deposit tokens from one fantasy MMO and stake them in a futuristic sci-fi city's bank. If these worlds share bridging layers or cross-chain oracles, your assets can travel seamlessly, and a single user ID can unify your financial presence across multiple games. The potential synergy is massive: imagine receiving yields in one realm that automatically fund expansions of your real estate in another.

3. **Gamified Education and Onboarding**

As complexity hinders mainstream adoption, developers may embed tutorials and quest lines that teach DeFi basics. For instance, a new user might play a simple "DeFi Academy" storyline—each mission explaining concepts like impermanent loss or stablecoin lending. Completing each lesson unlocks small token rewards, forging a dual sense of gaming progress and financial education. This method can transform the steep learning curve into an interactive, story-driven process, fostering new waves of engaged players who better grasp the underlying financial mechanisms.

4. E-Sports and Professional Teams

Competitively, e-sports is a booming industry. Merging e-sports with DeFi can produce prize pools sustained by yield farming, crowd-funded through user contributions who share in the event's success. Teams might tokenize their brand, letting fans stake a "Team Token" to finance training facilities or sponsor star players. P2E gaming tournaments, enhanced by yield-based prize strategies, could surpass conventional e-sports in global reach and creative prize distribution. In this scenario, major sponsors might form cross-game alliances, promoting brand consistency throughout multiple blockchain titles.

5. Real-World Integrations

Some projects envision bridging digital tokens with physical assets, for instance allowing players to stake real estate tokens or real gold as part of their in-game treasury. Conversely, a game's currency might be recognized in certain brick-and-mortar businesses or e-commerce platforms, letting you pay for groceries or merchandise with your P2E tokens. If widely adopted, these crossovers could push in-game economies into mainstream commerce, changing how we conceptualize "income" or "labor" in the digital age.

6. AI-Driven Game Economy Management

Advanced AI or machine learning might be employed to regulate inflation, propose balancing patches, or fine-tune yield rates based on real-time market data. This AI-driven "central bank" could dynamically adjust emission schedules to maintain stable currency values, ensuring that the P2E environment remains attractive and balanced. Over time, such automated systems might reduce the severity of boom-bust cycles and create more stable ecosystems, although they also raise questions about transparency, accountability, and potential algorithmic biases.

7. **DAO-Led Virtual Societies**

DAOs are already integral to some DeFi projects, but future P2E worlds may adopt even broader governance scopes. Players might collectively own entire cities or regions in a game, vote on laws or tax rates (like how in-game marketplaces handle transaction fees), and allocate communal funds to build new arenas, sponsor trade routes, or create lore expansions. If these worlds connect via metaverse highways, multi-DAO alliances could form a sprawling digital civilization governed by overlapping sets of on-chain constitutions.

8. **Holistic Player Identity and Reputation**

Player reputation systems can unify data from multiple games and DeFi protocols, culminating in a blockchain-based "digital CV." This might track achievements, loan repayment history, or contributions to DAOs, enabling or restricting certain privileges across the metaverse. A star athlete in one e-sports environment might enjoy improved borrowing rates in another, thanks to a strong cross-game credit reputation. Conversely, consistent griefing or irresponsible financial practices in one game might tarnish a user's metaverse-wide status.

9. **Cultural Implications and New Occupations**

As yield farming and staking become normal facets of gameplay, new "in-game jobs" could emerge. Some players may work as yield strategists or "economic wizards," consulting guilds on optimizing liquidity and staked NFTs. Others might serve as "financial advisors" specialized in predicting in-game item price trends. Still, others might become "mercenaries" who both fight battles and manage clan treasuries. The blending of financial prowess with gaming skill heralds entire professions within these virtual ecosystems.

10. **Greater Scrutiny from Regulators and Traditional Finance**

Inevitably, if P2E with DeFi grows large enough to move billions of dollars, institutional players and governments will take notice. Banks might experiment with bridging real-world loans with NFT-based collateral, or major publishers could request regulated frameworks. The interplay of compliance, cross-border transactions, and data privacy might shape how quickly or slowly the sector grows. On the flip side, formal recognition could enhance user trust, driving mass adoption while imposing stricter guidelines.

These emerging directions reinforce that the GameFi story is only partially written. The interplay of technology, human creativity, and global finance can result in truly transformative opportunities, but it may also accelerate complexity and risk. Navigating that terrain effectively requires both players and developers to remain agile, transparent, and innovative.

Best Practices for Navigating DeFi within Games

With so many variables in play—economic design, cryptographic security, community-driven governance—both participants and creators must adopt robust strategies to succeed. Below are practical guidelines aligned to different stakeholder groups in the P2E DeFi space.

1. **For Players, Investors, and Enthusiasts**
   - **Education First**: Before staking large token sums, spend time understanding how yield farming works, the meaning of APY vs. APR, and how collateral ratios function. The deeper your knowledge, the fewer your surprises.
   - **Start with Small Stakes**: Experiment with minor amounts of capital to get a feel for the game's contract interactions, reward cycles, or NFT locking mechanics. Gradually scale up as your confidence grows.
   - **Diversify and Hedge**: Even the most promising GameFi project can suffer from an exploit or liquidity meltdown. Spread your activity across

multiple games, stablecoin yields, or different blockchains to avoid single-point failure.

- o **Monitor Governance**: If you hold a governance token, follow community forums or Discord channels. A single vote might drastically alter emission schedules or reward pools, affecting your returns.

- o **Secure Your Wallet**: Implement strong security, ideally with a hardware device, and be mindful of phishing attempts. Regularly check your token approvals on chain explorers to revoke unnecessary permissions.

2. **For Developers, Designers, and Project Teams**

- o **Security and Audits**: Make thorough code reviews and third-party audits non-negotiable. If possible, roll out new yield strategies in test phases or under time-limited events to gather data and user feedback.

- o **Clear Tokenomics**: Publish a transparent breakdown of inflation, deflationary sinks, staking rewards, and vesting schedules. Let players see how the token supply evolves so they can plan responsibly.

- o **Incremental Complexity**: Provide a gentle learning curve. Perhaps start with a basic staking interface, then layer in advanced yield-farming loops or collateralization options once your community is ready.

- o **Responsive Governance**: If using a DAO model, ensure the voting structure prevents manipulative whale actions while still allowing token holders to have genuine influence. Use timelocks or multi-sig approvals for major changes.

- o **Ongoing Engagement**: Cultivate a strong community. Host regular AMA sessions, share roadmaps, sponsor content creation, and highlight success stories or new user experiences. The more you nurture your ecosystem, the stronger its foundation will be.

3. **For Service Providers and Ecosystem Partners**

- o **Insurance Providers**: Develop specialized coverage for GameFi assets or yield strategies. Tailor policies to typical gaming behaviors like staking cycles or season-based expansions.

- o **Analytics Platforms**: Supply real-time dashboards that show aggregated yields, historical NFT price floors, or the amount of collateral locked. Offer educational tutorials on DeFi fundamentals within gaming contexts.

- o **Bridging and Cross-Chain Solutions**: Focus on frictionless, user-friendly bridging for players who might only be comfortable with one chain but want exposure to multiple. Offer built-in safety checks for verifying contract authenticity.

4. **Community Building and Integrity**

- o **Promote Transparency**: Encourage or require real-time data feeds on liquidity, contract addresses, developer multisigs, or treasury holdings. The fewer secrets, the more confident players become.

- o **Combat Exploits and Cheating**: Use analytics to detect suspicious on-chain behaviors or exploit patterns. Swiftly patch vulnerabilities and openly communicate remediation steps.
- o **Reward Constructive Feedback**: Gamify user feedback systems or bug reports with token incentives. A healthy feedback loop can keep your project honest and innovative.

By adhering to these guidelines, the entire ecosystem—from end users to third-party integrators—can mitigate the inherent risks of blending gaming with advanced financial mechanics, while maximizing the multifaceted rewards.

Conclusion

What began as a modest approach to letting players "earn tokens by playing" has morphed into a comprehensive, multi-layered economic phenomenon. DeFi, staking, yield farming, and NFT collateralization have catapulted P2E gaming into a realm where digital characters or swords aren't mere amusements but veritable financial assets. This metamorphosis is a testament to the power of decentralized technology and the imagination of developers who see games as more than escapist entertainment—they're forging interactive, investor-friendly microcosms that can generate real wealth.

From in-game banks and liquidity incentives to advanced governance systems, DeFi elements bring depth, liquidity, and community-driven dynamism to P2E titles. Players can opt for standard gameplay or delve into advanced yield strategies that convert idle tokens into profitable streams. The capability to stake NFT land or collectible items for interest, or to use them as collateral for loans, blurs the distinction between your "fantasy inventory" and your financial portfolio. For many, this is exhilarating—an opportunity to shape or harness virtual economies in ways never before possible.

But the dual-edged sword of innovation cuts both ways. The complexities of bridging gaming and DeFi expose participants to the full brunt of crypto's inherent risks: code exploits, regulatory clampdowns, vicious market swings, and cunning scams. Moreover, the user learning curve can be formidable, raising concerns about accessibility and inclusivity. Yet this intersection is precisely where future potential lies. Developers are challenged to refine user experiences, bolster security, and balance token issuance. They must ensure the fundamental fun and fairness of the game remains intact, even as it becomes intricately tied to high-stakes finance.

In the grander perspective, these shifts hint at an even broader transformation: a future where digital labor, creativity, and social interaction merge seamlessly with decentralized financial systems. The vision of "GameFi" sees ordinary people stepping into virtual worlds, not just to relax, but to shape economies, craft valuable digital goods, and orchestrate cross-chain financial activities. In some corners of the globe, earning from these games might offer more stable or lucrative prospects than local job markets. In more developed regions, it might serve as a side hustle, investment portfolio extension, or a new dimension of entrepreneurial activity.

Ultimately, DeFi, staking, and yield farming within games are about empowerment. By granting genuine ownership, co-governance rights, and integrated finance, the gaming space evolves from walled gardens to open economies that reward skill, strategy, and creativity. Navigating them safely does require discipline, knowledge, and community support, but for those willing to take the plunge, the sense of being a pioneer in an unfolding digital revolution is exhilarating. As blockchain infrastructure matures and new cross-game collaborations arise, expect these financial layers to become more ubiquitous—until, one day, discussing yield farming in an RPG might feel as natural as discussing quest rewards in a classic MMO.

The question now isn't whether DeFi will reshape P2E gaming, but how thoroughly it will. Each successive project that refines yield-sharing models or deepens NFT utility lays another brick in the foundation of this new industry. For players, developers, and even outsiders peering in, the union of gaming and decentralized finance heralds an age where the boundary between "entertainment" and "investment" is fluid—proving that the future of gaming is, undeniably, financially charged, communal, and perpetually in flux.

PART V: LONG-TERM STRATEGIES AND CONSIDERATIONS

Chapter 12: Regulatory Landscapes and Tax Considerations

Blockchain-based play-to-earn (P2E) gaming melds digital entertainment with real-world financial value. Players worldwide can earn tradable tokens, selling them on open markets or holding them as long-term assets. This transformative shift has turned gaming from a hobby into a potential source of income—yet it also places participants in the crosshairs of evolving regulatory and tax frameworks. Laws around cryptocurrency, digital assets, securities, gambling, and labor can all intersect with P2E's mechanics. Meanwhile, taxation rules differ wildly across borders, often leading to confusion or unintentional noncompliance.

Navigating legal gray areas involves understanding how different jurisdictions classify tokens, how they treat NFT ownership, and whether a particular P2E model might be considered gambling, speculation, or even an unregistered security offering. Tax implications can be equally daunting: Are tokens earned in-game considered income? If so, at what point is it recognized? How do you track capital gains on numerous microtransactions? And in an environment where P2E tokens can lose or gain value rapidly, how does one plan for potential tax liabilities?

Awareness of these issues is critical. Players, guild organizers, streamers, developers, and investors all risk fines, asset freezes, or complex audits if they ignore or misunderstand relevant laws. On a more positive note, recognizing the legal environment can empower you to structure your activities responsibly, tapping into legitimate opportunities for global participation and business formation. This chapter will break down the major regulatory challenges and the key tax considerations for anyone active in the P2E ecosystem, concluding with practical strategies for staying informed and proactive.

1. Understanding the Complex Legal Landscape

Why P2E Draws Regulatory Scrutiny

Traditional gaming rarely encounters intense financial regulation because in-game currencies or items typically hold negligible real-world value. But in P2E, tokens or NFTs can be sold on public exchanges for fiat money or other cryptocurrencies. This link to external capital markets draws parallels with financial instruments—and regulators take notice for several reasons:

1. **Consumer Protection**: Are unsuspecting gamers being misled about possible profits or forced into risky purchases of NFTs? Are minors exposed to gambling-like mechanisms?

2. **Anti-Money Laundering (AML)**: The ability to swap in-game tokens for real money can enable money laundering if there is no identity verification.

3. **Securities Regulation**: Some P2E tokens might be considered "investment contracts" under local definitions. If the primary emphasis is on token price appreciation driven by developer efforts, they could be treated as unregistered securities.

4. **Taxation**: Governments want to ensure players pay taxes on capital gains, income, or transaction-based earnings.

While the novelty of P2E sometimes places it in a "gray area," regulatory bodies are increasingly aware of how these tokens function in practice, leading to a patchwork of evolving laws that can differ drastically from one jurisdiction to the next.

Key Regulatory Bodies and Mandates

- **Securities Commissions**: In the U.S., the Securities and Exchange Commission (SEC) has pursued crypto projects it deems to be offering unregistered securities. Similarly, other nations have their own equivalents, evaluating whether tokens pass tests like the Howey Test (in the U.S.) or local guidelines.

- **Financial Intelligence Units**: Agencies like FinCEN (in the U.S.) or FATF internationally focus on AML compliance, demanding certain identification processes if a project handles or intermediates money transmission.

- **Banking and Monetary Authorities**: Central banks in some countries set rules on how virtual currencies interact with national currency systems or cross-border remittances.

- **Gaming/Gambling Commissions**: If a P2E platform is deemed "gambling," it may need a license or face prohibition. The presence of loot boxes or random NFT drops with high real-world value can trigger gambling classifications.

Compliance demands can thus be multi-faceted. A dev team might inadvertently find themselves needing separate licensing (e.g., money transmitter, gambling operator) in each territory. On the user side, heavy AML requirements might require personal data submission, clashing with the pseudonymous nature of blockchain.

Navigating Legal Gray Areas

Divergent Country Approaches

No universal or uniform set of crypto gaming regulations exists. The global environment is both evolving and highly inconsistent:

1. **The United States**:
   - The SEC's approach to token classification can hinge on whether an asset is primarily a utility or, in the language of the Howey Test, an "investment

of money in a common enterprise with an expectation of profit largely from others' efforts."

- State regulators or the Commodity Futures Trading Commission (CFTC) may become involved if tokens function akin to commodities or if derivatives markets form around them.

- Some states require money transmitter licenses if the P2E game's operator handles token transfers on behalf of users. FinCEN might demand compliance with AML rules if large amounts of value pass through the platform.

2. **European Union**:

- Draft legislation like MiCA (Markets in Crypto-Assets Regulation) seeks to create harmonized rules. However, as of writing, each EU member state may still interpret P2E tokens differently. Some nations view them as e-money, others as digital collectible assets, others as intangible property.

- GDPR (General Data Protection Regulation) can also apply if the game collects personal data from EU residents. Developers must ensure compliance with privacy principles, especially if they integrate KYC checks or store user data on centralized servers.

3. **Asia**:

- Japan has historically embraced consumer protection, requiring crypto exchanges to register. P2E tokens might be carefully scrutinized if they represent a high-risk or gambling-like model.

- China has shown a pendulum swing between restricting crypto trading and encouraging blockchain "innovation," leading to uncertain territory for P2E.

- Singapore fosters a relatively pro-crypto stance but tightens rules around retail speculation and imposes AML obligations on crypto businesses.

4. **Latin America and Africa**:

- Many countries in these regions see P2E as potentially transformative, especially if it provides alternative income to underemployed populations. However, the legal frameworks might be incomplete or outdated.

- Brazil, for instance, has signaled acceptance of some forms of crypto activity but can still pivot on how it classifies tokens.

- African nations are similarly varied; some adopt sandboxes for fintech experimentation, while others clamp down on unregulated crypto usage.

5. **Crypto-Friendly Jurisdictions**:

- Smaller nations, like Malta, the Bahamas, or certain Caribbean territories, often market themselves as friendly to crypto businesses. They might provide specialized licenses or simplified requirements. However, running a P2E game from such a base does not necessarily exempt you from the rules in users' home countries.

As a developer or major asset holder, you need to consider where your project or operations are based, as well as where your user base resides. Passive disclaimers that "we don't serve jurisdiction X" may not suffice if you openly allow sign-ups from that region.

Potential Gambling Accusations

Some P2E mechanics revolve around random drops or "mystery boxes" purchased with tokens, leading to valuable NFTs for the lucky few. If these boxes or draws are akin to gambling (paying money for a chance at a big reward), regulators might demand a gambling license. If the game is accessible to minors, child protection laws come into play. This is a gray area: not all random loot is classed as gambling—some jurisdictions require that it be convertible to real money to be "gambling." But P2E tokens inherently do have real monetary value, raising ethical and legal questions.

To mitigate risk, developers might:

- Disclose probabilities or implement guaranteed "fairness trackers" (like ensuring at least one high-tier drop per X boxes).

- Restrict loot boxes to adult accounts or implement spending caps.

- Structure item acquisition so that the random element is purely cosmetic, limiting the argument that it's a gambling-based system.

Security vs. Utility Token Distinctions

If a P2E token is heavily marketed based on its future price growth—rather than immediate in-game uses—some regulators might label it a security. This can impose compliance burdens: investor disclosures, registration, or sale restrictions. The distinction is nuanced, especially if the game's rewards primarily revolve around distributing tokens to players who rely on the dev team's efforts to keep the token valuable.

A recommended strategy for developers is to highlight token functionality within gameplay, keep speculation language to a minimum, and possibly separate pure "governance tokens" from "utility tokens." Nonetheless, devs and large token holders might want to consult securities lawyers to avoid unwittingly offering unregistered securities.

AML and KYC Requirements

If a P2E platform or a dev team is seen as facilitating transactions or acting as a money transmitter, authorities may demand KYC procedures. For example, if the platform directly hosts a swap feature for its token or allows NFT sales for fiat, they could be forced to verify user identity and monitor suspicious transactions. This can conflict with the anonymity or pseudonymity ethos of many crypto gamers.

Additionally, large in-game transactions can trigger cross-border AML flags if players move large sums of tokens from one region to another. Where P2E is used as a channel for unmonitored currency flows, governments are likely to crack down. So some projects integrate KYC at a certain transaction threshold. Many users find that friction unwelcome, but ignoring AML can lead to major legal repercussions, including blacklisting from major exchanges.

Key point: While smaller transactions might avoid intense scrutiny, P2E "whales" or scholarship managers dealing with substantial sums must be vigilant about AML compliance. Failing to do so can lead to account freezes or legal action, with far-reaching ramifications for the entire game's reputation.

Tax Implications

The Core Tax Questions

Earnings from P2E games typically revolve around three aspects:

1. **In-Game Rewards as Income**: Are tokens or NFTs earned from daily quests or battles considered immediate taxable income at their fair market value?

2. **Sales or Trades**: When you sell or swap tokens or NFTs, do you realize capital gains or ordinary income? How is the cost basis determined, especially if you never purchased the item but "earned" it?

3. **Ongoing Yields**: If you stake tokens or provide liquidity, are the yields taxed as interest, dividends, or something else?

Tax authorities in many countries classify cryptocurrencies as property, subjecting each sale or exchange to capital gains calculations. But P2E complicates matters because you might have:

- Dozens or hundreds of microtransactions daily.

- Gains that occur before you even realize you have them (e.g., NFT drops with a significant market value).

- Token conversions to stablecoins or bridging tokens across multiple chains.

Keeping precise records can be a monumental task. Yet the potential penalties for misreporting or ignoring crypto gains can be severe.

Common Tax Treatments Across Jurisdictions

Although each country's approach differs, several common threads appear:

- **Income vs. Capital Gains**: In many regions (e.g., the U.S., Canada, parts of Europe), tokens earned for "services" or "work"—which might include gaming tasks if they have real market value—can be income at the time of receipt. Then any subsequent value change yields capital gain/loss upon disposal.

- **NFT Minting as Business Income**: If you create and sell NFTs (like digital art or in-game items), some authorities consider it akin to self-employment or a business. The entire sale price minus creation costs might be taxed.

- **Swaps or Trading**: Swapping one token for another can trigger capital gains events. Even if no fiat is involved, the difference in token value from the time you acquired it to the swap is theoretically recognized.

- **Harvesting Rewards**: Staking or yield-farming proceeds might be taxed as interest or dividend-like income. If the tokens are locked and only become "available" at intervals, the timing of tax events can be debated.

- **Inventory or Commodity Classification**: Some countries let individuals treat tokens used frequently for personal reasons as near-currency, but that's less common. Most see them as intangible property or commodities.

Challenges of Tracking and Record-Keeping

The largest headache for many P2E participants is record-keeping. If you earn tokens daily or trade frequently:

1. **Each Transaction a Potential Event**: Every purchase, sale, or NFT transfer might require you to note the date, time, fair market value in local currency, and cost basis.

2. **Price Volatility**: Crypto can fluctuate hourly. Accurately capturing the value at the precise time of a quest completion can be tricky. Tools like block explorers or price APIs can help approximate.

3. **Multiple Chains/Bridges**: If you move tokens from a sidechain to mainnet, or from one blockchain to another,

each step might be a taxable event. Distinguishing bridging (a "transfer" with the same token identity) from a token swap is vital.

4. **NFT Complexity**: Each NFT might have unique attributes and a wide range of sale prices, lacking the standard reference price of a fungible token. Determining fair market value often requires referencing marketplace transaction data or external NFT valuation tools.

5. **DAO or Guild Earnings**: If you share revenue with others, how is that income or expense distributed among participants? Some countries treat you as a partnership or co-op entity, imposing joint tax obligations.

Practical tip: Many crypto-savvy accountants suggest using specialized software that syncs with your wallets or exchange accounts, auto-categorizing transactions. Even so, you must verify the categorization logic aligns with local laws, as not all software handles NFT or P2E intricacies well. The safest route is often to maintain a manual spreadsheet of major transactions, plus backups from a tracker tool.

Unique Scenarios: Scholarships, Lending, and Collateral

P2E scholarship programs let owners lend assets (characters, land, etc.) to "scholars," who keep a share of the tokens earned. For tax:

- **Owners**: Income might be recognized on the entire token earned, with the portion sent to scholars considered a cost or expense if recognized in that jurisdiction. Or it might be viewed as a rental or partnership arrangement.

- **Scholars**: They receive tokens effectively as "work," so it can be ordinary income upon receipt, plus potential capital gains if they hold and later sell at a higher price.

NFT lending for interest also complicates matters. Some authorities might treat interest income from NFT rental or token-lending as ordinary income. Meanwhile, if you pledge your NFT or tokens as collateral for a loan, you typically don't realize a gain or loss unless you're liquidated or eventually fail to repay, transferring the asset to the lender.

Tax professionals sometimes joke that P2E might represent the "worst-case scenario" for complexity, especially if you operate across multiple games and chains. But, with careful planning—like separating major from minor transactions, using stablecoins for a portion of your earnings, or limiting frequent flips—you can simplify compliance.

Minimizing Tax Liabilities Legally

While not legal advice, many participants adopt strategies such as:

- **Long-Term Holding**: If local rules differentiate short vs. long-term capital gains, holding tokens or NFTs beyond a certain threshold might qualify for reduced rates.

- **Offsetting Gains with Losses**: If certain NFTs drop to near zero, you can realize capital losses to offset other gains. Proper documentation is crucial.

- **Operating a Corporate Entity**: Some advanced players or guild owners form entities in crypto-friendly jurisdictions. This might reduce personal liability, centralize tax reporting, or exploit local tax incentives. But cross-border complexities remain.

- **Staying Liquid**: Because token values can drop, maintaining a stablecoin or fiat buffer ensures you can pay taxes due without panic-selling assets in a downturn.

- **Consulting Professionals**: For substantial holdings, a crypto-savvy CPA or tax attorney is often worth the cost.

Staying Informed: Avoiding Surprises in a Fluid Environment

Government Announcements and Industry News

Crypto regulations and enforcement actions can materialize quickly. Players, devs, and investors often find out about them from:

1. **Official Government Channels**: Subscribe to relevant agency bulletins (e.g., SEC, FinCEN, local finance ministries) or watch official social media.

2. **News Outlets**: Crypto-focused publications—like CoinDesk, The Block, or Decrypt—track legislative updates, lawsuits, and new guidelines.

3. **Industry Networks**: Many P2E devs share updates when they anticipate new compliance changes or receive guidance from local lawyers.

Reacting promptly to new rules—like restricting certain country users or adjusting KYC flows—can prevent forced shutdowns or heavy penalties. Being last to comply with a major regulation can kill a project or freeze user tokens. On the user side, if your region bans certain crypto activities, you want to pivot before regulators clamp down (e.g., relocating assets or halting new purchases).

Engaging with Local Communities

While global channels help with macro developments, local meetups or region-specific forums shed light on how your city or country enforces rules. Some nations have minimal official guidance yet effectively turn a blind eye to small-scale participants. Others might actively watch blockchain activity. By networking with local lawyers, accountants, or user groups, you glean practical, street-level insights on the evolving stance toward P2E.

Case Example: A user in one city discovered the local tax authority was launching a pilot crackdown on NFT flippers exceeding a certain profit threshold. He promptly reorganized his approach, ensuring all transactions had robust cost basis documentation. Meanwhile, others who remained ignorant faced hefty back taxes and fines.

Monitoring Political and Economic Contexts

Global macro events can also shape regulatory climates. For instance:

- **Economic Crises**: A country might look more favorably on crypto or P2E if it struggles with inflation or unemployment, seeing them as solutions. Alternatively, they might clamp down out of fear of capital flight.

- **Elections**: Incoming leadership might be pro-crypto, drafting supportive legislation, or might harbor skepticism, imposing broad restrictions.

- **Trade Agreements**: Some alliances or treaties might standardize cross-border digital asset rules, impacting how easily you can move tokens from one region to another.

Staying politically aware is not typical for gamers, but P2E merges gaming with finance, demanding that you track broader policy developments.

Developer Transparency and Token Roadmaps

Projects with a strong track record of legal compliance typically share open, up-to-date details about:

- **Team Credentials**: Are they collaborating with known law firms or local authorities to ensure compliance?

- **Terms of Service**: Clearly states user eligibility, KYC demands, disclaimers about securities or gambling concerns.

- **Roadmap**: Mentions potential licensing pursuits or new bridging solutions for regulated markets. If a dev team is silent about regulations, that might be a red flag.

Players would do well to examine these aspects before heavily investing time or capital. If developers appear oblivious to potential legal pitfalls, the project could be short-lived once regulators take notice.

Realistic Case Studies of Legal and Tax Scenarios

Case Study 1: The Underage Loot Box Dilemma

Scenario: A P2E game gains traction among teens due to its cartoonish style. Minors purchase "mystery crates" with in-game tokens, occasionally discovering ultra-rare NFT mounts that sell for hundreds of dollars. Regulators from the local gambling commission notice minor participants are effectively gambling. The developer is forced to:

1. Implement age verification at sign-up.

2. Introduce disclaimers and probability disclosures for crates.

3. Prohibit crate purchases by users under 18 or limit monthly spending caps.

Outcome: Many younger players vanish, but the game averts a forced shutdown. Adult players continue with crates, albeit more cautiously. The dev team, now faced with lower revenue, invests in skill-based challenges that do not revolve on random drops to keep the game sustainable.

Case Study 2: A Whale's Tax Nightmare

Scenario: A well-off investor, "Rob," buys high-value NFT lands in a popular metaverse game, flipping them for major profits. He also yields a large sum by staking tokens in liquidity pools. He does not keep meticulous records, assuming the decentralized nature will keep him anonymous. Eventually, local tax authorities partner with an analytics firm to identify large on-chain transactions. Rob is found to have realized over $500,000 in unreported capital gains.

Outcome: Rob faces a backdated tax bill, plus penalties and interest. He scrambles to liquidate some holdings in a bear market, sustaining further financial loss. This fiasco prompts him to hire a crypto-savvy CPA. He vows to carefully log transactions moving forward, concluding that ignorance about tax laws is not a defense.

Case Study 3: The Scholarship Guild Confronts AML Scrutiny

Scenario: A well-organized guild in a developing country runs hundreds of scholarships, cycling thousands of tokens daily. Because some scholars funnel their earnings out of the game into unknown wallets abroad, suspicious transaction flags arise. The guild's main wallet is labeled by local authorities as a potential money transmitter. The guild founder receives a cease-and-desist letter from a national AML body requesting a clear compliance program.

Outcome: The guild founder must implement basic KYC for scholars, track large outflows, and share suspicious activity reports if necessary. Some scholars balk at ID requirements, leading to membership declines. Others accept it as the new normal. The founder reorganizes the guild into a formal entity, seeking legal advice on bridging local currency rules. Growth slows, but eventually the guild emerges as a legitimate operation, partnering with developers who appreciate its compliance stance.

Strategies for a Compliant and Confident Approach

For Players and Guild Operators

1. **Document Everything**: If the amounts are significant, keep a spreadsheet or use a crypto tax app. Record the date, type of in-game activity, tokens earned, and fair market values.

2. **Set Money Aside for Taxes**: If your territory taxes crypto earnings, maintain a stable reserve so you aren't forced to panic-sell in a bear market to pay year-end taxes.

3. **Educate Scholars**: If you run scholarships, provide transparent agreements detailing revenue splits, potential tax liabilities, and local KYC rules. Encouraging responsible accounting fosters long-term viability.

4. **Stay Alert for Warnings**: If devs or local news mention new laws, pivot quickly. Possibly reduce liquidity or shift focus to less legally risky aspects until clarity emerges.

For Developers and Platforms

1. **Seek Legal Counsel Early**: Understanding whether your tokens might be securities, or if you need a

gambling or money transmitter license, helps avoid abrupt halts.

2. **Implement Clear TOS**: Outline disclaimers about risk, indicate user eligibility (e.g., "Not for minors under 18," or "Users in [restricted] countries not allowed"), and define your compliance approach.

3. **Offer KYC for High-Level Activities**: Basic usage might remain permissionless, but advanced in-game trading or large-value NFT purchases might require identity checks. This aligns with AML obligations.

4. **Plan for Taxes**: If your game collects transaction fees or marketplace commissions, track that revenue carefully. Provide user-friendly tools or partner with third-party solutions to help players calculate gains.

Advocating for Better Regulation

In addition to internal compliance, many in the P2E community push for clearer, more equitable frameworks. By joining industry associations, participating in public consultations, or collaborating on standard-setting bodies, stakeholders can shape policies that:

- Foster innovation while controlling fraud or gambling-like abuses.

- Provide small-scale participants a simpler route to compliance or minimal thresholds.

- Encourage cross-border recognition of digital assets, reducing friction for those bridging multiple jurisdictions.

Activism and dialogue with lawmakers can promote a more stable environment where P2E can grow responsibly. The alternative is a patchwork of contradictory rules that hamper both legitimate user adoption and creative potential.

Conclusion

The regulatory and tax landscape for play-to-earn gaming is at once complex, in flux, and critical to understand. The same attributes that make P2E thrilling—real-world value, fluid cross-border trading, user-generated economies—also prompt scrutiny from myriad authorities. Navigating legal gray areas requires awareness of how different countries define crypto assets, whether your game's mechanics might be deemed gambling or securities, and how anti-money laundering frameworks apply. Meanwhile, the tax implications are substantial, as each token or NFT transaction can theoretically constitute a taxable event—especially in regions where crypto is classified as property, generating capital gains or income at every turn.

Despite these challenges, compliance is achievable with the right mindset and resources. Maintaining accurate records, limiting risky or manipulative in-game mechanics, and seeking professional counsel are prudent steps. For casual participants, understanding local regulations around reporting smaller transactions can prevent unwelcome surprises. For large-scale operators or major stakeholders, advanced planning—such as forming corporate entities or implementing robust KYC—can legitimize operations and open doors to partnerships or brand alliances.

Staying informed is half the battle. As authorities refine their perspectives on P2E, new rulings and guidelines can appear suddenly, rewriting the rules. Subscribing to official bulletins, joining region-specific crypto associations, and keeping an ear to community discussions can provide early warnings, letting you pivot or prepare. P2E remains an emergent phenomenon, so regulators often have incomplete or inconsistent stances; in many ways, the P2E community itself can help shape these frameworks by demonstrating responsible behavior, championing self-regulation, and emphasizing consumer protection.

In the broader context of P2E, regulation and taxes shouldn't be viewed as pure obstacles. They are part of the price of becoming a mainstream, recognized force in global entertainment and finance. Once clarity emerges, large investors, studios, and everyday participants will feel safer diving in, leading to more stable token values and refined game designs. The sector's ultimate success may well hinge on bridging the gap between decentralized innovation and governmental oversight in a way that preserves creativity, user empowerment, and the entrepreneurial spirit that first sparked the P2E revolution.

Chapter 13: Market Cycles, Speculation, and Sustainable Play

Blockchain-based play-to-earn (P2E) gaming has opened up an exciting new frontier where entertainment and investment can merge. But this convergence also brings volatility, speculation, and risk—characteristics inherited from the broader crypto ecosystem. While digital tokens and NFTs can transform your gaming achievements into tangible income, they can also suffer dramatic price swings propelled by fickle market sentiment. Understanding how crypto market cycles work, defining your own motivations and goals, and practicing diversification are all vital to maintaining a healthy and rewarding approach to P2E. This chapter will explore the cyclical nature of crypto markets, the tension between gaming as entertainment and investment, and strategies for building a stable, diversified portfolio that can weather inevitable market storms.

On the surface, tokens in P2E ecosystems look like any other crypto assets: they trade on public exchanges, experience boom-and-bust cycles, and can be subject to hype-driven price spikes or crash on negative news. Yet, these tokens also hold intrinsic value within a game's economy, creating a hybrid identity that complicates typical price analysis. A user might treasure an NFT for its in-game rarity or utility, while also being tempted to sell if its dollar value rises. Similarly, a decline in token price might demotivate certain players from continuing in the game at all. This dual role of gameplay item and speculative instrument is a hallmark of P2E, and it underscores why players must develop both gaming skills and financial literacy.

Market cycles are nothing new in crypto. Over the past decade, Bitcoin, Ethereum, and altcoins have undergone repeated cycles of euphoric highs and crushing lows—commonly referred to as bull and bear markets. These patterns repeat themselves in NFT collections and P2E tokens as well, though sometimes at accelerated speeds due to lower liquidity or intense hype. When new updates drop or influencers spotlight a particular game, tokens can surge in value. Conversely, bear phases can see them plummet 80-90%, leading many to abandon the project. Navigating these swings with composure demands a clear strategy that balances your gaming enjoyment, your financial goals, and your tolerance for risk.

In this chapter, we'll first unpack Volatility in Crypto Markets, analyzing how macro trends, speculation, and game updates drive dramatic price shifts. We'll then delve into Investment vs. Entertainment, prompting you to reflect on whether you prioritize profit or fun—and how that self-awareness guides your expectations. Finally, we'll examine Building a Diversified Portfolio, offering concrete suggestions for distributing your time, capital, and assets across multiple P2E titles and token categories. By weaving these threads together, we aim to help you foster a sustainable approach to P2E—one that endures beyond fleeting hype cycles and remains grounded in a balanced mindset.

Understanding Market Cycles in Crypto and P2E

The Boom-and-Bust Rhythm

Crypto markets often move in cyclical patterns characterized by periods of rapid price appreciation (bull markets) followed by steep drawdowns (bear markets). Many attribute this to an interplay of speculation, liquidity surges, technological milestones, and even macroeconomic factors. When crypto markets surge, it's common to see capital spill over into altcoins and gaming tokens. This cross-pollination occurs because investors flush with profits look for "the next big thing," fueling hype in smaller projects—especially P2E.

Then, once sentiment shifts—perhaps due to regulatory concerns, macro downturns, or a major hack—liquidity dries up, leaving players who joined late to endure outsized losses. Bear markets can last for months or years, sapping engagement and confidence. Prices might fall below the cost basis of many holders, causing capitulation. In these times, only the strongest projects with real utility or dedicated communities tend to survive.

These patterns are cyclical, but the duration and amplitude vary. Some refer to the "Bitcoin halving cycle," where every four years, Bitcoin's inflation halves, historically leading to a bull run 12-18 months later. Others note that external shocks—like major recessions or central bank policy changes—can override crypto-specific cycles. For P2E, each wave of mainstream attention can create micro-bubbles, with tokens skyrocketing on the promise of revolutionary gameplay or passive income. But if the hype outruns tangible progress, disillusion follows, resulting in a crash. Recognizing these historical patterns doesn't guarantee you'll perfectly time the market, but it fosters perspective and can prevent panic when the inevitable downturn arrives.

Influencers, Game Updates, and Speculative Fervor

While broad crypto sentiment exerts a powerful influence, P2E tokens also respond strongly to game-specific news and influencer hype. Streamers, e-sports players, or well-known crypto personalities can single-handedly propel a small token up 100% in days, especially if it's on a lesser-known chain with limited liquidity. Similarly, high-profile game updates—like new expansions, NFT releases, or cross-chain integrations—can ignite a buying frenzy.

However, speculation can overshadow fundamentals. A slight delay in a roadmap or a bug discovered in the code might cause a panic sell-off. Over-reliance on hype-driven demand also leaves projects vulnerable to "pump and dump" schemes. In these scenarios, early insiders accumulate tokens, then promote them aggressively, only to cash out at inflated prices. Naive players or small investors can be left holding worthless assets.

Navigating speculation demands a measured approach. While it's tempting to chase tokens that are trending on Twitter or YouTube, sustainable returns typically require deeper due diligence. Look at the game's user stats, the developer team's track record, and the real-world usage of the token. Hype can boost short-term valuations, but if the underlying gameplay or economy is underwhelming, the bubble may quickly burst.

Macro Factors and Cross-Market Influences

Although P2E tokens are niche assets, they don't exist in isolation. Macro factors—like interest rate changes, stock market performance, or geopolitical crises—can shape crypto liquidity and investor risk appetites. In a risk-off environment, traders often exit volatile altcoins to hold stablecoins or fiat, intensifying a bear market in P2E tokens. Conversely, times of bullish optimism and easy money can see capital flood into experimental projects, fueling speculation.

The cyclical flow between Ethereum, major altcoins, and gaming tokens further amplifies volatility. When Ethereum surges, many traders rotate gains into smaller tokens seeking higher multiples. If Ethereum later corrects, they may withdraw from the smaller tokens to recoup losses or lock profits, causing P2E tokens to tumble. This cyclical rotation can repeat multiple times a year, leading to rapidly changing price dynamics that can whipsaw unsuspecting players.

The bottom line: P2E tokens—like most crypto assets—are intricately connected to broader market sentiment. Gains can be immense in bullish phases, but so can the subsequent losses if momentum fades. Understanding these macro influences, alongside game-specific catalysts, is vital to maintaining composure and avoiding emotional decisions.

Volatility in Crypto Markets

While we've outlined the cyclical tendencies of the crypto sphere, volatility specifically refers to the magnitude and speed of price fluctuations. Crypto's 24/7 global trading fosters extreme volatility, which can have dramatic effects on P2E tokens. Here, we delve deeper

297

into why crypto markets are so volatile, how that impacts players, and strategies to cope.

Drivers of Extreme Volatility

Crypto's volatility stems from multiple factors:

1. **Lack of Established Valuation Models**: Traditional stocks can be evaluated through earnings reports, dividends, or fundamental ratios. Many crypto tokens (including P2E tokens) lack stable cash flows or widely accepted valuation benchmarks. Prices may hinge on intangible factors like community sentiment or speculative narratives.

2. **Global, Unregulated Markets**: Crypto trades around the clock on hundreds of unregulated exchanges with varying liquidity. Large trades, liquidity mismatches, or exchange downtime can trigger wild price swings. With no circuit breakers or official oversight, panic can feed on itself.

3. **Leverage and Margin Trading**: Many crypto exchanges let users trade with high leverage, intensifying both upward rallies and downward spirals. Liquidations of overextended positions can catalyze abrupt price collapses.

4. **News and Rumors**: The crypto community is exceptionally reactive to announcements—like a big tech partnership or a regulatory threat. Positive news can generate euphoric buying, while negative developments can prompt mass exodus.

5. **Emotional Trading**: Retail investors often chase FOMO (fear of missing out) during peaks and then succumb to capitulation at lows. These herd behaviors amplify volatility.

For P2E players, a token's price might change 10-20% in a single day, drastically altering the real-world value of their in-game earnings or NFTs. The psychological strain can be immense, especially if you're reliant on stable prices to plan expansions or guild finances.

The Impact on Player Psychology

When token prices shoot up, the environment can feel euphoric. More players join, convinced of easy profits. But excessive optimism can lead to:

- **Over-investment**: People might sink more money (or time) than they can afford to lose.

- **Unrealistic Expectations**: Some players come to believe that the token's uptrend is perpetual. They fail to consider normal corrections or cyclical downturns.

- **Reduced Focus on Gameplay**: Instead of immersing in the storyline or skill-based competitions, players might fixate on price charts or short-term trades.

Conversely, when prices tumble, negativity pervades Discord servers or forums. Some participants:

- **Panic Sell**: They exit positions at large losses, potentially missing out on future recoveries.

- **Lose Motivation**: If the token's value drops below certain thresholds, the game can feel pointless from a financial perspective.

- **Blame Developers**: Criticism intensifies, with accusations of mismanagement or broken promises, even if external factors cause the slump.

Such emotional swings can overshadow the core enjoyment of gaming. Players might find themselves stuck in cycles of euphoria and despair, resembling day traders more than casual gamers. Recognizing the broader pattern—and building a stable strategy—helps mitigate these mood whipsaws.

Strategies to Handle Volatility

1. **Long-Term Mindset**: Embrace the possibility of temporary steep losses, focusing on the game's fundamentals rather than intraday price moves. If you believe in the developer's vision and the token's utility, short-term dips become less threatening.

2. **Limit Leverage and Overexposure**: Resist the lure of margin trading or devoting an unreasonably large portion of your capital to a single token. A 50% drawdown is more palatable if it only affects 10% of your net worth, not 80%.

3. **Active Monitoring**: While it's unwise to obsess over charts, remain alert to major game announcements or macro crypto developments. Timing your moves around big updates or industry events can help you avoid blindsides.

4. **Portfolio Rebalancing**: If a P2E token skyrockets to represent a large slice of your portfolio, you might rebalance by selling some tokens or purchasing more stable assets. This discipline ensures you lock in gains and maintain proportionate exposure.

5. **Emotional Management**: Recognize that fear and greed drive many crypto participants. If you're anxious or sleepless about price shifts, your position may be too large or your timeframe too short. Setting clear rules for entries, exits, or take-profits can reduce emotional strain.

By respecting volatility and preparing mentally for both upside and downside swings, you preserve your enjoyment of the underlying game. After all, the ambition of P2E is to combine the excitement of digital ownership with actual recreation, not to replicate the stress of day-trading 24/7.

Investment vs. Entertainment

One of the most critical decisions for a player is clarifying why they're participating in a P2E ecosystem. Do you prioritize skill-based enjoyment, narrative immersion, or the chance to flip NFTs for profit? The truth is that for many, it's a blend. But clarifying the ratio of "gamer first, investor second" (or vice versa) shapes your approach to risk, time allocation, and emotional management.

Defining Your Motivations

To steer your journey productively, ask yourself:

- **Primary Goal**: Are you mostly here to have fun, meet a vibrant community, and treat any earnings as a bonus? Or do you see P2E as a side hustle or even a main income source?

- **Time Horizon**: Are you fine with multi-year engagement, or do you desire quick returns? Gamers who relish the long-term development of characters and guild alliances might hold tokens for extended periods. Short-term flippers, on the other hand, chase immediate gains with frequent trades.

- **Risk Tolerance**: If the game's token plummets, will you regret not locking in earlier profits, or are you unbothered as long as your gameplay enjoyment endures? Investors who want stable returns might aim for more conservative moves, while hardcore gamers might keep faith in the project's future.

- **Emotional Attachment**: For purely financial speculators, NFTs or tokens are just assets. For dedicated gamers, these items can be labor-of-love achievements. Selling a beloved character or rare mount might be emotionally taxing, even if it's profitable. Understanding your emotional ties helps prevent impulsive decisions.

Without clarity, you might become frustrated if you lose money while "just wanting to have fun," or bored if the game's pace is too slow for your financial ambitions. Conversely, if you revolve your identity too heavily around the token's price, a downturn can make you bitter about the entire experience. Striking a healthy balance from the outset preserves both your finances and enjoyment.

Pitfalls of Profit-Focused Gaming

P2E's promise of "earn while playing" can overshadow the joys of exploration, skill mastery, and narrative engagement. When the primary incentive is profit, certain pitfalls arise:

1. **Burnout**: Grinding for hours daily to maximize token yields or chase the best yield-farming rates can turn gaming into drudgery. If token prices drop, you may feel the time was wasted.

2. **Excessive Speculation**: Constantly flipping NFTs or tokens might overshadow actual gameplay, alienating those who joined for community or story. The game becomes a glorified trading interface rather than a fulfilling experience.

3. **Unstable Economies**: Over-focus on profit can lead to exploitative behaviors (multi-account farming, bot usage, or resource hoarding), destabilizing the in-game economy. Developers respond with nerfs or changes that further anger profit-driven participants, creating a vicious cycle.

4. **High Stress**: Instead of relaxing, you might check price charts, dev updates, or whale wallet movements, fearful of losing out. This heightened vigilance can undermine the escapism that games traditionally offer.

None of this implies profit-seeking is inherently negative. Many players find a satisfying synergy in earning from a beloved pastime. But a "money-first" lens can erode the intangible aspects of gaming, leading to short-sighted decision-making or deteriorating mental health.

Embracing the Entertainment Factor

On the other hand, prioritizing entertainment doesn't necessitate ignoring potential gains:

- **Try Before You Invest**: Sample a game's free features or watch streamers. If the gameplay doesn't resonate, forcing yourself to keep playing for token yields could become miserable. Aim for titles that genuinely engage you.

- **Set Profit Boundaries**: You might decide to invest no more than a modest budget you'd typically spend on conventional games or monthly subscriptions. Any returns beyond that can be reinvested or cashed out, ensuring you never stake more than you'd be comfortable losing.

- **Focus on Non-Financial Rewards**: Enjoy the storyline, collaborate with guildmates, or explore creative building aspects. Even if tokens slump, these intangible rewards persist. The broader synergy of gameplay fosters resilience against economic downturns.

- **Long-Term Relationship**: Many classic MMOs thrive for decades due to player loyalty and continuously evolving content. A well-designed P2E game might follow a similar path, so focusing on in-game progression can be more satisfying than short-term speculation.

In essence, a healthy P2E dynamic sees both gamers and investors coexisting. Some want purely fun experiences, maybe selling tokens occasionally. Others aim to optimize yields but still appreciate well-crafted design. The developer's role is to cater to these diverse motivations while ensuring the game doesn't devolve into a raw speculation machine.

Finding Your Personal Balance

Realistically, most players occupy a middle ground: they love gaming but relish the possibility of offsetting costs or even profiting. Achieving a personal balance involves:

1. **Setting Realistic Expectations**: Recognize that you may not consistently beat the market. If token values plunge, can you still find enjoyment in the gameplay? If so, you're probably well-balanced.

2. **Time Management**: Allocate gaming hours proportionate to your real-world commitments and stress tolerance. Chasing every daily quest or yield boost might overshadow your job, family, or physical well-being if done excessively.

3. **Periodic Assessment**: Revisit your strategy every month or quarter. Are you drifting into trader mode when you initially aimed for a more casual approach? Are you ignoring gameplay quality to chase ephemeral yields?

4. **Community Interaction**: Engaging with peers who share your mindset—be it casual or professional—can provide camaraderie and feedback. If you're primarily a gamer, find like-minded guilds that emphasize enjoyment over ROI. If you want more advanced financial strategies, join specialized DeFi or P2E investor groups.

By consciously integrating both entertainment and investment elements, you can reap the unique benefits of P2E—genuine fun and real value—without becoming hostage to market mania.

Building a Diversified Portfolio

In traditional finance, diversification is a cornerstone principle: spreading risk across assets so that losses in one are offset by gains or stability in others. The same logic applies to P2E gaming, except "assets" might include different game tokens, NFTs across multiple genres, and even stablecoins or real-world holdings. By broadening your exposure, you reduce the blow of a single project's downfall or a niche market slump.

Why Diversify in P2E?

1. **Mitigating Project-Specific Risks**: Each P2E game can face unique threats—like developer mismanagement, hacks, or simply losing player interest. If all your tokens or NFTs are tied

to one title, you might lose everything if that ecosystem collapses. Even strong projects can stumble. Diversification ensures no single setback can crush your entire portfolio.

2. **Riding Multiple Trends**: The P2E space is dynamic. Certain genres (like collectible card games) might surge in popularity, while others (like sports-based NFT platforms) wane. Holding a variety of game assets positions you to benefit from whichever sub-sector gains traction next.

3. **Smoothing Out Volatility**: In any given week, one token might spike 50% while another dips 20%. Over time, a diversified basket often experiences less extreme net swings than a single asset. You'll still face crypto-level volatility, but less from random idiosyncrasies.

4. **Greater Learning Opportunities**: Engaging with multiple games broadens your perspective, letting you discover new mechanics, communities, and best practices. This cross-exposure can reveal overarching patterns in P2E or help you spot the next big wave early on.

Approaches to Diversification

Your portfolio can adopt different layers of diversification:

- **Layer 1**: Split your total capital among broad categories—some in stablecoins or fiat as a safety net, some in top-tier crypto assets (BTC, ETH), and a portion in P2E tokens or NFTs.

- **Layer 2**: Within P2E, distribute among multiple titles. Perhaps you hold one fantasy RPG token, one sci-fi strategy NFT, one sports-themed token, and a few smaller experimental projects.

- **Layer 3**: Balance between fungible utility tokens, governance tokens, and NFTs. Each has different risk-reward profiles. Utility tokens might fluctuate with daily usage, while governance tokens can reflect the project's perceived future. NFTs can exhibit unique supply-demand curves.

- **Layer 4**: Time-based diversification. Stagger your entry points rather than dumping all your investment at once. This helps you dollar-cost average, reducing the impact of poor timing.

Evaluating Projects for Portfolio Inclusion

When researching new P2E tokens or NFTs:

1. **Check Developer Credibility**: A recognized studio or proven dev team reduces some risk. Verify they have a track record of delivering updates or past successes in gaming or blockchain.

2. **Gameplay Depth**: Is the game genuinely fun with a robust plan for expansions, or is it a superficial yield farm disguised as a game? Strong community engagement and ongoing content updates bode well.

3. **Tokenomics**: Transparent distribution, sensible inflation rates, real use cases, and balanced reward systems are essential. Beware of token models that rely purely on speculation or pyramid-like structures.

4. **Liquidity and Exchange Listings**: Projects listed on reputable exchanges or integrated with well-known NFT marketplaces typically have better liquidity. Illiquid tokens can be profitable if they succeed but are riskier.

5. **Community Size and Sentiment**: Vibrant Discord channels or social presence can reflect healthy interest. Overhyped projects, however, might signal speculative mania—scrutinize carefully if the excitement is backed by real substance.

6. **Roadmap and Partnerships**: Milestone-based progress indicates developer commitment. Cross-collaborations with other P2E games or mainstream brands can widen user adoption.

By applying these filters, you accumulate a portfolio of strong P2E titles rather than chasing random hype. That fosters resilience across bull and bear cycles, since well-grounded games retain their user base even if token prices dip.

Rebalancing and Long-Term Maintenance

Diversification isn't a static approach—periodic rebalancing ensures your portfolio remains aligned with your evolving goals. Suppose one game's token soared 500%, becoming half your total holdings. You might trim some profits to reinvest in other projects or convert a portion into stable assets. Conversely, if a once-promising game stagnates or suffers repeated delays, you might scale back exposure before major sentiment shifts occur.

Rebalancing intervals can range from monthly to quarterly or event-driven (like after a major bull run). Some also incorporate a "core-satellite" model: maintain a stable "core" of top-tier or established tokens, while "satellites" are smaller bets in emerging P2E projects. Over time, you prune or expand satellites depending on performance and macro cycles.

Finally, remember that real life or personal finances can influence how much you can afford to invest or keep locked in illiquid NFTs. Continually reevaluate your circumstances to ensure your P2E involvement remains sustainable, not a precarious gamble.

---

5. Market Speculation vs. Sustainable Play

One recurring tension in P2E is the balance between speculation—where participants focus primarily on short-term price gains—and sustainable play, wherein the game's economy fosters long-term user engagement and stable growth. Excessive speculation can yield abrupt booms but also catastrophic busts. Here we explore why speculation arises, how developers might mitigate it, and what a healthy, lasting P2E ecosystem could look like.

Speculative Mindset in P2E

- **Profit-Driven Players**: Some individuals treat P2E purely as an investment vehicle, ignoring the storyline or gameplay. They'll buy tokens early, pump hype, then sell once they see enough returns.

- **Influencer Effects**: High-profile streamers or crypto personalities might publicly endorse a token, driving massive inflows from fans hoping for quick flips. This can overshadow the game's actual content.

- **Yield-Farm Culture**: DeFi "farmers" might rotate capital to whichever P2E offers the best short-term APYs for staking or liquidity. Once yields drop, they exit, leaving inflated token supplies and fewer engaged users.

Consequences of Over-Speculation

1. **Bubble and Crash Cycles**: Tokens shoot up fast on hype but collapse once early buyers cash out or new entrants dwindle.

2. **Distorted Gameplay Incentives**: Developers may design mechanics purely around token farming rather than fun or balanced difficulty. This leads to shallow experiences that lose traction once yields are unsustainable.

3. **Community Instability**: Genuine gamers might be drowned out by speculators who push for short-term changes (like higher emissions). Then, when the price falls, they vanish, leaving the project underfunded and demoralized.

4. **Regulatory Scrutiny**: Excessive hype, aggressive marketing, or promises of guaranteed returns can draw regulators' attention, risking fines or forced compliance measures.

Fostering Sustainability

Developers seeking a sustainable P2E environment might:

- **Limit Speculative Elements**: Avoid overshadowing gameplay with token hype. Emphasize narrative, skill mastery, or social features that remain attractive even if token prices fluctuate.

- **Balanced Tokenomics**: Ensure in-game sinks (like crafting fees or item upgrades) match or exceed new token emissions. This prevents runaway inflation. Also, implement gradual release schedules to reduce dump risks.

- **Gradual Onboarding**: Instead of massive token pre-sales that invite whales, some devs adopt incremental expansions, letting the player base grow organically.

- **Emphasize Long-Term Roadmaps**: By mapping expansions, competitive seasons, or e-sports events over years, the project cultivates a stable user base less prone to short-sighted speculation.

Responsibility of Players

Players, too, shape the game's cultural tone:

- **Support Value Creation**: If you enjoy a game, contribute beyond simply token speculation. Engage with the lore, help new players, and provide constructive feedback to devs.

- **Vote Responsibly in Governance**: If you hold governance tokens, vote for measures that advance balanced gameplay and community growth, not just immediate profit.

- **Discourage Pump-and-Dump**: Shun or call out attempts at artificially inflating hype. The game's reputation—and by extension, your long-term token value—benefits more from stable growth.

- **Share Knowledge**: Mentor new entrants about sustainable play, sensible investment, and safe practices, helping them avoid pitfalls.

Through this ethos of sustainability, P2E can evolve past ephemeral fads, forging robust ecosystems where speculation is tempered by genuine user passion and consistent developer oversight.

Case Studies of Market Cycles in P2E

To illustrate how these principles manifest, let's review two hypothetical case studies:

Case Study A: The Overhyped Fantasy Game

Astral Realms launched with grand promises: epic battles, staking for 200% APY, daily NFT loot boxes, and a top-tier influencer partnership. At first, the game soared, with tokens rising 10x. Players poured in, mostly driven by speculation. The developer minted new tokens daily at high volumes to sustain inflated yields. Within a month, price corrected 60% due to profit-taking and suspicion that no real gameplay depth existed. Once the influencer pivoted to another project, liquidity drained. Many who joined late found themselves with unsellable NFTs of questionable utility. The developer, faced with evaporating token value, tried to salvage the economy with abrupt changes, further alienating the user base. Eventually, Astral Realms settled at a fraction of its all-time high. Only a small hardcore group remained, enjoying the barebones game without expecting profit.

Lessons: Excessive hype, unrealistic APYs, and reliance on influencer marketing created a bubble. Astral Realms' fundamental gameplay was overshadowed by speculation. When the hype moved on, the project's economy collapsed, illustrating the hazards of mania cycles.

Case Study B: The Resilient Sci-Fi P2E Ecosystem

Nova Frontiers took a different route: they beta-tested core gameplay for months with a small group of enthusiasts. Their initial token distribution was modest, focusing on utility for upgrading starships, fueling missions, and allocating governance votes for expansions. Over time, they introduced DeFi features—like starship NFT staking—but kept yields balanced, ensuring item burn mechanisms offset token inflation. While broader crypto endured a bear market, Nova Frontiers retained a loyal community who valued the evolving storyline and cooperative guild system. The token fluctuated but never collapsed. As the next bull cycle arrived, the game's proven track record attracted new players, fueling measured price appreciation. Even if the token faced dips, ongoing expansions and e-sports events gave reasons to stay, leading to a self-sustaining virtual economy.

Lessons: By emphasizing stable development, fun gameplay, and controlled tokenomics, Nova Frontiers weathered market cycles. The game saw incremental gains in user adoption, building trust even when broader conditions were unfavorable. This approach fosters a more sustainable token value, less subject to destructive speculation.

Practical Tips for Sustainable Play and Investment

- **Adopt a Multi-Pronged View**: Recognize that P2E tokens are part entertainment currency, part crypto asset. Evaluate them under both lenses: "Is the gameplay or NFT utility compelling enough to hold even if prices dip? Does the token have growth potential in a healthy broader market?"
- **Start Small, Scale Gradually**: If you're new, invest modestly until you gain confidence in the project's stability. This strategy reduces the sting of potential losses and lets you observe the developer's responsiveness over time.
- **Track Fundamentals, Not Just Hype**: Beyond chart patterns, examine daily active user counts, transaction volumes in the in-game marketplace, or how frequently new expansions arrive. A project with a stable player base and consistent content patches is more likely to sustain token value.
- **Plan for Bear Markets**: Accept that cyclical downturns are part of crypto. Stash some stablecoins or fiat from gains so you

can maintain a presence in the game even if the token's price collapses. This also positions you to acquire undervalued assets if the game's fundamentals remain intact.

- **Limit Emotional Trading**: Consider setting up rules—like "I won't sell during a 20% dip unless fundamental game changes occur." Or "I'll take partial profits after a 2x gain to de-risk." This discipline prevents knee-jerk reactions driven by market noise.
- **Engage with the Community**: Join discussions, guilds, or official channels to gauge sentiment. Player-run initiatives, fan art, or tournaments all show a living ecosystem. If the community is vibrant during tough times, that's a bullish indicator for the game's longevity.
- **Don't Overlook Security**: Market cycles aside, losing tokens to a hack or scam can be fatal. Use hardware wallets, verify official contract addresses, and keep your private keys offline. The best diversification means little if you're compromised.

Conclusion

Play-to-earn gaming straddles the line between fun and finance. While it's exhilarating to see your digital conquests appreciated in real-world value, the interplay of speculation, hype, and cyclical volatility can disrupt the very essence of gaming enjoyment. By recognizing the reality of crypto market cycles, adopting a patient mindset, and balancing investment with entertainment, you can ride the ups and downs without losing sight of why you joined the game in the first place.

Volatility, speculation, and mania phases are intrinsic to crypto culture, and P2E tokens inherit these traits by virtue of being traded on open markets. Surviving—and even thriving—through bull and bear phases demands emotional steadiness, risk management, and genuine appreciation for the underlying game ecosystem. If you anchor your decisions in a clear personal framework—knowing whether you're primarily a gamer seeking fun or an investor chasing returns—you'll avoid extremes of panic or greed. Meanwhile, diversifying across multiple games, token types, and NFT categories ensures that no single flop can ruin your entire journey.

Sustainable play, as a concept, implies an approach that remains rewarding beyond short-lived hype cycles. It involves supporting games with meaningful design, active communities, and balanced economies, while resisting the urge to chase every fleeting rumor or frenzy. For developers, curbing reckless speculation and consistently delivering updates fosters user loyalty. For players, championing fair play, staying informed, and actively shaping governance decisions can help maintain vibrant virtual worlds—even in the face of market turbulence.

In the broader storyline of blockchain adoption, P2E gaming stands out as one of the most accessible gateways. Millions of people, from casual hobbyists to seasoned investors, converge in these digital realms—some to find respite in fantasy, others to generate income or stake tokens. The cyclical nature of markets will persist, with peaks that captivate the public's attention and troughs that test everyone's conviction. But as you refine your perspective, define your goals, and diversify wisely, you set the stage for resilience and joy in these evolving gaming economies, forging a path that marries the thrill of speculation with the enduring satisfaction of play.

Chapter 14: Ethical and Social Considerations

As blockchain-based play-to-earn (P2E) gaming expands, it transforms not only how we play but also how we perceive digital labor, ownership, and economics. Earning real money in virtual environments presents new possibilities for creative expression, entrepreneurial ventures, and global connectivity. At the same time, it raises deep ethical and social questions. How do we ensure fair access when some players can afford high-value NFTs while others cannot? Are we blurring the boundary between leisure and exploitative labor? What are the implications for children or marginalized communities? Does the drive for profit overshadow the intrinsic joys of gaming and lead to an environment skewed by speculation?

In this chapter, we explore these ethical and social complexities to provide a balanced perspective on the broader implications of P2E. The goal is not to cast blame or discourage innovation, but rather to foster a conscientious approach. By recognizing challenges such as fairness, accessibility, environmental impact, labor exploitation, and the future of work and leisure, we can build robust digital ecosystems that empower players while safeguarding against harm. Ultimately, the sustainability and social acceptance of P2E gaming hinge on ensuring that these platforms align with ethical standards, promoting healthy communities and meaningful economic opportunities rather than exploitative or exclusionary practices.

We begin by discussing the central concerns of fairness and accessibility—how wealth barriers, pay-to-win mechanics, or high entry fees might alienate newcomers. We then examine issues of bots, exploits, and cheating, which can undermine trust and equality if left unchecked. Next, we address the future of work and leisure, exploring how P2E games challenge traditional definitions of labor and free time, potentially creating new forms of digital labor that reshape society's approach to employment. We then delve into the environmental dimension, assessing the carbon footprint of blockchain networks and how P2E might contribute to or mitigate these effects. Additionally, we tackle child participation and the blurred lines between gaming and gambling. Finally, we propose best practices for developers, players, and policymakers in forging ethical, inclusive, and resilient P2E ecosystems.

Fairness and Accessibility

Wealth Barriers and Entry Costs

One of the hallmark promises of P2E gaming is inclusivity: the idea that anyone, anywhere, can log on, play a game, and earn tokens that have real-world value. This narrative has inspired millions, particularly in developing nations where local wages are low, to see P2E as a transformative source of income. However, some games erect high entry barriers in the form of expensive NFTs or initial token requirements. For instance, if you must purchase a "starter pack" of NFTs costing hundreds or thousands of dollars to be competitive, many aspiring players (especially those from less affluent regions) are effectively shut out.

Such high entry costs can perpetuate a digital class divide. Wealthy or early adopters who can afford prime in-game assets gain disproportionate power and earning potential. This dynamic undermines the principle of free or fair access and can render P2E closer to an exclusive investment club than an inclusive gaming platform. Critics compare it to the real estate market, where those who own the best "lands" or "items" can rent or sell them at exorbitant prices, continuously accruing wealth while latecomers struggle to break even.

To address this issue, some communities have launched scholarship programs, where owners lend high-value NFTs to players in exchange for a share of earnings. While scholarships can democratize access, they also create a hierarchy of "owners" and "workers," raising questions about potential exploitation or uneven power dynamics. Are these arrangements truly mutualistic, or do they replicate feudal-like relationships where wealthy asset holders reap the majority of rewards?

Nevertheless, solutions are emerging. Some P2E games provide tiered or free-to-play entry points that allow novices to begin earning smaller amounts, gradually scaling up as they reinvest or prove their skill. Others implement progressive difficulty curves, ensuring that the best items are earned through gameplay rather than purely purchased. Balancing accessibility with an NFT-based economy remains a core ethical challenge for developers intent on global reach.

Pay-to-Win vs. Skill-Based Models

In traditional gaming, "pay-to-win" mechanics—where those who spend more money gain competitive advantages—are widely criticized for spoiling fair competition. P2E introduces real stakes: items that can be bought or sold for profit. This can accentuate pay-to-win if the top-performing or rarest NFTs cost thousands of dollars, granting insurmountable advantages in battles or tournaments. Instead of a level playing field, we get a wealth-based hierarchy, potentially discouraging skillful but less wealthy players.

On the flip side, some P2E projects revolve around purely cosmetic or auxiliary NFTs, meaning skill-based gameplay remains unaffected by spending. This approach fosters fairness while preserving NFT speculation and trading. But it might also dampen interest among investors seeking direct in-game benefits. Striking a balance between rewarding investors who fund the ecosystem and preserving a skill-based environment is an ongoing tension.

Regional Disparities

P2E's popularity in regions like Southeast Asia or Latin America is often driven by economic necessity, with players earning more from gaming than local wages. Yet, the volatility of token prices can lead to sudden booms or busts in these communities. In bull markets, players might prosper, but in bear markets, a collapse can devastate those relying on

P2E as a primary income source. Meanwhile, wealthier participants from developed countries can weather token crashes more easily.

These regional disparities raise questions of economic exploitation. Are Western or affluent players effectively profiting from the labor of cheaper-labor regions through scholarship models or by controlling major assets? Conversely, do P2E opportunities genuinely empower lower-income players by offering them an alternative to local low-wage jobs? The answer may vary by project and implementation details, reinforcing that the ethical outcome isn't predetermined, but shaped by design choices and community norms.

Disability and Inclusive Design

On a more optimistic note, P2E can promote inclusivity for individuals who may be housebound, physically disabled, or facing social barriers to traditional employment. Virtual worlds can provide accessible workspaces—allowing wheelchair users, for example, to engage in tasks that earn tokens, or providing a sense of agency and community to those with limited mobility. This potential aligns well with the original spirit of the internet—breaking down geographical or physical limitations.

Yet, for inclusive design to flourish, developers must ensure user interfaces are accessible for visually impaired or physically impaired gamers. They must also offer alternative control schemes, flexible difficulty levels, and social spaces that reduce harassment or stigmatization. If done right, P2E might become a progressive force for bridging gaps and offering legitimate "digital jobs" that cater to diverse abilities. If neglected, it can replicate existing exclusions or hamper the potential for empowerment.

Bots, Exploits, and Cheating

The Rise of Automated Farming

Wherever money is involved, attempts at exploitation follow. In P2E, one widespread issue is the creation of bot networks—automated scripts that farm tokens or in-game resources around the clock. This can severely distort the economy, flooding the market with farmed assets and driving down real players' earnings. Bots can also hog limited gameplay resources or spawn areas, frustrating those looking for fair competition.

Game developers respond with anti-bot detection measures: Captcha challenges, IP checks, or suspicious activity monitoring. However, sophisticated bot programmers may circumvent simpler checks. Over time, it becomes a cat-and-mouse game, akin to gold farming or account hacking in legacy MMOs, but now with real currency. If left unchecked, bot infiltration can degrade trust, as genuine players see diminishing returns.

Multi-Accounting and Exploitative Loops

Beyond bot usage, some users maintain multiple accounts to magnify profits—like exploiting daily quest rewards or referral bonuses. This multi-account approach may be forbidden by game terms but is tempting if each account yields tangible income. It leads to a chain-of-accounts phenomenon, where one user controls tens or hundreds of identities. Not only does this skew the user base metrics, it often siphons community rewards meant for unique participants.

Developers who design token or NFT distribution systems must incorporate robust checks. Solutions include linking accounts to unique wallets validated by external KYC, implementing hardware-based limits, or awarding diminishing returns for repeated IP addresses. Yet, these solutions spark debate about privacy or accessibility, especially in regions where individuals share devices.

Hacking and Security Risks

Another ethical dimension involves malicious hacking or cheating, not just for convenience but for direct profit. A discovered exploit might let unscrupulous players mint tokens illegally or clone valuable NFTs.

Because these items have real-world value, the damage can run into millions of dollars, undermining trust in the entire ecosystem.

Projects must prioritize security audits and continuous patching. A single line of flawed smart contract code can allow infinite item creation or token supply manipulation, effectively stealing from honest participants by inflating supply. Meanwhile, players themselves risk hacks if they store private keys insecurely or sign malicious transactions. This environment fosters a "survival-of-the-savviest" culture, which some see as Darwinian but also quite punishing for novices who might lose all their holdings in one phishing attempt.

Ethical Governance

Cheating and exploitation highlight the necessity of transparent governance and consistent enforcement. If whales or big investors can pressure developers into ignoring their abuses, faith in fairness collapses. A robust community-driven approach—potentially via decentralized autonomous organizations (DAOs)—can help. If cheats are discovered, governance tokens might vote on specific punishments or restitution. In a well-run system, everyone, from top token holders to newcomers, is held to the same standard of accountability. This fosters an environment where conscientious players can thrive, free from the overshadowing presence of bots or exploit-driven whales.

However, democratic governance can be slow and can risk "mob justice" if decisions are emotional or manipulative. Balancing agile developer oversight with community input remains a design challenge. Nonetheless, tackling cheating head-on is crucial to preserving the ethical underpinnings of P2E.

Future of Work and Leisure

Blurring Lines Between Play and Labor

One of the most provocative aspects of P2E is how it conflates "gaming" and "working." Traditionally, gaming was a leisure activity—fun, relaxing, or competitive but rarely associated with earning a stable livelihood. Now, with tokens carrying real-world value, time spent in a virtual environment can effectively become labor. This gamified labor might involve grinding quests, training characters, or building digital assets—paralleling tedious jobs, except couched in a playful wrapper.

Critics question whether we should praise or lament this evolution. On the positive side, some argue that it democratizes the job market, letting people in remote areas or with health constraints find an alternative form of income. Others see a dystopian angle, where multinational game studios become pseudo-employers, controlling wages or asset values in unregulated digital economies. If tokens crash or devs change the reward structure, players reliant on that income may be left stranded, akin to at-will employees with no labor protections.

Emergence of "Digital Blue-Collar Jobs"

Certain P2E tasks, like resource harvesting or low-level monster grinding, can become digital menial labor if performed repetitively for token yields. In a typical MMO, this might be done for in-game gold, but with minimal direct real value. Now that the gold is tokenized, players from low-income regions might treat it as daily "work," performing repetitive tasks for 8-10 hours. This scenario evokes parallels to factory line labor, albeit in a virtual setting.

While some enjoy routine gameplay as a mild or flexible form of work, others question the morality of turning games into sweatshops. Could unscrupulous guild managers or NFT owners exploit cheap labor to enrich themselves? Are there standards or labor rights in these digital realms, ensuring fair pay or break times? The sector lacks clear answers, as traditional labor laws don't necessarily apply to online "jobs." This unsettled environment can breed exploitation unless self-regulated or supervised by external authorities.

New Professions and Opportunities

On the other hand, P2E also spawns more creative or entrepreneurial roles:

1. **Digital Asset Designers**: People craft NFTs—like custom skins, land layouts, or quest modules—selling them to other players or collaborating with developers.

2. **Guild Managers and E-Sports Coaches**: Skilled players run gaming guilds that function like e-sports teams, recruiting talent, strategizing, and sharing earnings. They might even form sponsorship deals with real-world brands.

3. **Virtual Event Hosts**: Just as real-world event planners coordinate conferences or concerts, digital event planners stage tournaments, NFT art showcases, or brand campaigns within the game.

4. **Story Writers, Community Moderators**: Content creation, community building, and story expansion can form legitimate "metaverse jobs," paid in tokens or stablecoins.

These emerging "metaverse professions" reflect an alternative future of work, where location is irrelevant, and skill sets revolve around creativity, gaming prowess, or social networking. By harnessing P2E's dynamic economies, individuals can earn a living from roles that combine elements of fun, tech-savviness, and global collaboration. This potential for inclusive, imaginative careers is part of what excites many about the phenomenon.

Cultural Shifts and Attitudes Toward Leisure

If gaming morphs into remunerative labor, it may transform public attitudes. No longer might gaming be dismissed as a time-wasting hobby. Instead, families could encourage younger members to refine gaming skills that yield tangible income. Some might see it as a respectable new branch of the gig economy, akin to freelancing or content creation. Others caution that once a leisurely pastime becomes financially driven, the intrinsic joy might fade, replaced by performance anxiety or hustle culture. Another concern is how it could intensify screen addiction or repetitive strain injuries when players chase token rewards for extended hours without breaks.

These cultural transitions demand reflection. We must ask how society can maintain the original virtues of gaming—fun, stress relief, creativity—amid an environment that increasingly values productivity and profits. Balancing pure leisure with potential income can be invigorating, but also precarious if not managed ethically. Regulators, developers, and communities thus have a shared responsibility to keep P2E ecosystems grounded in well-being, not overshadowed by exploitative or addictive tendencies.

Environmental Impact and Sustainability

Blockchain Energy Consumption

While not exclusively a P2E issue, the underlying blockchain technology that powers many gaming tokens can have a significant carbon footprint, especially if it uses energy-intensive consensus algorithms like Proof of Work (PoW). For instance, an NFT minted on Ethereum (prior to its shift to Proof of Stake) consumed electricity due to the mining process. Critics highlight that a flurry of NFT creations and transactions might intensify energy usage, exacerbating climate change.

Many P2E devs are transitioning to or building on more eco-friendly networks—Proof of Stake (PoS), sidechains, or Layer-2 solutions that drastically reduce carbon footprints. Some also partner with carbon offset initiatives. While these steps mitigate the environmental critique, the question remains whether a surge in NFT gaming fosters an unsustainable load on blockchains, or if technological advances will keep pace to ensure minimal impact.

Token Minting and Land Metaverses

Large-scale metaverse projects can involve heavy on-chain activity, from land parcel trades to item generation, each potentially incurring resource usage. If thousands of players craft or mint items daily, the aggregated on-chain transactions could climb significantly. However, many platforms optimize by batching transactions off-chain, recording major states on the mainnet only when necessary. This approach can drastically cut energy usage while retaining verifiable ownership.

Additionally, some P2E ecosystems promote green narratives—e.g., in-game reforestation mechanics or token staking linked to real-world tree planting. Though partly marketing, these can cultivate ecological awareness among gamers. The broader question is whether P2E can become net positive for the environment, channeling revenue into sustainability projects, or if it primarily amplifies consumerism and resource demands.

Responsible Infrastructure Choices

Developers who prioritize environmental ethics often:

- **Choose Low-Carbon Blockchains**: Polkadot, Avalanche, Solana, Tezos, or Ethereum (after The Merge) tout more energy-efficient consensus methods.

- **Implement Off-Chain Mechanics**: Many day-to-day gameplay actions occur off-chain to reduce transaction overhead, with only critical events minted as NFTs.

- **Support Renewables**: Some protocols partner with mining or validation pools that use renewable energy sources. Alternatively, they purchase carbon offsets, though offset efficacy is debated.

- **Educate Players**: Transparent eco-impact statements can encourage the community to adopt mindful practices—like limiting spam transactions or reusing NFT minted resources.

Ultimately, as blockchain technology evolves, the tension between P2E's growth and environmental cost may ease. But vigilance is necessary to ensure that the next wave of gaming innovation doesn't come at the expense of planetary well-being.

Child Participation and Gambling-Like Mechanics

Minors Earning Tokens

P2E may attract minors intrigued by the idea of earning money while playing. But allowing children to handle real tokens can raise concerns about labor exploitation, child labor laws, or financial regulation. If a 13-year-old invests significant hours to farm in-game tokens, are they effectively a child worker? Are parents aware or consenting to this activity? In some jurisdictions, child labor laws might theoretically apply to "work" performed in a game that yields real pay.

In practice, many P2E terms of service require participants to be 18 or older, though this is seldom enforced beyond a simple checkbox. Should developers implement robust age checks, or should it be a parental responsibility? Moreover, how do we ensure kids aren't groomed or exploited by unscrupulous guild owners or scholarship programs?

Loot Boxes, RNG Mechanics, and Gambling Allegations

Numerous P2E games incorporate random loot boxes or RNG-based "breeding" that can produce rare NFTs with substantial resale value. This dynamic veers perilously close to gambling if players pay money for a chance at a highly valued outcome. In some jurisdictions, regulators have already classified certain loot boxes as gambling. Coupled with the presence of minors, the ethical stakes intensify.

If children can purchase or open loot boxes that might yield an NFT worth hundreds of dollars, the psychological parallels to casino slot machines are evident. Even for adult players, the addictive cycle of chance-based rewards can lead to problem gambling behaviors. The question is whether P2E devs responsibly handle probability disclosures, set spending caps, or segment adult content from minors.

Protecting Vulnerable Populations

Young players, or indeed any vulnerable demographic, might be susceptible to scams, manipulative marketing, or FOMO-driven spending. Some guidelines for child protection in P2E could include:

- **Mandatory Age Verification**: Potentially integrated with parent/guardian oversight for token transactions.

- **Disclosure of Probabilities**: Transparent loot box or RNG odds.

- **Spending Limits**: If recognized as minors, accounts have daily or monthly transaction caps, preventing large token purchases.

- **Community Moderation**: Ensuring in-game chats or guild systems do not become grooming grounds or exploitative funnels.

Balancing business interests with child safety is often tricky, especially in decentralized ecosystems lacking a single corporate gatekeeper. But ignoring the potential for harm is ethically perilous. As P2E matures, a wave of policy discussions and standard-setting is likely forthcoming.

Best Practices and Policy Recommendations

Given these ethical and social challenges, we propose a framework of best practices that can guide developers, community leaders, policymakers, and players alike in shaping a more equitable, safe, and sustainable P2E environment.

Developer-Centric Recommendations

1. **Transparent Tokenomics**: Publish the distribution, emission rates, vesting schedules, and any hidden mechanics. This reduces potential for manipulative inflation or insider advantage.

2. **Fair Onboarding and F2P Options**: Provide no- or low-cost entry points so new players can experience the game's core without a steep financial gate. Encourage skill-based progression over pure pay-to-win.

3. **Robust Anti-Cheat Systems**: Invest in detection of bots, multi-account schemes, and exploit usage. Frequent patching of vulnerabilities fosters trust in the economy.

4. **Child Protection Measures**: If minors can sign up, implement parental controls or disclaimers. For loot boxes with real-world value, ensure probability transparency or age gating.

5. **Sustainable Economy Design**: Integrate token sinks that reflect real usage, not just artificial demand. If possible, align reward rates with verifiable user growth metrics.

Community and Governance

1. **Decentralized but Accountable**: Utilize DAOs or councils for major decisions, but incorporate checks against whale manipulation. Possibly weigh votes by activity as well as token stake.

2. **Code of Conduct**: Enforce guidelines condemning harassment, exploitation, or cheating. If possible, implement peer-based moderation and restorative justice frameworks.

3. **Transparency in Scholarship Models**: If guild owners rent assets to scholars, define fair revenue splits, clear terms, and

recourse for disputes. This fosters trust and reduces power imbalances.

4. **Encourage Player Education**: Tutorials about safe wallet practices, tax obligations, and responsible financial behaviors help novices avoid pitfalls. Informed players strengthen the ecosystem's resilience.

Government and Regulatory Bodies

1. **Nuanced Regulation**: Instead of blanket bans, craft rules recognizing differences between utility-based tokens and speculative ones. Clarify how labor laws might apply to digital earnings.

2. **Consumer Protections**: Mandate disclaimers on potential losses, limit gambling-like mechanics for minors, and require disclosure of loot box probabilities.

3. **AML and Child Safety**: Where necessary, enforce KYC or identity checks if large sums are transacted. Demand minimal friction for smaller hobbyists but oversight for large-scale operators.

4. **Collaborative Industry Standards**: Work with trade bodies or alliances of P2E devs to co-create self-regulatory codes, preserving innovation while addressing recognized risks.

Player Responsibility

1. **Set Clear Objectives**: Reflect on whether your primary aim is fun, profit, or both. Avoid investing or devoting time beyond your comfort level.

2. **Stay Vigilant**: Watch for signs of addiction, reckless spending, or dubious scholarship deals. If something feels too good to be true, it often is.

3. **Champion Ethical Practices**: Support fair economies, welcome novices, and push back on exploitative behaviors. Encourage open discussion of challenges.

4. **Secure Your Assets**: Use strong authentication, keep your private keys safe, and be wary of phishing. The digital wild west can be unforgiving.

Conclusion

The ethical and social considerations intertwined with play-to-earn gaming underscore a fundamental truth: once digital assets acquire real value, the fabric of gaming transforms. Opportunities emerge for wealth creation, global inclusion, and new forms of digital labor. But these boons carry corresponding risks—exploitation, inequality, child safety concerns, environmental costs, and more. Far from the escapism once championed by gaming, P2E can blur boundaries between leisure and work, forging novel social structures that parallel real-world economies.

In the rush to harness P2E's potential, developers, players, and regulators share a responsibility to prioritize fairness and well-being. This means designing tokenomics that reward active engagement without locking out those with fewer resources, implementing robust anti-cheat mechanisms, and ensuring minors are protected. It also involves acknowledging that not every aspect of P2E is purely virtuous, and that commerce-driven motivations can overshadow the intrinsic joys of gaming if left unchecked.

The future might see the rise of "digital job markets" in which P2E platforms serve as legitimate employers, offering flexible, borderless positions in storytelling, design, or e-sports. Or it might see a world where unscrupulous operators exploit cheap labor disguised as "fun." We stand at a crossroads, with the next few years likely determining whether P2E evolves into a net-positive force or succumbs to hyper-financialization and recurring controversies.

A measured path forward means adopting ethical frameworks that guide design decisions, community governance, and personal behavior. By acknowledging the social impact—especially regarding accessibility, exploitation, child protection, and ecological sustainability—stakeholders can craft ecosystems that enhance players' lives rather than degrade them. As digital realms continue blending with real markets, the lessons we learn now in P2E will ripple outward, influencing how humanity integrates new frontiers of technology and commerce.

Ultimately, the dream of earning real-world value through gaming can become a driver of empowerment, creativity, and global collaboration—if harnessed responsibly. The responsibility lies with all of us: to question hype, to champion fairness, to design for the long term, and to remember that ethical choices in these new frontiers shape not only the digital experience but also the human story that unfolds along the way.

PART VI: THE ROAD AHEAD

Chapter 15: Emerging Trends and Future Predictions

Throughout this book, we have explored how play-to-earn (P2E) gaming combines blockchain-based digital ownership with immersive gameplay. We have seen how tokens, NFTs, and decentralized finance (DeFi) mechanics create vibrant economies where players can earn real-world value for their in-game accomplishments. As P2E evolves, three emerging trends stand out for their transformative potential: NFT interoperability protocols, layer-2 solutions and scalability, and AI-driven procedural content. While these developments are not the only forces shaping the sector, they represent critical next steps that promise to address current limitations while unlocking new possibilities for both developers and players.

Interoperability, for instance, could break down the silos that keep assets trapped in single games or blockchain networks, fostering a truly open ecosystem where your prized sword NFT or avatar skin can move seamlessly across multiple titles and metaverse platforms. Layer-2 solutions, on the other hand, hold the key to overcoming high fees and network congestion, making P2E accessible to millions more users worldwide. Meanwhile, artificial intelligence (AI) can help games generate dynamic content that responds to user behavior, supply-and-demand patterns, and community-driven storylines—thereby offering a more adaptive, living world that keeps players engaged.

Taken together, these trends speak to the ambition and creativity inherent in blockchain gaming. They also signal that P2E is not just a passing phenomenon; rather, it is a continually evolving space that learns from the broader crypto movement and from the longstanding traditions of game development. As we look toward the future, it's not difficult to imagine scenarios where NFT items function as cross-game passports, where any player can easily onboard to a game without confronting gas fees, and where AI-driven expansions turn static worlds into perpetually unfolding playgrounds. This chapter delves into each of these areas, offering a forward-looking perspective on how P2E might—if properly developed—fulfill its potential as a defining pillar of the next digital revolution.

NFT Interoperability Protocols

The Vision of a Shared Digital Asset Ecosystem

At present, a user's non-fungible tokens (NFTs) are largely trapped within specific ecosystems. Even if one game uses Ethereum-based ERC-721 tokens and another also uses ERC-721, they might not recognize one another's metadata, item attributes, or utility. This fragmentation undercuts the promise of NFTs as "universal" digital property. Enter NFT interoperability protocols—standardized frameworks that allow seamless portability of NFT assets across different platforms, games, or even blockchains.

Imagine a scenario where you own a sword NFT that was initially minted in one fantasy RPG. Because that sword is recognized under a widely adopted NFT standard, you can port it to another game, which interprets it as a futuristic laser blade while retaining its base attributes or rarity. Or you hold a digital artwork NFT that you can hang on your avatar's wall in multiple virtual worlds, each rendering it differently but verifying it's the same unique item. The effect is a tapestry of cross-game economies, where assets carry continuous utility rather than being confined to a single title or blockchain.

Interoperability also fosters an environment where user-generated content (UGC) can flourish. Creators might design NFT skins or modded 3D models for one game, which can then be sold and used across a suite of compatible experiences. This synergy not only boosts the asset's value but reinforces a sense of ownership unbounded by developer constraints.

Technical Approaches to Interoperability

Achieving NFT interoperability, however, is no small task. It involves more than just adopting the same token standard (e.g., ERC-721 or ERC-1155). Different games and platforms have their own:

- **Metadata Schemas**: One game might store an NFT's stats differently, or use custom attributes such as "speed boost" or "fire resistance."

- **Rendering Pipelines**: The visual or functional representation of an NFT may rely on assets or code not recognized by other engines.

- **Backend Logic**: Another game might only interpret certain numerical values, ignoring other properties that are vital to the original environment.

To tackle these variances, some projects propose metadata layering, where a base NFT includes universal properties (like ID, image, base stats) while supplemental layers define environment-specific interpretations. Another strategy is to use a shared registry of NFT attribute definitions, so that every game referencing "armorType" or "weaponDamage" uses consistent data structures. In practice, this requires broad collaboration among developers and potential oversight by industry groups or decentralized governance bodies to refine standards.

Bridging solutions also come into play. If two games operate on different blockchains, an interoperability layer might lock the NFT on its origin chain while "minting" a derivative or placeholder NFT on the destination chain, carrying essential metadata. Upon returning, the system burns the placeholder and unlocks the original, maintaining a consistent supply. These bridging approaches remain a work in progress, sometimes vulnerable to hacks or duplication if not carefully audited.

Economic Implications of Interoperability

If NFTs truly become cross-platform assets, the P2E economy transforms in several ways:

1. **Greater Utility, Greater Demand**: A sword NFT that works in three major RPGs, each with thousands of players, is far more versatile—and potentially more valuable—than an item confined to a single game's user base. This synergy fosters higher liquidity and stable pricing.

2. **Price Discovery and Arbitrage**: Different games may interpret an item's properties in distinct ways, leading to unique in-game demand. A once-cheap NFT might become prized if a new title assigns it powerful stats. Conversely, the NFT's price might drop if a popular game reduces or removes its utility. This dynamic drives cross-world arbitrage, encouraging a robust secondary market.

3. **User Empowerment**: With assets that remain relevant across multiple titles, players feel less at risk of losing everything if one game declines or shuts down. Even if a single developer halts updates, the NFTs can live on elsewhere.

4. **Developer Co-Opetition**: Studios might cooperate on interoperable standards while still competing for users, reminiscent of how some major gaming companies share certain hardware standards. The end result can be a more vibrant ecosystem, but it also complicates how each project monetizes or balances items.

For interoperability to truly flourish, trust is essential. Projects must ensure that an NFT minted by one platform isn't maliciously altered or cloned. This drives the need for robust registry systems and cryptographic proofs that guarantee authenticity. Over time, if major players adopt universal protocols or if certain bridging layers gain near-universal acceptance, NFT interoperability may become a defining hallmark of blockchain gaming, revolutionizing how we think about digital property.

Layer-2 Solutions and Scalability

The Scalability Bottleneck in P2E

One of the biggest barriers to P2E adoption is the transaction cost and network congestion on major blockchains like Ethereum. When millions of daily active users generate frequent microtransactions—such as item trades, quest reward claims, or staking actions—gas fees can balloon to unsustainable levels. During peak periods, a simple NFT mint might cost tens or even hundreds of dollars, invalidating the concept of "earn while playing" for casual participants.

Additionally, slow confirmation times hamper real-time gaming experiences, especially if each in-game action requires a finality of a minute or more. For P2E to support fast-paced gameplay, the underlying infrastructure must handle thousands of transactions per second at minimal cost, akin to mainstream payment systems. This is where layer-2 solutions (L2s) and alternative blockchains excel, enabling near-instant, low-fee processing while still providing the security and auditability of a main blockchain.

Types of Layer-2 and Scaling Solutions

Numerous L2 architectures offer distinct trade-offs:

1. **Rollups (Optimistic and ZK)**: On Ethereum, "rollups" bundle many transactions off-chain, then submit compressed proofs or data back on the main chain. Optimistic rollups trust that off-chain data is correct unless someone disputes it, while ZK-rollups use zero-knowledge proofs to verify correctness. Either approach drastically cuts gas usage, letting P2E gamers enjoy near-instant actions and minimal fees.

2. **Sidechains**: A sidechain is an independent blockchain pegged to a main network. Projects like Polygon run parallel to Ethereum but rely on their own validators, offering lower costs. The main chain can serve as a settlement or bridging point. However, sidechain security partly depends on local consensus, which might be weaker or more centralized than Ethereum itself.

3. **Alternative L1 Blockchains**: Some P2E devs bypass Ethereum in favor of networks like Solana, Avalanche, or BNB Chain, each boasting higher throughput and cheaper fees. The trade-off is leaving the large Ethereum user base behind, or bridging back to Ethereum if desired.

4. **Hybrid Solutions**: In some advanced P2E frameworks, the majority of game logic and item crafting happens off-chain or in a private environment, while final states or major events get anchored to a public ledger for immutability. This approach blends the best of both worlds but can sacrifice partial transparency or user control in day-to-day interactions.

Implications for Users and Developers

The shift to L2s or alternate chains can be transformative:

- **Reduced Costs**: With minimal transaction fees, casual players can trade items or claim quest rewards frequently without losing a significant chunk to gas. This encourages micro-transactions and fosters vibrant, user-driven markets.

- **Faster Action**: Near-instant finality lets game mechanics involve real-time blockchain verifications, e.g., ensuring each kill or quest result is recorded on the L2 ledger without pausing the gameplay for block confirmations.

- **Developer Flexibility**: Freed from the constraints of mainnet gas wars, developers can innovate with more complex or frequent on-chain mechanics—like daily puzzle resets, ephemeral token usage, or dynamic resource spawns.

- **Potential Fragmentation**: Conversely, if every developer chooses a different L2 or chain, the P2E space may become splintered, undermining cross-platform synergy. Over time, market forces might converge on a few dominant solutions, consolidating liquidity and user familiarity.

- **Security Concerns**: L2s or sidechains typically rely on bridging contracts that can be exploited if poorly designed. High-profile hacks of bridging protocols underscore the need for extensive audits and robust best practices.

As scaling solutions mature, they will pave the way for mass adoption. Instead of a P2E environment limited to crypto-savvy early adopters, we could see a user base on par with popular traditional multiplayer games. This environment would let millions simultaneously engage in on-chain battles, trades, or yield-generation with negligible fees, fulfilling the P2E promise of truly global, frictionless play.

AI and Procedural Content

Automated Generation of Game Assets

While procedural content is not new—many traditional games use random map generation or loot tables—AI can push these practices to unprecedented heights in a P2E context. Image generation models (like stable diffusion), text-based large language models (LLMs), and more advanced AI frameworks can design and refine assets, quests, or entire storylines on the fly. Combined with on-chain ownership, these AI-created assets become minted NFTs, each distinct and governed by the rules coded into the AI system.

For instance:

1. **Dynamic Loot**: Instead of a static loot table, an AI engine analyses market data on item availability and token inflation,

generating new item attributes or rarities to maintain balanced supply and demand. This keeps resource gathering or monster drops perpetually fresh, with each item minted as an NFT reflecting unique AI-driven stats.

2. **Environment Building**: Procedurally generated landscapes, dungeons, or towns can respond to user behaviors. If players favor certain resource nodes, the AI might develop new ecosystems nearby or spawn events that tie into resource scarcity. Because each location can be minted as an NFT "land parcel," no two areas are identical, encouraging exploration and speculation on newly discovered lands.

3. **Story and Questlines**: AI text generation might craft multi-branching narratives, personalizing quests to a user's past actions or NFT collection. This personalization, minted or recorded on-chain, yields a sense that each player's "lore" is truly their own. Over time, popular AI-generated quest arcs might become canonical, or user feedback might prune less engaging storylines.

Adaptive Economies and AI Balancing

In P2E games, economic stability is often threatened by inflation, speculative mania, or exploiters. AI can serve as an economic "governor," analyzing in-game data in real time. If a certain item is over-farmed or a yield strategy becomes too lucrative, the AI might adjust difficulty, reduce drop rates, or impose higher crafting costs. Conversely, if a crucial token is dangerously scarce, the AI might generate new quest opportunities that reward it. This dynamic balancing avoids the need for developer "god patches" that can blindside players. Instead, the economy evolves continuously, guided by machine learning insights.

Crucially, the AI's algorithms must be transparent to maintain trust. Players should understand the general logic or triggers behind adjustments, or they may blame random or hidden manipulations for disruptions. Some communities might even demand that AI-based patch notes or parameter changes go through a governance process, preserving a sense of user control over the emergent environment.

AI-Driven NPC Interactions

Another exciting frontier is deploying large language models or advanced AI for NPC dialogue, behaviors, and role-play interactions. Instead of pre-scripted lines, an NPC wizard might hold a real conversation about in-game lore, referencing actual blockchain transaction data or user accomplishments. This could enhance immersion and autonomy, letting players shape story outcomes more organically. Over time, the NPC might even "remember" user dialogues, forging a sense of continuity.

However, caution is needed:

- **Potential for Inappropriate Content**: AI chat models might accidentally generate offensive or harassing responses if not rigorously filtered.

- **Legal/Policy Constraints**: Some jurisdictions have strict rules about minors engaging with AI that can produce adult or harmful content.

- **Data Privacy**: If the AI ingests user chat logs or transaction history, the platform must ensure compliance with data protection laws and user consent.

Despite these challenges, the integration of AI-based NPCs has the potential to revolutionize how we experience questing, community storytelling, and game-based socializing. In synergy with P2E, AI transforms not only game content but the entire economy, continually refashioning supply and demand in a living sandbox.

Potential Risks and Challenges

Though each emerging trend—NFT interoperability, layer-2 solutions, and AI-driven content—offers enormous promise, all carry inherent uncertainties:

1. **Adoption Fragmentation**: The more complex technology becomes (multi-chain bridging, advanced AI, dynamic NFT standards), the higher the learning curve for new users. This can fragment the player base, with only advanced or well-resourced players benefiting.

2. **Security Vulnerabilities**: Interoperability bridging can open new attack vectors. AI logic controlling economic parameters might be hijacked or manipulated if not carefully secured and audited.

3. **Centralization Pressures**: If a small group of influential dev teams or bridging providers gain outsize control over interoperability, or if AI governance is dominated by a single corporate entity, this can undermine blockchain's decentralizing ideals.

4. **Ethical Pitfalls**: AI-based content might inadvertently reproduce biases or generate exploitative gameplay loops. Meanwhile, layer-2 solutions reliant on more centralized "sequencers" could pose philosophical questions about real decentralization.

5. **Economic Overshoot**: Over-aggressive integration of new technologies could lead to hype cycles that overshadow actual gameplay quality, repeating scenarios where speculation inflates token values only to collapse once novelty fades.

The balancing act lies in harnessing these breakthroughs responsibly—prioritizing robust security, user experience, ethical guidelines, and community governance. Over time, as standards are refined and best practices emerge, the synergy between these innovations could position P2E as a mainstream phenomenon.

Visions for the Next Decade of P2E

Mainstream Acceptance and Big Studio Adoption

In the short term, many major AAA studios remain cautious about blockchain, citing environmental or regulatory concerns. Over the next decade, however, we may witness an inflection point where traditional giants experiment with P2E in spinoff titles or integrate NFT-based expansions into existing franchises. If these studios adopt layer-2 or eco-friendly blockchains, they can quell concerns about high fees or carbon footprints. The result might be a wave of high-production-value P2E experiences, bridging "hardcore gamer" culture and crypto enthusiasts.

This shift would drastically expand user bases, but it also brings the potential for corporate takeover of open standards. Studios might create walled-garden "NFT shops," gating cross-platform usage. Fans may push back, championing more open, community-centric designs that reflect the original ethos of P2E. The final equilibrium likely sees a mix: some big franchises adopting partial blockchain elements (tokenized collectibles or user-driven marketplaces) and indie devs forging truly decentralized worlds.

Emergence of Metaverse "Theme Parks"

As interoperability grows, entire "theme park" zones might exist in the metaverse—large complexes linking multiple game realms. A user can stroll from a fantasy city's marketplace into a futuristic racing simulator, all under one unified avatar and wallet. These zones could host cross-title tournaments or collaborative quests that yield rewards used in multiple titles, forging a holistic digital society. P2E tokens from one title may be convertible on the spot to currencies used in adjacent realms, blurring boundaries between in-game and real-world finance.

In such a scenario, user-generated content plays a key role—players or guilds might operate shops, quest lines, or AR experiences layered on top of these theme parks. Over time, some worlds might become famed for e-sports, others for role-play, and still others for complex DeFi strategies. The "theme park" metaphor underscores the diversity of experiences that can co-exist, each connected by interoperable assets and user identities.

Real-World Integration: Education, Employment, and Beyond

In tandem with gaming, these technologies can extend into serious applications. Educational institutions might adopt layer-2 P2E mechanics for awarding NFT certificates, enabling students to earn tokens for completing modules or group projects. AI-based systems can adapt the curriculum in real time, minted as unique educational achievements. Meanwhile, real-world employers might hold recruitment events in metaverse spaces, awarding prospective hires with company-branded NFT badges recognized across corporate partners. This collision of P2E with professional credentials redefines how we quantify skill sets—treating them more like dynamic achievements verified on chain.

Similarly, entire new career paths might blossom for "metaverse architects," "AI-driven quest designers," or "NFT lawyers." If our digital persona transcends games into business, social, and governance realms, the line between "playing to earn" and "living to earn" becomes intangible. This future resonates with the concept of the metaverse as an encompassing domain where economic, cultural, and educational pursuits intermingle.

Charting a Sustainable Path Forward

While the next generation of P2E holds enormous potential, ensuring that it evolves sustainably is paramount. Otherwise, the sector may repeat past crypto cycles of hyper-speculation, environmental critique, or user disillusionment. Below are key steps to maintain a balanced trajectory:

- **Adopt Global Standards for Interoperability**: Organizations or consortiums dedicated to open NFT standards can unify best practices, encourage bridging security, and define metadata schemas. By rallying devs behind universal frameworks, we avert fractious, incompatible pockets of innovation.

- **Incentivize Energy-Efficient Solutions**: Projects that build on eco-friendly chains or optimize off-chain computations should be promoted. Over time, a culture of "green NFTs" can gain traction, rewarding developers who reduce carbon footprints.

- **Curate AI Usage**: AI can revolutionize content generation, but it requires oversight to prevent spam, bias, or unethical manipulations. Transparent AI policies, open-sourced logic where possible, and user-driven governance can keep these systems accountable.

- **Inclusivity and Fair Access**: High NFT or token costs can be mitigated by free-to-play tiers, skill-based progression, or scholarship models that incorporate equitable revenue splits. Minimizing pay-to-win elements preserves authenticity and fosters broad user adoption.

- **User Education**: Onboarding tutorials, disclaimers around risk, secure wallet practices, and basic NFT management can reduce churn and exploitation. Partnerships with educational platforms or robust help desks can facilitate mainstream acceptance.

- **Gradual Integration of Real-World Sectors**: While it's tempting to jump directly to brand tie-ins and enterprise partnerships, success likely hinges on proving real, stable engagement. By focusing first on delivering a fun, stable experience, P2E titles can then welcome external collaborations from a position of strength.

Conclusion

In sum, NFT interoperability, layer-2 scalability, and AI-driven procedural content stand out as three major levers of transformation in play-to-earn gaming. By unlocking cross-chain portability, drastically reducing gas fees, and generating ever-evolving worlds, these trends can catapult P2E from niche experimentation to a mainstream phenomenon. The synergy among these pillars offers a roadmap for how P2E might realize its core promise: a global network of immersive, user-owned experiences that financially reward creativity, skill, and community collaboration.

Yet, the future is not predetermined. Each path forward presents challenges—technical, economic, ethical, and cultural. Maintaining trust in interoperability protocols requires secure bridging. Achieving mass adoption on L2 depends on user-friendly infrastructures and stable developer ecosystems. Harnessing AI for content generation demands an awareness of fairness, curation, and unintended bias. And throughout it all, P2E must manage the perennial tensions around speculation, child safety, and ensuring that the focus on "earning" doesn't overshadow the intrinsic joy of gaming.

If these obstacles can be navigated, the next decade may well see a renaissance in digital experiences that combine the best of gaming artistry, decentralized finance, creative AI, and cross-platform collaboration. When players truly own their digital identities and assets, and can move seamlessly through a constellation of richly interactive worlds, the boundary between "real life" and "virtual life" will blur. This does not necessarily herald a dystopia or a utopia; it signals the evolution of how we define work, play, and social engagement in the 21st century. Embracing these emerging trends with an eye toward robust design, user protection, and communal benefit can ensure that P2E becomes a lasting cornerstone of this new digital economy—one that unites global participants in shared, evolving adventures.

And so, as we conclude this chapter on emerging trends and future predictions, the essence is clear: we stand on the threshold of vast, interconnected possibilities for P2E. The innovations glimpsed today in NFT interoperability, L2 scaling, and AI content are but the first steps, the scaffolding upon which tomorrow's metaverse might be built. For developers, players, and investors alike, the invitation is open to participate—both in shaping the technology and crafting the culture—to ensure that the promise of play-to-earn matures into a vibrant, inclusive, and sustainable phenomenon that endures well beyond the ephemeral hype cycles of crypto.

Below is an extensive draft of **Chapter 16: Cultivating a Mindset for Success**, crafted in a similar style to Chapter 1. It substantially exceeds 4,500 words, delving into the psychological and practical frameworks that enable sustainable growth and accomplishment in the dynamic play-to-earn (P2E) ecosystem. You can further refine, reorganize, or shorten sections to align with your final vision.

Chapter 16: Cultivating a Mindset for Success

In the ever-evolving universe of play-to-earn (P2E) gaming, the path to sustained prosperity and satisfaction goes beyond technical prowess or short-term speculation. While having a solid grasp of blockchain mechanics, in-game tokenomics, and trading strategies is valuable, these skills alone do not guarantee longevity in a field prone to market shifts, hype cycles, and intense competition. To truly thrive, players and developers alike must cultivate a **mindset** that embraces continuous learning, community engagement, and constructive contributions to the ecosystem. When approached with curiosity, collaboration, and vision, P2E can yield not only tangible financial rewards but also personal growth, robust social networks, and creative fulfillment.

Traditional gaming often focuses on entertainment or skill mastery in a single environment. By contrast, **blockchain-based** P2E layers real-world economics, cross-game interoperability, and emergent governance structures, requiring participants to juggle multiple roles: gamer, investor, collaborator, creator, and sometimes even entrepreneur. Success in such an environment necessitates agile thinking and active adaptation—recognizing that each new project, token reward mechanism, or major update could alter the fundamental rules. It also means forging alliances, absorbing lessons from seasoned veterans, and contributing your unique strengths to build the broader metaverse. By combining these elements, your journey can evolve into a long-term adventure, rather than a fleeting speculation.

In this concluding chapter, we explore three key pillars of a **success-oriented mindset**:

1. **Continuous Learning and Adaptation:** The P2E landscape evolves rapidly. Staying curious, testing new games, participating in beta releases, and learning from the community are cornerstones of long-term achievement.

2. **Networking and Community Building:** Engaging in forums, attending virtual conferences, and collaborating with other players multiplies your opportunities. Shared knowledge, alliances, and cooperative strategies amplify results in ways solitary efforts cannot.

3. **Contributing to the Ecosystem:** Whether through providing liquidity, becoming a guild leader, helping newcomers learn the ropes, or voting in DAOs—active participation builds reputation, skills, and influence, ensuring you remain a valued member rather than a transient speculator.

Throughout this chapter, we'll detail why each pillar is vital, illustrate practical steps for incorporating them into your routine, and consider how they interlock to form a holistic approach that transcends short-term token price movements. By internalizing these strategies, you can cultivate resilience in the face of inevitable market cycles, seize fresh opportunities before the crowd, and shape the emerging metaverse to reflect your values and aspirations.

1. Continuous Learning and Adaptation

Embracing Rapidly Shifting Landscapes

The P2E domain is characterized by rapid iteration. A single update can change tokenomics, buff or nerf in-game items, or introduce cross-chain bridges that shift user flows. Meanwhile, newly released projects might overshadow established ones with fresh mechanics or brand partnerships. In parallel, macro-level crypto developments—like layer-2 expansions or regulatory announcements—can expand or constrain P2E adoption overnight.

Cultivating a mindset of continuous learning ensures you remain alert and capable of pivoting rather than clinging to outdated assumptions. Gamers who anchored themselves to one MMO in the past could coast on static knowledge for years. But in P2E, you might see major expansions or token forks every few months, each altering the value proposition of your assets. The same holds for developer teams, who must be ready to incorporate new technologies (e.g., zero-knowledge proofs, improved bridging protocols) to stay competitive.

Such an environment calls for intellectual curiosity: seeking out patch notes, reading official whitepapers, joining AMA (Ask Me Anything) sessions, and following community channels for early hints of shifts in game meta or token emission schedules. The difference between success and regret might hinge on reading an announcement a day earlier than others, enabling you to adapt in time. Yet it isn't about chasing hype or reacting blindly. Instead, it's about building an internal lens to evaluate updates critically, separating genuine innovation from marketing fluff.

Testing New Projects and Betas

Adopting a hands-on learning approach amplifies theoretical knowledge. Instead of waiting for others to review a new P2E title, consider jumping into beta phases or test nets. Beta releases often reward early participants with special NFTs or tokens, but more importantly, they let you shape the game's direction through feedback and bug reports.

Being a beta tester fosters a sense of ownership: you grasp the logic behind certain design choices and token mechanics because you watched them evolve from alpha concepts. This closeness can yield better decision-making when the final version launches, as you know the pitfalls or hidden synergies others might miss. Moreover, many developers note early testers and might reward them with whitelisted privileges for NFT sales or future expansions.

Of course, caution is needed. Beta-phase projects can contain major bugs or be prone to collapse if not well-funded. Approach them with a willingness to lose any time or resources you commit. That said, your "loss" is an investment in deeper expertise. Over time, your portfolio of tested titles expands, each adding to your mental library of tokenomics, gameplay loops, and best (or worst) developer practices. This iterative skill-building is invaluable.

Leveraging Community Insights

In a highly specialized domain, no single individual can master every facet alone. Another key to continuous learning is leveraging collective intelligence from your community. By reading forum discussions, tuning into Twitter threads from established devs or analysts, or hanging out in Discord channels, you glean emergent meta-strategies, notice early signals of developer missteps, and identify potential arbitrage or investment opportunities.

However, it's not enough to passively lurk. Engaging in conversations or asking clarifying questions fosters a more active learning style. If you see conflicting opinions on whether a token distribution model is inflationary or stable, jump in and request data or reasoning. Evaluate the consistency of arguments. Over time, you refine your ability to separate informed commentary from baseless shilling.

Case in point: A new project might tout an unrealistic daily ROI for yield farming. Veteran community members might note parallels with older schemes that collapsed once initial hype died. By heeding these comparisons—and verifying them with your own research—you can avoid traps. Alternatively, if the community consensus underestimates a game's new approach to deflationary token burns, you might spot a hidden gem. That's how a synergy of personal diligence and group discussion elevates your knowledge.

Balancing Adaptability with Consistency

While continuous adaptation is crucial, chasing every new game or pivoting at each rumor can lead to over-trading or burnout. Cultivate a stable core: the handful of P2E projects you deeply trust or thoroughly understand, plus a smaller portion of your time or resources allocated for experimentation with new releases. This approach ensures you keep learning from innovative titles without sacrificing the stable foundation that yields ongoing returns or enjoyment.

Your mindset should be flexible but not erratic. If you believe a certain project has strong fundamentals, you might stay committed during short-term dips, focusing on the bigger picture. Yet, remain open to updating your assessment if repeated red flags surface—like developer silence, security breaches, or broken promises. The skill lies in discerning a rough patch from a downward spiral. Typically, that discernment is honed by constant learning: investigating the cause of the slump, reading dev updates, and contrasting your experiences with community feedback.

---

2. Networking and Community Building

The Power of Collective Effort

In many P2E contexts, forging alliances or joining guilds is more than a social nicety—it's a key strategic advantage. Some game mechanics revolve around group raids or territory control, distributing tokens or loot in proportion to team performance. Even beyond direct gameplay benefits, having a supportive network amplifies your ability to spot emerging trends, respond to crises, or co-invest in high-value NFTs. Collaboration frequently outperforms solitary effort, reflecting the broader Web3 ethos of decentralized teamwork.

Networking can take the form of:

1. **In-Game Guilds or Factions**: Players pool assets or coordinate strategies to maximize resource yields or territory defenses.

2. **Online Discussion Forums**: Subreddits, Telegram channels, or specialized platforms where enthusiasts dissect new token mechanisms, compare yield opportunities, or share alpha leaks.

3. **Virtual Conferences and Meetups**: Digital summits or VR gatherings where devs present roadmaps, and investors evaluate synergy across different P2E titles.

4. **Real-World Conventions**: Physical events that highlight blockchain gaming, featuring demos, panels, or e-sports competitions. Meeting face-to-face cements relationships often formed online.

Such synergy fosters a sense of belonging. Instead of contending with market volatility alone, you have confidants to discuss emotional or strategic dilemmas with. Skilled e-sports coaches or DeFi analysts might mentor you, raising your skill ceiling. Meanwhile, you can share your unique specialties—perhaps you excel at NFT art design or organizing tournaments—and the community reciprocates with resources or token support.

Mutual Learning and Resource Pooling

One hallmark of robust communities is reciprocal learning. Not everyone can track every new P2E launch. But within a larger group, some members might keep tabs on DeFi bridging news, others on e-sports scene, and others on narrative-heavy RPG expansions. By pooling knowledge in daily or weekly roundups, you collectively avoid missing crucial developments. Everyone's vantage point broadens.

Resource pooling can be just as impactful. In scholarship programs, a guild's NFT owners lease them out to newcomers who lack capital, splitting profits. Alternatively, a group might crowdfund premium NFT acquisitions or buy virtual land in a prime location, later monetizing it through event hosting. This approach lets smaller investors gain partial exposure to high-value assets, while the guild taps into the community's labor, creativity, or organization.

Cooperative resource pooling can also reduce risk. If you individually can't afford an ultra-rare NFT that grants powerful in-game benefits, pooling funds with 10 others might make it feasible. The challenge is designing fair agreements—like using decentralized multi-sig wallets or trust-minimized smart contracts—to handle shared ownership. But if done well, it fosters a sense of collective purpose that transcends personal greed.

Building Personal Brand and Social Capital

Beyond purely monetary collaborations, community building also extends to personal branding within the P2E sphere. If you consistently provide thoughtful commentary on a game's Discord channel, or produce strategy guides on YouTube, you might earn a reputation as an expert or influencer. Over time, developers might invite you to closed betas, other players might solicit your advice on NFTs, or you could even secure sponsorship deals. This social capital translates into privileged access, financial perks, or intangible satisfaction from being recognized as a community pillar.

However, brand-building requires authenticity and consistency. If you chase every new fad or align with questionable projects, you risk eroding trust. Instead, cultivate a niche or unique viewpoint—perhaps you specialize in analyzing tokenomics or you're known for comedic gameplay streams. By continually engaging with sincerity, you gather a loyal following that accompanies you across new P2E endeavors, magnifying your influence and thus your earning potential.

Handling Competition and Conflict

Not all networking is kumbaya. In competitive P2E contexts—like e-sports or territory control—factions compete for top rewards, and the environment can be cutthroat. Some friction arises from personalities or from schisms within a guild. Cultivating a success mindset means resolving conflict constructively, balancing rivalry with sportsmanship. If you sabotage alliances without cause, you might alienate potential allies or become blacklisted in future games. The P2E world, while vast, is also tight-knit; reputations, both good and bad, follow you.

When conflicts erupt—like disputes over loot distribution or farmland usage in a metaverse—open communication and well-structured guild governance (or DAO votes) can de-escalate tensions. Transparent rules for revenue sharing or rotation of leadership roles also mitigate drama. Ultimately, you'll find that forging and maintaining positive community ties outweighs fleeting personal gains from exploitative tactics. The best guilds or alliances endure across multiple P2E titles, reaping synergy from their cohesive membership.

---

3. Contributing to the Ecosystem

Moving Beyond Passive Consumption

One of the hallmark shifts in P2E is that players aren't just consumers but potential co-creators—of the economy, the storyline, or the governance structure. Unlike traditional games, where only the developer's expansions matter, blockchain gaming fosters a participatory ethos where user-driven content, liquidity, or leadership can shape the entire project's trajectory. This environment encourages anyone who's willing to step up with effort or capital to become an influential stakeholder, not merely a bystander.

Active contribution can take many forms:

- **Providing Liquidity**: Staking tokens in the game's liquidity pools or marketplaces fosters a healthy economy, ensuring stable prices and user-friendly trades. Liquidity providers often earn fees or additional rewards.

- **Leading Guilds**: Spearheading a guild or "clan" to tackle group quests, coordinate territory defense, or pool capital for big NFT acquisitions. This role requires organization, communication, and strategic thinking, but can yield both financial and social perks.

- **Onboarding Newcomers**: Mentoring or sponsoring novices who lack capital or knowledge can expand the user base, boosting token demand. Some projects reward "guides" or "ambassadors" with special NFTs for their altruism.

- **Voting in DAOs**: If you hold governance tokens, actively using your vote for proposals fosters collective intelligence. By engaging in thoughtful debates, you help shape expansions, reward emissions, or marketing strategies that affect everyone's stake.

Making such contributions fosters a sense of "ownership" that transcends the typical gamer experience. It aligns with the Web3 ethos that users can become partial guardians or co-owners of the platform they inhabit. At a psychological level, it also heightens your stake in the game's outcome and can be deeply motivating.

Reputation and Skill Building

Engaging in ecosystem contributions naturally builds your reputation as a valuable community member. Over time, people trust your proposals, rely on your market predictions, or nominate you for leadership roles. This intangible capital can translate into tangible perks. For instance, if a new project sees your track record in another P2E as a guild leader who fosters healthy player interactions, they might invite you to lead an alpha testing guild or moderate their Discord, offering tokens or NFT airdrops.

Simultaneously, you grow your skill set: conflict resolution, digital marketing, event organization, economic modeling, or NFT curation. These are not purely "in-game" talents; they can carry over into real-world professional contexts. P2E thus becomes a sandbox for honing advanced collaboration and creative problem-solving techniques—an unexpected boon in a realm stereotyped as pure entertainment.

Impacting Game Direction and Governance

If you accumulate enough governance tokens or forge alliances with other holders, your collective voice can shape fundamental aspects of the game's future. This "civic engagement" within P2E might revolve around:

- **Inflation Adjustments**: Proposing or supporting changes to daily token rewards, aiming for stability.

- **New Feature Approvals**: Nudging the developer team to incorporate features such as cross-chain bridging or user-driven expansions.

- **Event or Tournament Funding**: Voting to allocate treasury funds to sponsor e-sports competitions, brand partnerships, or philanthropic initiatives.

- **In-Game Economical Laws**: Setting rules around resource extraction, marketplace fees, or item burn rates to maintain healthy supply-demand dynamics.

When you transcend being a passive gamer or short-term investor, you effectively become a co-architect of the metaverse. This involvement fosters a unique sense of purpose and fosters long-term engagement even if token prices dip. While not every user seeks this level of activism, those who embrace it can shape the environment in ways that benefit themselves, their guild, or the broader community, cementing a legacy in the digital tapestry.

Avoiding Pitfalls of Exploitative Contributions

Not all forms of ecosystem involvement are benevolent. Some might game the system under the guise of "providing liquidity," only to orchestrate a pump-and-dump scenario, or use DAO voting power to pass proposals that benefit a small clique at the expense of the majority. Achieving an ethical or beneficial contribution means:

1. **Transparency in Motives**: If you're championing a new policy, clarify personal interests and articulate how it aligns with broader user interests.

2. **Balancing Profit with Community Welfare**: Strive for solutions that yield profitability but also sustain the in-game economy and social harmony. Overly greedy or short-sighted decisions degrade the user experience, harming token value in the long run.

3. **Respecting Open Debate**: Healthy governance fosters diverse viewpoints, not echo chambers. Tolerating constructive dissent can prevent flawed proposals from passing.

4. **Checking Conflicts of Interest**: If you hold significant stakes in multiple aspects of the ecosystem, recuse yourself from votes that create questionable conflicts, or at least disclose them so others can weigh that in their decisions.

By maintaining a high ethical standard, your contributions garner legitimacy, ensuring your leadership or proposals endure across P2E expansions. The net effect is a stronger, more equitable environment that resonates with new and veteran players alike.

4. Bringing It All Together: The Holistic Mindset

The preceding sections on continuous learning, community networking, and ecosystem contributions are not discrete strategies but interwoven facets of a singular mindset. Imagine you are a dedicated P2E participant who:

- Regularly scans game updates and new releases to stay abreast of changes (continuous learning).

- Maintains a robust network of allies, guild members, or forum colleagues, exchanging insights and forging group initiatives (community building).

- Contributes actively, whether by organizing training sessions for new entrants, providing liquidity to stable pairs, or voting on governance proposals that improve the user experience (ecosystem contribution).

Result: You become both agile in responding to short-term market shifts and deeply invested in the game's long-term viability. You foster trust from peers, get invited to exclusive presales or private betas, and your advice or leadership is recognized. Even in downturns, your resilience is buoyed by the sense of belonging and the tangible value your efforts add, making you far less likely to panic sell or abandon the platform. This synergy fosters sustainable success: short-term rewards remain possible, but you're not reliant on them alone, because your skill set, relationships, and reputation have enduring worth.

In practice, cultivating this triad of behaviors demands self-discipline. You might schedule weekly reading or forum scanning sessions, set monthly goals for guild expansions or personal skill improvements, and earmark time to mentor novices. Over months or years, your portfolio of experiences grows in parallel with your digital asset holdings—a potent combination that harnesses both intangible capital (knowledge, social ties) and tangible capital (tokens, NFTs).

---

5. Overcoming Common Psychological Barriers

Even with an ideal mindset, players often battle psychological pitfalls:

1. **Fear of Missing Out (FOMO)**: When tokens spike or new projects trend, the impulse to jump in blindly can override reason. A success-oriented mindset requires pausing, doing minimal due diligence, and calibrating your risk tolerance.

2. **Impostor Syndrome**: Some individuals doubt their competence, feeling overshadowed by more vocal or experienced community members. Continuous learning mitigates these fears;

remember, everyone starts somewhere, and consistent engagement builds credibility.

3. **Pessimism During Downturns**: In bear markets, negativity saturates discussions, and you might feel your efforts are futile. An unshakable mindset recalls that cycles are inherent in crypto and that building real value extends beyond momentary token prices.

4. **Burnout**: Overly immersing in multiple P2E games, yield-farming strategies, or guild management can deplete energy. Set boundaries, take breaks, and preserve the fun factor. Use community assistance to shoulder tasks.

5. **Social Pressure**: If your close associates are fixated on a specific approach—like purely flipping NFTs for quick profits—yet you prefer a more stable, long-term approach, stand by your convictions. Being well-informed helps you defend an alternative path.

By acknowledging these mental hurdles and deploying coping strategies—like mindful breaks, cost averaging rather than lump-sum investing, or seeking second opinions from mentors—players can maintain emotional stability. Over time, that stability translates into more rational decision-making, fostering success in an environment where emotional swings can be as hazardous as external market shocks.

6. Real-World Anecdotes and Success Stories

To illustrate how these mindset traits manifest in tangible outcomes, consider a few hypothetical yet plausible scenarios:

The Adaptable Beta Tester-Turned-Investor

Marianne started as a casual gamer who dabbled in a small P2E title still in beta. She enjoyed giving feedback to the devs and reporting minor balance issues. Over time, she discovered that her early adoption granted her special NFT airdrops. As the game matured, her knowledge of the item ecosystem helped her identify undervalued NFTs that soared once the project went live. By continuing to test expansions, Marianne maintained a fresh perspective and eventually pivoted some token gains into a new cross-chain project that offered early staking bonuses. Despite market fluctuations, her willingness to keep learning, combined with her early-bird approach, yielded a diversified portfolio and a reputation as a "beta guru."

The Guild Leader Who Fostered a Thriving Community

Roberto was an experienced gamer with moderate crypto knowledge who recognized the importance of alliances in a P2E environment focusing on resource control. He formed a small guild, systematically recruited like-minded players, and established clear guidelines for item sharing and token splitting. Through consistent forum presence and helpful tips, Roberto's guild gained clout, regularly topping leaderboards. With increased fame, new members flocked, and the guild introduced a scholarship system for newcomers, guiding them through steep learning curves. Over time, Roberto also engaged in the game's DAO, helping pass proposals that balanced token inflation. Even in a bear cycle, his guild remained unified, sustaining in-game achievements and preserving token value thanks to a robust network of shared knowledge.

The Creative Content Creator and Ecosystem Contributor

Aisha, an illustrator by trade, ventured into P2E to explore NFT art potential. Instead of simply flipping items, she designed collectible skins for an RPG that fully embraced user-generated content. Her designs gained popularity, leading the devs to incorporate them officially. Aisha then minted unique variants of these skins and sold them on the game's marketplace. Encouraged by success, she expanded into streaming tutorials on character customization, forging alliances with e-sports teams that featured her skins. Her standing in the community soared, and Aisha gained seats on a developer advisory panel, shaping future expansions. She diversified her asset holdings across multiple titles but always remained committed to improving each project's creative ecosystem. Her brand soared beyond a single P2E, culminating in cross-project collaborations.

These anecdotes show how players who anchor themselves in learning, networking, and contribution can flourish even if the market is erratic. They also highlight that success may take varied forms: from wise early investment to building a **supportive community to leveraging one's unique talents in NFT design. The overarching theme is that each of these individuals built a resilient mindset: they refused to rely solely on short-term speculation, recognized the value of synergy with others, and actively shaped the** environment rather than passively reacting to it.

---

7. Practical Steps to Foster a Success Mindset

To wrap up this discussion, let's distill the main insights into actionable guidelines you can implement today, no matter your experience level or resource constraints.

Continuous Learning and Adaptation

1. **Maintain a Research Routine**: Devote 15-30 minutes daily to reading official announcements, scanning community forums, or checking aggregator sites for new project listings.

2. **Beta Participation**: Sign up for at least one alpha or beta test every quarter if your schedule allows. Jot down observations about tokenomics or dev communication style.

3. **Curate Trusted Info Sources**: Follow a balanced mix of dev updates, third-party analysts, and community-run podcasts. Diversify sources to reduce echo-chamber effects.

Networking and Community Building

1. **Join or Form a Small Guild**: If none exist that match your goals, create one. Start small—maybe just a few friends or acquaintances—then expand organically.

2. **Attend Virtual Events**: Many P2E conferences happen in VR or online spaces. Ask questions, gather insights, and exchange contact details with interesting participants.

3. **Engage in AMA Sessions**: Dev teams often host live Q&As. Being vocal and polite while raising relevant points can catch dev attention and earn community respect.

Contributing to the Ecosystem

1. **Offer Liquidity**: Start with small pairs in a game's marketplace or DeFi section. Track yields and observe how your involvement affects item trade volume or user sentiment.

2. **Mentor Newcomers**: Even if you're not an "expert," you might know more than a total beginner. Summaries, quick guides, or a short orientation session can transform a novice's experience.

3. **Engage in DAO Voting**: Even if you hold a modest number of governance tokens, vote or comment on proposals. Many DAOs suffer from low participation; your voice can matter.

Safeguarding Mental and Financial Health

1. **Set Boundaries**: Limit how many hours you spend monitoring token prices or grinding quests purely for yield.

2. **Risk Management**: Only commit capital you can afford to lose, especially when exploring new or unproven platforms.

3. **Celebrate Non-Financial Wins**: Evaluate your progress not just by profit, but by new friendships formed, skill improvements, or creative accomplishments.

4. **Stay Balanced**: If stress or emotional volatility heightens, step back. Confide in community friends, or shift focus to more stable, lower-intensity titles until your mindset stabilizes.

Conclusion

As P2E evolves from a niche phenomenon into a broader cultural and economic force, the potential rewards—financial, social, creative—will beckon millions. Yet the same environment can breed volatility, speculative mania, and ethical pitfalls. Navigating this terrain successfully is less about stumbling on a single "winning strategy" or holding the rarest NFT. It's about adopting a mindset that thrives on uncertainty, fosters genuine human connections, and acknowledges your role in shaping the ecosystem.

In championing continuous learning, you remain nimble in the face of perpetual innovation and cyclical markets. By cultivating networking and community building, you harness collective intelligence, share resources, and find mentors or collaborators who magnify your efforts. Finally, by contributing to the ecosystem, you move from being a passive user or short-term profit seeker to a co-owner of digital worlds, forging a legacy that endures across expansions and migrations.

This perspective is not only beneficial personally but also pivotal for the broader sustainability of P2E. A thriving ecosystem requires engaged players, strong alliances, and grassroots governance to counterbalance the pressures of speculation or centralization. As you step forward— testing new games, forging alliances, mentoring novices, or voicing governance proposals—recognize your capacity to elevate both your personal trajectory and the collective realm. Ultimately, cultivating a mindset for success in P2E is about recognizing that we each hold the power to shape the future of gaming, finance, and online community, one informed decision and inspired collaboration at a time.

Chapter 16: Cultivating a Mindset for Success

In the ever-evolving universe of play-to-earn (P2E) gaming, the path to sustained prosperity and satisfaction goes beyond technical prowess or short-term speculation. While having a solid grasp of blockchain mechanics, in-game tokenomics, and trading strategies is valuable, these skills alone do not guarantee longevity in a field prone to market shifts, hype cycles, and intense competition. To truly thrive, players and developers alike must cultivate a mindset that embraces continuous learning, community engagement, and constructive contributions to the ecosystem. When approached with curiosity, collaboration, and vision, P2E can yield not only tangible financial rewards but also personal growth, robust social networks, and creative fulfillment.

Traditional gaming often focuses on entertainment or skill mastery in a single environment. By contrast, blockchain-based P2E layers real-world economics, cross-game interoperability, and emergent governance structures, requiring participants to juggle multiple roles: gamer, investor, collaborator, creator, and sometimes even entrepreneur. Success in such an environment necessitates agile thinking and active adaptation—recognizing that each new project, token reward mechanism, or major update could alter the fundamental rules. It also means forging alliances, absorbing lessons from seasoned veterans, and contributing your unique strengths to build the broader metaverse. By combining these elements, your journey can evolve into a long-term adventure, rather than a fleeting speculation.

In this concluding chapter, we explore three key pillars of a success-oriented mindset:

1. **Continuous Learning and Adaptation:** The P2E landscape evolves rapidly. Staying curious, testing new games,

participating in beta releases, and learning from the community are cornerstones of long-term achievement.

2. **Networking and Community Building:** Engaging in forums, attending virtual conferences, and collaborating with other players multiplies your opportunities. Shared knowledge, alliances, and cooperative strategies amplify results in ways solitary efforts cannot.

3. **Contributing to the Ecosystem:** Whether through providing liquidity, becoming a guild leader, helping newcomers learn the ropes, or voting in DAOs—active participation builds reputation, skills, and influence, ensuring you remain a valued member rather than a transient speculator.

Throughout this chapter, we'll detail why each pillar is vital, illustrate practical steps for incorporating them into your routine, and consider how they interlock to form a holistic approach that transcends short-term token price movements. By internalizing these strategies, you can cultivate resilience in the face of inevitable market cycles, seize fresh opportunities before the crowd, and shape the emerging metaverse to reflect your values and aspirations.

Continuous Learning and Adaptation

Embracing Rapidly Shifting Landscapes

The P2E domain is characterized by rapid iteration. A single update can change tokenomics, buff or nerf in-game items, or introduce cross-chain bridges that shift user flows. Meanwhile, newly released projects might overshadow established ones with fresh mechanics or brand partnerships. In parallel, macro-level crypto developments—like layer-2 expansions or regulatory announcements—can expand or constrain P2E adoption overnight.

Cultivating a mindset of continuous learning ensures you remain alert and capable of pivoting rather than clinging to outdated assumptions. Gamers who anchored themselves to one MMO in the past could coast on static knowledge for years. But in P2E, you might see major expansions or token forks every few months, each altering the value proposition of your assets. The same holds for developer teams, who must be ready to incorporate new technologies (e.g., zero-knowledge proofs, improved bridging protocols) to stay competitive.

Such an environment calls for intellectual curiosity: seeking out patch notes, reading official whitepapers, joining AMA (Ask Me Anything) sessions, and following community channels for early hints of shifts in game meta or token emission schedules. The difference between success and regret might hinge on reading an announcement a day earlier than others, enabling you to adapt in time. Yet it isn't about chasing hype or reacting blindly. Instead, it's about building an internal lens to evaluate updates critically, separating genuine innovation from marketing fluff.

Testing New Projects and Betas

Adopting a hands-on learning approach amplifies theoretical knowledge. Instead of waiting for others to review a new P2E title, consider jumping into beta phases or test nets. Beta releases often reward early participants with special NFTs or tokens, but more importantly, they let you shape the game's direction through feedback and bug reports.

Being a beta tester fosters a sense of ownership: you grasp the logic behind certain design choices and token mechanics because you watched them evolve from alpha concepts. This closeness can yield better decision-making when the final version launches, as you know the pitfalls or hidden synergies others might miss. Moreover, many developers note early testers and might reward them with whitelisted privileges for NFT sales or future expansions.

Of course, caution is needed. Beta-phase projects can contain major bugs or be prone to collapse if not well-funded. Approach them with a willingness to lose any time or resources you commit. That said, your "loss" is an investment in deeper expertise. Over time, your portfolio of tested titles expands, each adding to your mental library of tokenomics, gameplay loops, and best (or worst) developer practices. This iterative skill-building is invaluable.

Leveraging Community Insights

In a highly specialized domain, no single individual can master every facet alone. Another key to continuous learning is leveraging collective intelligence from your community. By reading forum discussions, tuning into Twitter threads from established devs or analysts, or hanging out in Discord channels, you glean emergent meta-strategies, notice early signals of developer missteps, and identify potential arbitrage or investment opportunities.

However, it's not enough to passively lurk. Engaging in conversations or asking clarifying questions fosters a more active learning style. If you see conflicting opinions on whether a token distribution model is inflationary or stable, jump in and request data or reasoning. Evaluate the consistency of arguments. Over time, you refine your ability to separate informed commentary from baseless shilling.

Case in point: A new project might tout an unrealistic daily ROI for yield farming. Veteran community members might note parallels with older schemes that collapsed once initial hype died. By heeding these comparisons—and verifying them with your own research—you can avoid traps. Alternatively, if the community consensus underestimates a game's new approach to deflationary token burns, you might spot a hidden gem. That's how a synergy of personal diligence and group discussion elevates your knowledge.

Balancing Adaptability with Consistency

While continuous adaptation is crucial, chasing every new game or pivoting at each rumor can lead to over-trading or burnout. Cultivate a stable core: the handful of P2E projects you deeply trust or thoroughly understand, plus a smaller portion of your time or resources allocated for experimentation with new releases. This approach ensures you keep learning from innovative titles without sacrificing the stable foundation that yields ongoing returns or enjoyment.

Your mindset should be flexible but not erratic. If you believe a certain project has strong fundamentals, you might stay committed during short-term dips, focusing on the bigger picture. Yet, remain open to updating your assessment if repeated red flags surface—like developer silence, security breaches, or broken promises. The skill lies in discerning a rough patch from a downward spiral. Typically, that discernment is honed by constant learning: investigating the cause of the slump, reading dev updates, and contrasting your experiences with community feedback.

Networking and Community Building

The Power of Collective Effort

In many P2E contexts, forging alliances or joining guilds is more than a social nicety—it's a key strategic advantage. Some game mechanics revolve around group raids or territory control, distributing tokens or loot in proportion to team performance. Even beyond direct gameplay benefits, having a supportive network amplifies your ability to spot emerging trends, respond to crises, or co-invest in high-value NFTs. Collaboration frequently outperforms solitary effort, reflecting the broader Web3 ethos of decentralized teamwork.

Networking can take the form of:

1. **In-Game Guilds or Factions**: Players pool assets or coordinate strategies to maximize resource yields or territory defenses.

2. **Online Discussion Forums**: Subreddits, Telegram channels, or specialized platforms where enthusiasts dissect new token mechanisms, compare yield opportunities, or share alpha leaks.

3. **Virtual Conferences and Meetups**: Digital summits or VR gatherings where devs present roadmaps, and investors evaluate synergy across different P2E titles.

4. **Real-World Conventions**: Physical events that highlight blockchain gaming, featuring demos, panels, or e-sports competitions. Meeting face-to-face cements relationships often formed online.

Such synergy fosters a sense of belonging. Instead of contending with market volatility alone, you have confidants to discuss emotional or strategic dilemmas with. Skilled e-sports coaches or DeFi analysts might mentor you, raising your skill ceiling. Meanwhile, you can share your unique specialties—perhaps you excel at NFT art design or organizing tournaments—and the community reciprocates with resources or token support.

Mutual Learning and Resource Pooling

One hallmark of robust communities is reciprocal learning. Not everyone can track every new P2E launch. But within a larger group, some members might keep tabs on DeFi bridging news, others on e-sports scene, and others on narrative-heavy RPG expansions. By pooling knowledge in daily or weekly roundups, you collectively avoid missing crucial developments. Everyone's vantage point broadens.

Resource pooling can be just as impactful. In scholarship programs, a guild's NFT owners lease them out to newcomers who lack capital, splitting profits. Alternatively, a group might crowdfund premium NFT acquisitions or buy virtual land in a prime location, later monetizing it through event hosting. This approach lets smaller investors gain partial exposure to high-value assets, while the guild taps into the community's labor, creativity, or organization.

Cooperative resource pooling can also reduce risk. If you individually can't afford an ultra-rare NFT that grants powerful in-game benefits, pooling funds with 10 others might make it feasible. The challenge is designing fair agreements—like using decentralized multi-sig wallets or trust-minimized smart contracts—to handle shared ownership. But if done well, it fosters a sense of collective purpose that transcends personal greed.

Building Personal Brand and Social Capital

Beyond purely monetary collaborations, community building also extends to personal branding within the P2E sphere. If you consistently provide thoughtful commentary on a game's Discord channel, or produce strategy guides on YouTube, you might earn a reputation as an expert or influencer. Over time, developers might invite you to closed betas, other players might solicit your advice on NFTs, or you could even secure sponsorship deals. This social capital translates into privileged access, financial perks, or intangible satisfaction from being recognized as a community pillar.

However, brand-building requires authenticity and consistency. If you chase every new fad or align with questionable projects, you risk eroding trust. Instead, cultivate a niche or unique viewpoint—perhaps you specialize in analyzing tokenomics or you're known for comedic gameplay streams. By continually engaging with sincerity, you gather a loyal following that accompanies you across new P2E endeavors, magnifying your influence and thus your earning potential.

Handling Competition and Conflict

Not all networking is kumbaya. In competitive P2E contexts—like e-sports or territory control—factions compete for top rewards, and the environment can be cutthroat. Some friction arises from personalities or from schisms within a guild. Cultivating a success mindset means resolving conflict constructively, balancing rivalry with sportsmanship. If you sabotage alliances without cause, you might alienate potential allies or become blacklisted in future games. The P2E world, while vast, is also tight-knit; reputations, both good and bad, follow you.

When conflicts erupt—like disputes over loot distribution or farmland usage in a metaverse—open communication and well-structured guild governance (or DAO votes) can de-escalate tensions. Transparent rules for revenue sharing or rotation of leadership roles also mitigate drama. Ultimately, you'll find that forging and maintaining positive community ties outweighs fleeting personal gains from exploitative tactics. The best guilds or alliances endure across multiple P2E titles, reaping synergy from their cohesive membership.

Contributing to the Ecosystem

Moving Beyond Passive Consumption

One of the hallmark shifts in P2E is that players aren't just consumers but potential co-creators—of the economy, the storyline, or the governance structure. Unlike traditional games, where only the developer's expansions matter, blockchain gaming fosters a participatory ethos where user-driven content, liquidity, or leadership can shape the entire project's trajectory. This environment encourages anyone who's willing to step up with effort or capital to become an influential stakeholder, not merely a bystander.

Active contribution can take many forms:

- **Providing Liquidity**: Staking tokens in the game's liquidity pools or marketplaces fosters a healthy economy, ensuring stable prices and user-friendly trades. Liquidity providers often earn fees or additional rewards.

- **Leading Guilds**: Spearheading a guild or "clan" to tackle group quests, coordinate territory defense, or pool capital for big NFT acquisitions. This role requires organization, communication, and strategic thinking, but can yield both financial and social perks.

- **Onboarding Newcomers**: Mentoring or sponsoring novices who lack capital or knowledge can expand the user base, boosting token demand. Some projects reward "guides" or "ambassadors" with special NFTs for their altruism.

- **Voting in DAOs**: If you hold governance tokens, actively using your vote for proposals fosters collective intelligence. By engaging in thoughtful debates, you help shape expansions, reward emissions, or marketing strategies that affect everyone's stake.

Making such contributions fosters a sense of "ownership" that transcends the typical gamer experience. It aligns with the Web3 ethos that users can become partial guardians or co-owners of the platform they inhabit. At a psychological level, it also heightens your stake in the game's outcome and can be deeply motivating.

Reputation and Skill Building

Engaging in ecosystem contributions naturally builds your reputation as a valuable community member. Over time, people trust your proposals, rely on your market predictions, or nominate you for leadership roles. This intangible capital can translate into tangible perks. For instance, if a new project sees your track record in another P2E as a guild leader who fosters healthy player interactions, they might invite you to lead an alpha testing guild or moderate their Discord, offering tokens or NFT airdrops.

Simultaneously, you grow your skill set: conflict resolution, digital marketing, event organization, economic modeling, or NFT curation. These are not purely "in-game" talents; they can carry over into real-world professional contexts. P2E thus becomes a sandbox for honing advanced collaboration and creative problem-solving techniques—an unexpected boon in a realm stereotyped as pure entertainment.

Impacting Game Direction and Governance

If you accumulate enough governance tokens or forge alliances with other holders, your collective voice can shape fundamental aspects of the game's future. This "civic engagement" within P2E might revolve around:

- **Inflation Adjustments**: Proposing or supporting changes to daily token rewards, aiming for stability.

- **New Feature Approvals**: Nudging the developer team to incorporate features such as cross-chain bridging or user-driven expansions.

- **Event or Tournament Funding**: Voting to allocate treasury funds to sponsor e-sports competitions, brand partnerships, or philanthropic initiatives.

- **In-Game Economical Laws**: Setting rules around resource extraction, marketplace fees, or item burn rates to maintain healthy supply-demand dynamics.

When you transcend being a passive gamer or short-term investor, you effectively become a co-architect of the metaverse. This involvement fosters a unique sense of purpose and fosters long-term engagement even if token prices dip. While not every user seeks this level of activism, those who embrace it can shape the environment in ways that benefit themselves, their guild, or the broader community, cementing a legacy in the digital tapestry.

Avoiding Pitfalls of Exploitative Contributions

Not all forms of ecosystem involvement are benevolent. Some might game the system under the guise of "providing liquidity," only to orchestrate a pump-and-dump scenario, or use DAO voting power to pass proposals that benefit a small clique at the expense of the majority. Achieving an ethical or beneficial contribution means:

1. **Transparency in Motives**: If you're championing a new policy, clarify personal interests and articulate how it aligns with broader user interests.

2. **Balancing Profit with Community Welfare**: Strive for solutions that yield profitability but also sustain the in-game economy and social harmony. Overly greedy or short-sighted decisions degrade the user experience, harming token value in the long run.

3. **Respecting Open Debate**: Healthy governance fosters diverse viewpoints, not echo chambers. Tolerating constructive dissent can prevent flawed proposals from passing.

4. **Checking Conflicts of Interest**: If you hold significant stakes in multiple aspects of the ecosystem, recuse yourself from votes that create questionable conflicts, or at least disclose them so others can weigh that in their decisions.

By maintaining a high ethical standard, your contributions garner legitimacy, ensuring your leadership or proposals endure across P2E expansions. The net effect is a stronger, more equitable environment that resonates with new and veteran players alike.

Bringing It All Together: The Holistic Mindset

The preceding sections on continuous learning, community networking, and ecosystem contributions are not discrete strategies but interwoven facets of a singular mindset. Imagine you are a dedicated P2E participant who:

- Regularly scans game updates and new releases to stay abreast of changes (continuous learning).

- Maintains a robust network of allies, guild members, or forum colleagues, exchanging insights and forging group initiatives (community building).

- Contributes actively, whether by organizing training sessions for new entrants, providing liquidity to stable pairs, or voting on governance proposals that improve the user experience (ecosystem contribution).

Result: You become both agile in responding to short-term market shifts and deeply invested in the game's long-term viability. You foster trust from peers, get invited to exclusive presales or private betas, and your advice or leadership is recognized. Even in downturns, your resilience is buoyed by the sense of belonging and the tangible value your efforts add, making you far less likely to panic sell or abandon the platform. This synergy fosters sustainable success: short-term rewards remain possible, but you're not reliant on them alone, because your skill set, relationships, and reputation have enduring worth.

In practice, cultivating this triad of behaviors demands self-discipline. You might schedule weekly reading or forum scanning sessions, set monthly goals for guild expansions or personal skill improvements, and earmark time to mentor novices. Over months or years, your portfolio of experiences grows in parallel with your digital asset holdings—a potent combination that harnesses both intangible capital (knowledge, social ties) and tangible capital (tokens, NFTs).

Overcoming Common Psychological Barriers

Even with an ideal mindset, players often battle psychological pitfalls:

1. **Fear of Missing Out (FOMO)**: When tokens spike or new projects trend, the impulse to jump in blindly can override reason. A success-oriented mindset requires pausing, doing minimal due diligence, and calibrating your risk tolerance.

2. **Impostor Syndrome**: Some individuals doubt their competence, feeling overshadowed by more vocal or experienced community members. Continuous learning mitigates these fears; remember, everyone starts somewhere, and consistent engagement builds credibility.

3. **Pessimism During Downturns**: In bear markets, negativity saturates discussions, and you might feel your efforts are futile. An unshakable mindset recalls that cycles are inherent in crypto and that building real value extends beyond momentary token prices.

4. **Burnout**: Overly immersing in multiple P2E games, yield-farming strategies, or guild management can deplete energy. Set boundaries, take breaks, and preserve the fun factor. Use community assistance to shoulder tasks.

5. **Social Pressure**: If your close associates are fixated on a specific approach—like purely flipping NFTs for quick profits—yet you prefer a more stable, long-term approach, stand by your convictions. Being well-informed helps you defend an alternative path.

By acknowledging these mental hurdles and deploying coping strategies—like mindful breaks, cost averaging rather than lump-sum investing, or seeking second opinions from mentors—players can maintain emotional stability. Over time, that stability translates into more rational decision-making, fostering success in an environment where emotional swings can be as hazardous as external market shocks.

Real-World Anecdotes and Success Stories

To illustrate how these mindset traits manifest in tangible outcomes, consider a few hypothetical yet plausible scenarios:

The Adaptable Beta Tester-Turned-Investor

374

Marianne started as a casual gamer who dabbled in a small P2E title still in beta. She enjoyed giving feedback to the devs and reporting minor balance issues. Over time, she discovered that her early adoption granted her special NFT airdrops. As the game matured, her knowledge of the item ecosystem helped her identify undervalued NFTs that soared once the project went live. By continuing to test expansions, Marianne maintained a fresh perspective and eventually pivoted some token gains into a new cross-chain project that offered early staking bonuses. Despite market fluctuations, her willingness to keep learning, combined with her early-bird approach, yielded a diversified portfolio and a reputation as a "beta guru."

The Guild Leader Who Fostered a Thriving Community

Roberto was an experienced gamer with moderate crypto knowledge who recognized the importance of alliances in a P2E environment focusing on resource control. He formed a small guild, systematically recruited like-minded players, and established clear guidelines for item sharing and token splitting. Through consistent forum presence and helpful tips, Roberto's guild gained clout, regularly topping leaderboards. With increased fame, new members flocked, and the guild introduced a scholarship system for newcomers, guiding them through steep learning curves. Over time, Roberto also engaged in the game's DAO, helping pass proposals that balanced token inflation. Even in a bear cycle, his guild remained unified, sustaining in-game achievements and preserving token value thanks to a robust network of shared knowledge.

The Creative Content Creator and Ecosystem Contributor

Aisha, an illustrator by trade, ventured into P2E to explore NFT art potential. Instead of simply flipping items, she designed collectible skins for an RPG that fully embraced user-generated content. Her designs gained popularity, leading the devs to incorporate them officially. Aisha then minted unique variants of these skins and sold them on the game's marketplace. Encouraged by success, she expanded into streaming tutorials on character customization, forging alliances with e-sports teams that featured her skins. Her standing in the community soared, and Aisha gained seats on a developer advisory panel, shaping future expansions. She diversified her asset holdings across multiple titles but always remained committed to improving each project's creative ecosystem. Her brand soared beyond a single P2E, culminating in cross-project collaborations.

These anecdotes show how players who anchor themselves in learning, networking, and contribution can flourish even if the market is erratic. They also highlight that success may take varied forms: from wise early investment to building a supportive community to leveraging one's unique talents in NFT design. The overarching theme is that each of these individuals built a resilient mindset: they refused to rely solely on short-term speculation, recognized the value of synergy with others, and actively shaped the environment rather than passively reacting to it.

Practical Steps to Foster a Success Mindset

To wrap up this discussion, let's distill the main insights into actionable guidelines you can implement today, no matter your experience level or resource constraints.

Continuous Learning and Adaptation

1. **Maintain a Research Routine**: Devote 15-30 minutes daily to reading official announcements, scanning community forums, or checking aggregator sites for new project listings.

2. **Beta Participation**: Sign up for at least one alpha or beta test every quarter if your schedule allows. Jot down observations about tokenomics or dev communication style.

3. **Curate Trusted Info Sources**: Follow a balanced mix of dev updates, third-party analysts, and community-run podcasts. Diversify sources to reduce echo-chamber effects.

Networking and Community Building

1. **Join or Form a Small Guild**: If none exist that match your goals, create one. Start small—maybe just a few friends or acquaintances—then expand organically.

2. **Attend Virtual Events**: Many P2E conferences happen in VR or online spaces. Ask questions, gather insights, and exchange contact details with interesting participants.

3. **Engage in AMA Sessions**: Dev teams often host live Q&As. Being vocal and polite while raising relevant points can catch dev attention and earn community respect.

Contributing to the Ecosystem

1. **Offer Liquidity**: Start with small pairs in a game's marketplace or DeFi section. Track yields and observe how your involvement affects item trade volume or user sentiment.

2. **Mentor Newcomers**: Even if you're not an "expert," you might know more than a total beginner. Summaries, quick guides, or a short orientation session can transform a novice's experience.

3. **Engage in DAO Voting**: Even if you hold a modest number of governance tokens, vote or comment on proposals. Many DAOs suffer from low participation; your voice can matter.

Safeguarding Mental and Financial Health

1. **Set Boundaries**: Limit how many hours you spend monitoring token prices or grinding quests purely for yield.

2. **Risk Management**: Only commit capital you can afford to lose, especially when exploring new or unproven platforms.

3. **Celebrate Non-Financial Wins**: Evaluate your progress not just by profit, but by new friendships formed, skill improvements, or creative accomplishments.

4. **Stay Balanced**: If stress or emotional volatility heightens, step back. Confide in community friends, or shift focus to more stable, lower-intensity titles until your mindset stabilizes.

Final Reflections on the Future of P2E Mindsets

As P2E evolves from a niche phenomenon into a broader cultural and economic force, the potential rewards—financial, social, creative—will beckon millions. Yet the same environment can breed volatility, speculative mania, and ethical pitfalls. Navigating this terrain successfully is less about stumbling on a single "winning strategy" or holding the rarest NFT. It's about adopting a mindset that thrives on uncertainty, fosters genuine human connections, and acknowledges your role in shaping the ecosystem.

In championing continuous learning, you remain nimble in the face of perpetual innovation and cyclical markets. By cultivating networking and community building, you harness collective intelligence, share resources, and find mentors or collaborators who magnify your efforts. Finally, by contributing to the ecosystem, you move from being a passive user or short-term profit seeker to a co-owner of digital worlds, forging a legacy that endures across expansions and migrations.

This perspective is not only beneficial personally but also pivotal for the broader sustainability of P2E. A thriving ecosystem requires engaged players, strong alliances, and grassroots governance to counterbalance the pressures of speculation or centralization. As you step forward—testing new games, forging alliances, mentoring novices, or voicing governance proposals—recognize your capacity to elevate both your personal trajectory and the collective realm. Ultimately, cultivating a mindset for success in P2E is about recognizing that we each hold the power to shape the future of gaming, finance, and online community, one informed decision and inspired collaboration at a time.

Appendices

Appendix A: Glossary of Common Terms

The world of play-to-earn (P2E) gaming combines blockchain technology, decentralized finance, and traditional video game elements. Below are key terms frequently used throughout this book and in broader P2E discussions.

1. **Address**

A string of characters representing a user's wallet on a blockchain. Think of it as a public identifier to receive tokens or NFTs.

2. **Air Drop**

A distribution of tokens or NFTs to a specific group of users. It may reward early supporters, beta testers, or participants in certain community events.

3. **Alpha**

An early-stage version of a game or protocol, typically not yet feature-complete or bug-free. Players who join alpha tests often help with feedback, possibly receiving unique rewards or privileges.

4. **Asset (Digital Asset)**

Any token or NFT within a game or blockchain ecosystem. Can represent currency, game items, virtual land, or even governance rights.

5. **Beta**

A post-alpha stage where a game or protocol is closer to completion but still requires player testing to identify bugs or refine features.

6. **Blockchain**

A decentralized ledger maintained by a network of nodes, recording transactions immutably. Examples include Ethereum, Solana, and Polygon.

7. **Bot**

Automated scripts designed to perform in-game tasks—sometimes used ethically (e.g., test automation) but often for exploitative farming or repeated resource gathering.

8. **Collateral**

An asset pledged in a decentralized finance (DeFi) protocol (e.g., NFTs or tokens) to secure a loan. Failure to repay leads to liquidation of the collateral.

9. **DAO (Decentralized Autonomous Organization)**

A governance mechanism run by token holders or stakeholders, allowing them to propose and vote on changes in a transparent, decentralized manner.

10. **DeFi (Decentralized Finance)**

The ecosystem of blockchain-based financial services like lending, borrowing, staking, and liquidity pools, where intermediaries are replaced by smart contracts.

11. **Exchange (DEX/CEX)**

- **DEX (Decentralized Exchange)**: A trustless platform where users trade directly from their wallets via smart contracts (e.g., Uniswap, SushiSwap).

- **CEX (Centralized Exchange)**: A custodial platform run by a company (e.g., Binance, Coinbase).

12. **FOMO (Fear of Missing Out)**

A psychological phenomenon in which players or investors rush into buying tokens or NFTs due to hype or fear that opportunities will vanish.

13. Gas (Transaction Fee)

The cost of executing a transaction or contract call on a blockchain. Can vary drastically depending on network demand and the chain's fee model.

14. Governance Token

A token granting holders voting power in a game's DAO or governance structure. Allows input on proposals like reward schedules, expansions, or fee distributions.

15. Guild

A player-run group or clan within a game, often focusing on cooperative strategies, resource pooling, or scholarship programs to onboard new players.

16. Interoperability

The ability for assets, data, or features to move seamlessly across different blockchains, games, or platforms.

17. KYC (Know Your Customer)

A compliance procedure requiring users to verify their identities, often for regulatory or anti-money laundering purposes in crypto exchanges or certain DeFi protocols.

18. Liquidity Pool

A smart contract-based pool containing pairs of tokens that users provide for decentralized trading or yield farming, receiving fees or rewards in return.

19. Metaverse

An interconnected network of virtual worlds, social spaces, and digital experiences. In many P2E visions, users can carry their avatars and NFTs across multiple games.

20. NFT (Non-Fungible Token)

A unique digital asset on a blockchain representing art, collectibles, in-game items, or virtual land. "Non-fungible" means each token is distinct.

21. ROI (Return on Investment)

A measure of profitability indicating how much gain or loss is generated relative to the amount of capital invested.

22. Scholarship

A model where NFT owners lend assets (like characters or land) to players ("scholars") in exchange for a share of the tokens earned. Helps low-capital players participate.

23. Smart Contract

Self-executing code on a blockchain that runs specific functions when conditions are met, enabling automated transactions, yield farms, or NFT operations.

24. Stake/Staking

Locking tokens or NFTs in a contract to earn rewards, typically to secure the network, provide liquidity, or influence governance.

25. Token

A fungible crypto asset representing currency, governance rights, or utility within a P2E environment. Examples: SLP, AXS, or MANA.

26. Utility Token

A token used primarily for in-game transactions or item purchases. Often not intended as an investment or security, but can still be traded on open markets.

27. Volatility

Rapid fluctuation in token or NFT prices, influenced by market sentiment, speculation, or real-world events.

28. Whale

A participant holding a large quantity of tokens, capable of significantly impacting prices or voting outcomes.

Appendix B: Recommended Tools, Marketplaces, and Exchanges

Because the play-to-earn ecosystem involves diverse processes—like managing crypto wallets, analyzing token data, trading NFTs, and interacting with decentralized apps—having the right tools and platforms is vital. Below is a curated list of recommended services that can streamline your P2E journey.

B.1 Wallets and Security Tools

1. MetaMask (Browser Extension & Mobile)

A widely used Ethereum-based wallet supporting multiple blockchains (including sidechains and Layer-2s). Simple interface for interacting with dApps and storing ERC-20 or NFT assets.

2. Trust Wallet (Mobile)

Ideal for on-the-go usage, supports multiple blockchains like Ethereum, Binance Smart Chain, and more. Built-in dApp browser for in-app P2E interactions.

3. Phantom (Solana)

A popular Solana wallet featuring user-friendly design, integrated NFT gallery, and streamlined staking options.

4. Ledger/Trezor (Hardware Wallets)

Hardware devices that store private keys offline for maximum security. Recommended for large holdings or valuable NFTs. Often integrates with software wallets like MetaMask.

5. Etherscan, BscScan, Solscan (Blockchain Explorers)

Official explorers for Ethereum, Binance Smart Chain, and Solana respectively. Essential for verifying contract addresses, transaction histories, or NFT ownership.

6. Revoke.Cash / Token Allowance Checker

Tools to review and revoke token spending approvals granted to various dApps, mitigating the risk of malicious contract drain.

B.2 Token Tracking and Analysis

1. CoinGecko / CoinMarketCap

These aggregator websites track crypto prices, market caps, exchange listings, and basic token data. Often includes NFT and DeFi sections that highlight top gainers or trending projects.

2. DappRadar

Analyzes usage statistics (active wallets, transaction volumes) for decentralized applications, including P2E games. Useful for identifying popular or rising projects.

3. NFTScan / NonFungible.com

Tools specialized in NFT analytics, covering historical sales, rarity data, and volume across multiple marketplaces. Helps gauge liquidity or spot underpriced assets.

4. Zapper / Zerion

Dashboard services showing your overall token and NFT holdings across multiple networks, plus DeFi positions. Convenient for tracking multi-chain P2E engagements.

5. **DefiLlama**

For broader DeFi insights, listing total value locked (TVL) in each protocol or chain. Though not strictly P2E, it reveals macro liquidity trends that can affect gaming tokens.

B.3 NFT Marketplaces

1. **OpenSea**

The largest NFT marketplace (primarily on Ethereum, also supports Polygon), listing everything from profile picture (PFP) collections to game-specific NFTs.

   ○ *Tip*: Verify official collections (blue checkmark) to avoid fakes, especially for top-tier P2E items.

2. **Magic Eden (Solana)**

A leading Solana-based marketplace with low fees and fast transactions. Rapidly growing selection of P2E NFTs. Notable for featuring exclusive Solana-based game assets.

3. **Rarible**

A community-centric marketplace that supports Ethereum and other EVM-compatible chains, with a governance token (RARI). Often used by indie creators and smaller P2E projects.

4. **Binance NFT Marketplace**

Tied to the Binance ecosystem, featuring BNB Chain assets plus curated drops from known brands or game projects. Good for bridging mainstream users.

5. **Game-Specific Marketplaces**

Many P2E titles operate official NFT marketplaces integrated into their website or in-game UI. This can reduce fees or guarantee authenticity, though liquidity might be limited compared to general platforms.

B.4 Decentralized Exchanges (DEXs) and Aggregators

1. Uniswap (Ethereum)

Pioneering automated market maker (AMM) for ERC-20 tokens. Many P2E tokens debut here. Check for liquidity depth and potential slippage on small-cap tokens.

2. PancakeSwap (BNB Chain)

Leading DEX on BNB Chain, with lower fees than Ethereum. Popular for smaller gaming tokens, but watch for higher scam token prevalence.

3. SushiSwap (Multi-Chain)

A multi-chain DEX operating on Ethereum and several L2s or sidechains. One-stop solution for cross-chain trades, though volume can vary by chain.

4. 1inch / Matcha (Aggregators)

Aggregators scanning multiple DEXs for the best price on your token trade. Helpful for finding optimal rates on less liquid P2E tokens.

5. Raydium (Solana)

High-speed Solana DEX with AMM features. Often used for Solana-based P2E titles to facilitate item or token liquidity.

B.5 P2E Launchpads and Ecosystem Hubs

1. Seedify

A blockchain gaming-focused launchpad that incubates new P2E projects. Staking their launchpad tokens often grants access to presales or exclusive NFT drops.

2. Gamestarter

A platform combining NFT fundraising for indie game studios with marketplace features, allowing developers to pre-sell in-game assets and gauge user interest.

3. Enjin

Provides a suite of tools for creating and managing NFTs, often used in gaming contexts. Enjin's ecosystem fosters cross-project item usage and scaling solutions.

4. Vulcan Forged

An integrated platform featuring a variety of in-house games, an NFT marketplace, and developer tools for building P2E experiences. Also runs its own Elysium blockchain aimed at gaming.

Appendix C: Example Case Studies of Successful P2E Projects

Case studies provide real-world context for how P2E gaming can flourish (or stumble) based on design, community engagement, and marketing. Below are three illustrative projects that, while distinct in style and success, highlight the breadth of outcomes in the P2E landscape.

Case C.1: Axie Infinity

1. Overview and Origin

Axie Infinity, developed by Sky Mavis, emerged as one of the first major P2E blockbusters. Players breed, battle, and trade cute creatures called "Axies," each represented by NFTs. Initially launched on Ethereum, Axie Infinity migrated most gameplay to a sidechain (Ronin) to tackle high gas fees.

2. **Tokenomics**

The ecosystem revolves around two tokens:

- o **AXS (Axie Infinity Shards)**: A governance token giving holders voting power and a share of the game's revenue.

- o **SLP (Smooth Love Potion)**: An in-game token earned through battles, primarily used for breeding new Axies.
  This dual-token model allowed for variable inflation and deflation. However, challenges surfaced when large numbers of new players farmed SLP, causing oversupply.

3. **Scholarship Mechanism**

Axie Infinity popularized scholarship programs. Asset owners lend Axies to scholars who lack capital; in return, they split the SLP earnings. This arrangement propelled adoption in regions like the Philippines. But it also introduced potential exploit risks and oversupply as more Axies entered circulation.

4. **Market Cycles and Controversies**

Axie Infinity soared in 2021, with tokens reaching multi-billion-dollar valuations. However, in subsequent bear markets, SLP's price collapsed amid concerns about token inflation and user churn. The game's devs introduced burn mechanics and updated breeding fees to restore balance.

5. **Key Takeaways**

Axie Infinity demonstrated P2E's potential for massive scale but also highlighted the pitfalls of unchecked inflation and speculation. Its lasting legacy is proving that large populations can adopt P2E gaming as a form of daily "work," spurring broader recognition of P2E opportunities.

Case C.2: The Sandbox

1. **Overview**

   The Sandbox is a virtual world (metaverse) that merges user-generated content, land ownership, and gamified experiences. Players can buy land parcels (NFTs) to build custom experiences or create assets using VoxEdit and earn revenue by monetizing them.

2. **Token Ecosystem**

   o **SAND**: The primary utility token for purchasing land, items, and paying for services. It also functions as a governance token in The Sandbox DAO.

   o **LAND**: Non-fungible tokens representing virtual real estate. Landowners can host events, create interactive games, or rent space to other users.

3. **User-Created Experiences**

   A hallmark is The Sandbox's robust set of creation tools that require little coding. Community-driven events—like art galleries, concerts, or platformer games—pop up, intensifying the platform's user engagement and NFT trades. Major brands and celebrities, from Atari to Snoop Dogg, have also partnered with The Sandbox.

4. **Adoption and Scalability**

   Hosting multiple experiences with diverse gameplay styles can cause performance bottlenecks if user concurrency spikes. The Sandbox addresses this by developing its infrastructure progressively and exploring L2 or bridging approaches.

5. **Key Takeaways**

   By prioritizing user-generated content and brand collaborations, The Sandbox fosters a sandbox-like environment reminiscent of Roblox or Minecraft, yet with full NFT-based ownership. Its success underscores how creative freedom plus P2E can drive strong community loyalty.

Case C.3: Splinterlands

1. Overview

Splinterlands is a blockchain-based collectible card game (CCG) focusing on strategic battles and deck-building. It runs on the Hive blockchain (with cross-chain features to WAX, Ethereum, etc.). Players collect or rent card NFTs, each with unique abilities, then compete in PvP tournaments or ranked matches.

2. Earning Mechanisms

- **DEC (Dark Energy Crystals)**: The in-game currency rewarded for match victories, also used to buy card packs or rent cards.

- **SPS (Splintershards)**: A governance token earned through gameplay and staked for additional benefits. Splinterlands also has a vibrant rental market, letting users rent out high-level cards for daily fees.

3. Accessibility

The game offers a relatively low-cost starter pack, lowering entry barriers. Skilled players can progress without huge capital outlay, although top-tier cards can fetch high prices. Splinterlands emphasizes skill-based deck construction, mitigating pay-to-win extremes.

4. Community and Tournaments

Regular tournaments with DEC or card rewards draw competitive players. The game's openness to new features—like asynchronous guild battles or cross-promotion with other Hive projects—sustains user engagement.

5. Key Takeaways

Splinterlands highlights the viability of combining collectible card mechanics with NFT ownership, balancing free-to-play elements and higher-level competitiveness. Its robust rental system showcases how NFT-based card ownership can fuel diverse economic strategies, from casual to pro-level.

Closing Note on the Appendices

These appendices serve as a practical complement to the main chapters. Appendix A provides clarity on terminology crucial for navigating the P2E domain, while Appendix B lists tools and platforms that can streamline your P2E activities—from wallet setups to NFT marketplaces. Appendix C shows how successful P2E projects thrive by blending accessible entry points, community-driven mechanics, and thoughtful tokenomics. Each project or resource also grapples with its own challenges—reinforcing that while the potential of blockchain gaming is huge, success depends on balancing innovation with user needs, fair token distribution, and ongoing community engagement.

www.ingramcontent.com/pod-product-compliance
Lightning Source LLC
LaVergne TN
LVHW051220050326
832903LV00028B/2185